Connecting
Mathematics and Science
to Workplace Contexts

T E R C

Connecting Mathematics and Science to Workplace Contexts

A GUIDE to Curriculum Materials

Edward Britton

Mary Ann Huntley

Gloria Jacobs

Amy Shulman Weinberg

CORWIN PRESS, INC.
A Sage Publications Company
Thousand Oaks, California

This book is a project of the National Center for Improving Science Education (NCISE), a division of WestEd, of Washington, D.C., in collaboration with and supported by a subcontract from TERC of Cambridge, Massachusetts. Work was sponsored by a grant from the Pew Charitable Trusts. The opinions expressed in this report are those of the authors and do not necessarily reflect the views of the Pew Charitable Trusts, TERC, or WestEd.

For information address:

Corwin Press, Inc.
A Sage Publications Company
2455 Teller Road
Thousand Oaks, California 91320
E-mail: order@corwinpress.com

SAGE Publications Ltd.
6 Bonhill Street
London EC2A 4PU
United Kingdom

SAGE Publications India Pvt. Ltd.
M-32 Market
Greater Kailash I
New Delhi 110 048 India

Printed in the United States of America

Library of Congress Cataloging-in-Publication Data

Britton, Edward D.
    Connecting mathematics and science to workplace contexts: A guide to curriculum materials / Edward Britton, et al.
    p. cm.
    Includes bibliographical references.
    ISBN 0-8039-6866-3 (cloth)
    ISBN 0-8039-6867-1 (pbk.)
    1. Mathematics — Study and teaching (Secondary) 2. Science — Study and teaching (Secondary) 3. School-to-work transition. I. Huntley, Mary Ann. II. Jacobs, Gloria. III. Weinberg, Amy Shulman. IV. Title.
    QA11.B814 1999
    507.1'2 — dc21

                                                                99-6183

This book is printed on acid-free paper.

99 00 01 02 03 04 05 10 9 8 7 6 5 4 3 2 1

Production Editor: S. Marlene Head
Editorial Assistant: Julia Parnell
Cover Designer: Tracy E. Miller

Contents

References

Appendixes

Foreword

This guide is, first of all, for science and mathematics educators. It is full of tangible ideas for connecting their instruction to the real-world context of industries and occupations. Educators in school-to-work and tech prep programs will also find ideas for integrating rigorous academic subject matter with their workplace-oriented curricula.

Why should science and mathematics educators be interested in making connections to the world of work? We are not arguing for yet another "movement" to add to the burden of paying attention to standards, integrating subject matter across disciplines, incorporating science-technology-society (STS) topics, and other important curriculum trends. Rather, we urge educators to tap movements that exist already to further their own goals. We believe that the best of school-to-work and similar programs address goals that are central to science and mathematics education, such as engaging all types of students in active learning and by making their time in school more relevant to their lives after graduation. This holds true for all students—whether they plan to seek immediate employment or to enter a postsecondary institution.

In fact, we believe mathematics and science educators will shortchange themselves and their students if they automatically discount these programs and the ideas in the curricula reviewed in this guide as inappropriate for college-bound students. Done well, and rigorously, curricula that are connected to the workplace can encourage more students to take more science and mathematics than they otherwise would. It is no accident that employers complain about newly minted graduates as being out of touch with the realities of work demands—and that holds for university graduates as well as high school graduates! Indeed, the typical secondary and postsecondary academic course of study rarely provides time or opportunity to think about applications of scientific and mathematical knowledge. As a result, even Ph.D. graduates often get a rude awakening when first employed in industry, and more and more complaints are heard from industry leaders that they are having to invest too much in the "training" of doctoral graduates. Does this sound familiar?

Another argument in favor of work-related curricula derives from the different ways of organizing knowledge. The phenomena that surround us in the natural and human-designed worlds are not in themselves broken down into the large numbers of scientific and mathematical subfields in which people specialize. However, in order to study and deal effectively with the complexities of these phenomena, academic institutions create ever more areas of specialization and courses that match them. We forget that this makes it difficult for students—and sometimes for ourselves—to understand the patterns, make the connections and see the applications. We argue that a curriculum relating to workplace contexts can help many students make better sense of the world than a traditional, exclusively theory-based approach.

This guide goes well beyond making arguments for linking science and mathematics instruction to the workplace. In chapter 2, the authors have sorted the included curriculum materials into six types of linkages. There isn't anything profound about these six ways; and one could come up with a different set of categories. However, the ones the authors have chosen give you some lenses useful for examining materials that claim links to the workplace. The guide also provides rich descriptions of the curriculum materials the authors have selected for inclusion, using the same lenses. These two aspects of the guide make it a practical tool for educators confronted with a plethora of materials and sometimes conflicting advice about how to choose effective science and mathematics curricula for their students.

The selection of materials for this guide posed some difficulties for the authors. A determining criterion was the connection of the curriculum to the workplace, but we also asked them whether the materials were pedagogically sound, contained solid science and mathematics, and addressed the national curriculum standards. Addressing all these criteria is a daunting challenge for curriculum developers, not only because it is complex to weave all these important features into one product adeptly, but also because each require different knowledge or expertise, so that it's difficult to find people who are sufficiently expert in all of them. Hence, few of even the selected products address all of these desired features well. Some of them are somewhat weak in one or another dimension. These still were included because they offered good examples of making connections to the workplace—the primary criterion. The authors found about 200 products that connected mathematics and science to workplace contexts; the choice of the 23 included in the guide was based on addressing our multiple criteria in as balanced a way as possible.

So we ask you to consider connecting school science and mathematics to workplace contexts. Take a look at the descriptions of curriculum materials in this book, including the sample pages of each product. Some of you might want to replace your traditional textbook or part of your instruction with curricula in the guide; others might use it for ideas on how to connect the science you already teach to workplace contexts. In either case, the purposes of the guide will be amply served.

December 1998
Senta Raizen
Director
National Center for Improving Science Education

Margaret Vickers
Senior Scientist
TERC

Preface

Purpose and Evolution of This Book

In the last 5 to 10 years, many educators have become interested in connecting mathematics, science, and technology to workplace contexts, but there has been little practical guidance available to help them begin. Unlike traditional approaches to academic subject matter, making workplace connections engages students by providing real-world contexts, helps more students learn mathematics and science, addresses important goals of the national curriculum standards, better prepares all types of students for their ultimate employment, provides teachers with a rewarding opportunity to expand their own expertise, and helps the school curriculum to better address the dramatically changing needs of U.S. workplaces. For these reasons, policymakers and professional organizations have very strongly urged vocational/technical teachers to infuse more academic mathematics and science into their curriculum to explain the concepts that underlie the processes used in their workplace-oriented curricula. This is giving rise to a movement to integrate academic and vocational education, and create school-to-work, tech prep, and similar programs that emphasize academic-workplace connections. Similarly, teachers of science, mathematics, and technology should seriously consider the value of using workplace connections to illustrate real-world applications of the theoretical concepts they teach. This new emphasis and interest has created a burgeoning demand for curriculum materials that connect science and mathematics to workplace contexts.

In the course of researching this book, we met with hundreds of different educators, many of whose comments became an oft-repeated refrain: "Give us real stuff that we can use as is, or use to get started." At a meeting convened in 1997 by the American Chemical Society to discuss this issue, tech prep directors from state departments of education said they only knew of a handful of curriculum materials that made the kinds of connections being sought and that could be used or adapted on a national basis. In 1995, Margaret Vickers and Amy Weinberg of TERC, in a precursor effort supported by the Massachusetts Office of School to Work, produced guides to curriculum materials that connect science, mathematics, and social studies to workplace learning. They found few candidates and, of necessity, included some that were less progressive in content or pedagogy than they had been seeking.

For this effort, the Pew Charitable Trusts enabled us to build on the earlier work by making a more exhaustive search in a more fertile time. The escalating interest in making workplace connections has led to the very recent development of many new candidate materials. In fact, half of the 23 curricula reviewed in this guide have been released in 1998 or will be completed in 1999; only seven were published in 1995 or earlier.

In researching this book, we obtained and reviewed about 200 candidate sets of curriculum materials from all over the country. They ranged from one unit that a mathematics teacher and a vocational teacher at a local school created about the use of mathematics in plumbing; to a series of 15 modules used to supplement the middle school science curriculum for a week or two at a time; to materials that comprise a two-year course in the physics and technology involved in mechanical, fluid, electrical, and thermal systems. Our exhaustive search drew on personal contacts with dozens of experts who gave us invaluable referrals. We also attended the annual meetings and conferences of the American Vocational Association, International Technology Education Association, National Council of Teachers of Mathematics, and the National Science Teachers Association; as well as the High Schools and Beyond conference of the Southern Regional Education Board. At these, we spoke with the exhibitors; listened to the presenters; and followed up by phone, e-mail, or letter on contacts we could not initiate during the conference proper. We obtained copies of curriculum materials funded by the National Science Foundation through its Instructional Materials Development and Advanced Technological Education programs. We requested and received draft materials from the dozen projects funded during the mid-1990s by the U.S. Department of Education to integrate academic subjects with vocational education. Finally, we continuously scanned the literature, especially the periodicals of the organizations named above.

While many of the collected materials were clever, innovative, and useful, most were rejected in accordance with the selection criteria we describe in chapter 3. Briefly, the materials we were seeking had to connect science, mathematics, or technology to workplace contexts, but also had to be sufficiently developed that teachers across the country could implement or adapt them. We did not limit ourselves to materials featuring full-blown integration in both design and execution. There just aren't very many of these available yet—at least not ones that can be readily used across the country. We gave preference to materials that used pedagogical practices called for in the national curriculum standards, although in some instances we retained curricula that did not use ideal instructional practices because their connections to workplace contexts were particularly strong. As long as our basic criteria were met, we did not preclude materials for having an unpolished appearance. Unfortunately, many materials that had been developed for local use could not be generalized to other areas: that is, their instructional activities depended so much upon workplace experiences particular to businesses in the local area that it would be difficult—if not impossible—for teachers elsewhere to adapt the experiences to careers available in their area. Other local materials did not provide sufficient instructional detail or guidance to permit adaptation by educators elsewhere.

The resulting portfolio of the 23 curricula reviewed in this guide and 10 others described in appendix A should empower teachers in mathematics, science, technology, or vocational/technical programs to either replace or augment their curriculum with instruction that links academic topics to workplace contexts. We hope this resource guide will help many interested educators to improve their curricula and to pique the curiosity of educators who may not previously have considered connecting academic subjects to workplace contexts.

Audiences for This Book

Science and Mathematics Teachers. This guide is designed to help the country's millions of teachers of academic science and mathematics move toward curricula that make content more relevant to students. There's very little that's more "real world"—an objective called for by the national curriculum standards in both science and mathematics—than workplace contexts. Using such materials, teachers will be better able to incorporate useful examples of their subjects, which will better engage students—all kinds of students— and more appropriately prepare them for the world of work and/or postsecondary study.

Teachers in School-to-Work, Tech Prep, Vocational Ed., and Related Programs. In recent years, policymakers have been demanding that vocational/technical programs offer as rigorous a curriculum as academic programs. They want all students, regardless of high school course of study, to be capable of postsecondary study if they so choose. An implication of this is that teachers of applied (as opposed to academic) courses should not just teach practical, workplace-relevant tasks and skills, but should further empower their students by explaining the underlying scientific and mathematical principles upon which those activities are based. Using the types of materials outlined in this book, teachers in these programs will be more able to accomplish this infusion of workplace activities with science and mathematics.

Curriculum Supervisors. State and district administrators responsible for curriculum materials in science, mathematics, and/or vocational and other workforce education programs should find this resource guide invaluable. All too often, busy administrators are aware of—and are knowledgeable about—only a small sample of the overwhelming number of curriculum materials available. Moreover, they rarely can dedicate the needed time and/or money to obtain and review products for comparison. The guide alleviates this burden by providing reviews of many curriculum materials and including sample pages of each.

Curriculum Developers. Curriculum developers in the public and private sectors should benefit from seeing the entire set of products reviewed in this guide. Like curriculum supervisors, developers seldom have the time or resources to keep track of, obtain, and review other products. Developers may want to consider the six ways that the reviewed materials connect to the workplace to see whether there are some new instructional treatments they could use. They might also consider how existing materials have connected specific science and mathematics to specific workplace contexts. This could prevent their inadvertently "reinventing the wheel" rather than developing a unique contribution.

Uniqueness of This Book

Although quite a number of good books already exist on the theory, principles, and process of connecting academic subjects to workplace contexts, this book may well be the only one devoted specifically to mathematics and science education, and to detailed illustration—by providing many examples of existing curriculum materials—rather than theoretical discussions of academic-workplace curricular integration. The first section of chapter 1 identifies some exemplary books that lay out the case for connecting school curricula to workplace contexts. While other books speak to all subject areas, this guide reviews those arguments in light of the specifics being faced by science, mathematics, and technology education. The majority of the guide then brings the issues to life by reviewing actual curriculum materials that make workplace connections.

Organization of This Book

Chapter 1 briefly reviews the literature that argues for connecting the school science and mathematics curriculum to workplace contexts, including how making such connections can fulfill aspects of the national curriculum standards. For the benefit of mathematics and science educators unfamiliar with applied courses of study, we then give a quick overview of programs such as school-to-work, tech prep, occupational clusters, and career academies. The chapter then gives a brief but explicit roster of who school mathematics and science education can benefit from making workplace connections. In closing, chapter 1 discusses barriers that often make it difficult for educators to connect mathematics and science to workplace contexts.

In chapter 2, we explain the different approaches the 23 reviewed curricula use to make workplace connections. The varied instructional treatments are sorted into six types of connections, and the types of connections used in each curricula are delineated. The six approaches are extensively illustrated with sample pages from the various curricula.

Chapter 3 explains how the 23 curricula described here were selected from among some 200 candidates reviewed. It then gives an overview of the 23 curricula, citing their publication dates; subject areas; funding sources; whether they are targeted for students in middle school, high school, or both; and self-described alignment with national curriculum standards. The chapter also gives an overview of the products' purposes, sizes, formats, components, media used, and costs. Finally, the chapter explains what kinds of information we provide in each of the dozen or more elements found in all 23 reviews.

Chapters 4 and 5 comprise the bulk of this guide. They provide the reviews, respectively, of 12 mathematics curricula and 11 that are for science or an integration of science with mathematics and/or technology education.

Appendix A provides paragraph-length descriptions of more curricula that we would like to have included but could not due to space limitations. Finally, if the reviewed curricula prompt some readers to consider creating curriculum materials for their own or—especially—others' use, they should look at Appendix B, which briefly mentions key points on developing curriculum materials that connect science and mathematics to workplace contexts.

Acknowledgments

We are grateful to the many people who made this book possible. Our two senior advisors, Senta Raizen and Margaret Vickers, offered sage insights throughout the development of this book and encapsulated these in a compelling foreword, wherein they briefly but forcefully make the case for connecting science and mathematics to workplace contexts.

LaDonna Dickerson, Donita Mitchell, and Steve Lewis provided conscientious assistance with administrative tasks and manuscript preparation. Nita Congress, who has edited several National Center for Improving Science Education books over the years, ever so nicely helped improve our communication throughout. Steve Waxman ably helped us design the format of the book, and JeAnne Waxman handled the page layouts within some extremely tight deadlines. Alice Foster at Corwin Press has taken on three NCISE projects in the last two years. We are particularly gratified that she and Corwin recognized the need for this book. The Pew Charitable Trusts funded this work as part of its considerable portfolio of efforts to promote connections between school mathematics and science and workplace contexts. We acknowledge the support of Robert Schwartz, formerly director of Education Programs at Pew, and of Janet Kroll, who assumed the responsibilities of monitoring our grant after his departure.

Hundreds of curriculum developers made this book possible by sharing their products with us; many graciously permitted us to look at works in progress. The authors and developers of the curriculum materials ultimately included in this book were most generous with their time and energy, providing prompt and detailed feedback on what we wrote and ensuring that permission was granted for us to reproduce sample pages from their work. Developing curriculum materials is always a conceptually challenging activity. In preparing this book, we are therefore especially indebted to, and appreciative of, those thousands of developers who, by endeavoring to create curriculum materials that connect school learning to the real-world contexts of jobs and careers, demonstrate their willingness to go beyond the usual intellectual boundaries of their fields.

The contributions of the following reviewers are gratefully acknowledged:

Brian C. Bertrand
New York, NY

Sandy Enger
The University of Alabama at Huntsville
Institute for Science Education
Huntsville, AL

Maria Found
Math Department Chair
Brewster Academy
Wolfeboro, NH

Michael Harmon
Research, Evaluation and Testing Division
Georgia Department of Education
Atlanta, GA

Michael Herman
Teacher
Mesa Verde Middle School
San Diego, CA

Jeanelle Bland Hodges
Doctoral Candidate
University of Alabama
Tuscaloosa, AL

Authors and Organizations

Authors

Edward Britton, author of chapters 1-3 and editor of the guide, is associate director of the National Center for Improving Science Education. Before joining NCISE in 1991, Dr. Britton taught secondary and postsecondary science courses, completed graduate work in analytical chemistry, and later developed and reviewed science curricula with the late Mary Budd Rowe. At NCISE, he has coauthored articles and books on curriculum issues in science and mathematics education that arose from several prominent national and international studies.

Mary Ann Huntley, author of reviews for the mathematics curricula, is a consultant to the National Center for Improving Science Education. Dr. Huntley's research addresses mathematics curricula, teacher preparation, and integrated mathematics and science education. She has worked as an applied mathematician in a variety of research settings, including the Eastman Kodak Company and NASA/Goddard Space Flight Center. Dr. Huntley also has taught mathematics at the secondary and undergraduate levels.

Gloria Jacobs, author of reviews for some of the science and integrated curricula, is a senior research associate at TERC. Over the past six years, Ms. Jacobs has provided curriculum research and evaluation for several TERC projects including the middle grades *National Geographic Kids Network*; *Classroom Feederwatch*; and *Science That Counts in the Workplace*, a curriculum that integrates challenging science subject matter with workplace and community contexts.

Amy Shulman Weinberg, coauthor and reviewer for some of the science and integrated curricula, is a senior research associate at TERC. Her work includes developing, reviewing, and evaluating science curricula. Along with Margaret Vickers, Ms. Weinberg produced three earlier guides for connecting science, mathematics, and social studies to workplace learning. She currently directs the evaluation of the National Science Foundation-funded *Science That Counts in the Workplace*.

Senta Raizen, project advisor and coauthor of the foreword, is director of the National Center for Improving Science Education. Ms. Raizen has been involved in science education for over three decades, and has led many projects aimed at curricular reform for the 1990s and beyond. She is coauthor of numerous books and reports on science education, including *Technology Education in the Classroom: Understanding the Designed World*, and several papers that provide a cognitive science perspective for experiential learning in school and the workplace.

Margaret Vickers, project advisor and coauthor of the foreword, was a senior scientist at TERC during this project. Dr. Vickers is director of the *Working to Learn* project, which promotes closer links between standards-based reform and school-to-career reform in part by developing new high school science curricula that integrate challenging science subject matter with workplace and community contexts. Dr. Vickers also is a coauthor of *Technology Education in the Classroom*.

Organizations

The National Center for Improving Science Education, established in 1987 and a division of WestEd since 1997, is a nonprofit organization dedicated to educational reform. The Center's mission is to promote change in state and local policies and practices in science curriculum, teaching, and assessment. To further this mission, NCISE conducts research and evaluation, and provides technical assistance.

TERC is a nonprofit organization dedicated to the improvement of mathematics, science, and technology teaching and learning. TERC works at the edges of current theory and practice to contribute to an understanding of learning and teaching, foster professional development, develop applications of new technologies, create curricula and other products, and support school reform.

Why Should 1 Mathematics and Science Connect to Workplace Contexts?

What are the advantages, the reasons, for connecting science, mathematics, and technology education to the workplace? In a nutshell, because the learning—and the teaching—of academic topics can be more effective, engaging, and powerful when it is connected with the daily job experiences of real people. Bringing the workplace to the classroom in these subjects will help educators meet some of their most prominent goals, as set forth by their professional communities.

- Science and mathematics educators will find that making such connections is a particularly appropriate way of developing "real-world" applications of theoretical topics that can engage students more effectively than traditional curricula, and a practicable way of integrating knowledge and subjects rather than teaching them in artificially separated domains.

- Educators in technical/vocational programs will also find that connecting their workplace-oriented curricula to the science and mathematics concepts that underpin them will better prepare students for what the modern workplace demands.

- Important goals of the national curriculum standards in mathematics, science, and technology education will be met, as will goals found in workplace performance standards for both general skills and those needed in specific industries.

- A connected curriculum meets the needs of all students, including those who are college-bound, by being consistent with what research tells us about how students learn most effectively and by better preparing them for their future in the workplace.

The chapter draws from the many existing articles and books that advance persuasive, detailed arguments for connecting school curricula to workplace contexts, although few of these make their case specific to the subjects of mathematics, science, or technology education. A particularly noteworthy source is *High School Mathematics at Work*, which includes essays by leading experts who explain in great detail how and why school mathematics instruction should be connected to workplace contexts

(MSEB, 1998). (*High School Mathematics at Work* is reviewed as a curriculum in chapter 4 because it contains some excellent workplace-connected tasks.) Because the purpose and unique contribution of the present resource guide is to review curriculum materials and include illustrative pages from them, the discussion here is limited to a very brief overview of the main reasons for making connections and the benefits to be gained from doing so. We refer the interested reader to the various sources cited herein for further information.

Definitions

We should begin by explaining what we mean by "workplace contexts" and by specifying the nature of the science, mathematics, and technology topics that can be connected to these contexts.

Workplace Context. We use the phrase "connecting to workplace contexts" as a convenient shorthand for referring to quite a variety of connections that can be used in curriculum materials: using workplace mathematics or science as a vehicle for explaining both the concepts and relevance of academic topics in the school curriculum, explaining some mathematics or science that is used in business or industry but seldom covered in the school curriculum, providing students with workplace experiences that use the science or mathematics studied in school, among many others. In all, we have identified six basic ways in which curriculum materials can connect to workplace contexts; these are presented and discussed in chapter 2. In researching this book, we looked for curriculum materials that connected to all types of jobs. While it was more common to find materials relating to occupations such as scientist, mathematician, doctor, technician, criminologist, and so on, we also found curriculum materials illustrating the use of science and mathematics in less technically oriented occupations such as firefighter, athletic coach, retail store manager, and building contractor, among others.

Mathematics, Science, and Technology Education Topics. All of the mathematics and science topics taught in school have workplace applications. Thus, the materials reviewed in this guide connect a great variety of mathematics and science topics to workplace contexts. The math ranges from general mathematics to calculus, with algebra and geometry being the most frequently addressed. All the sciences are also represented—albeit at different levels of specificity—including general life, earth, and physical sciences as well as biology, chemistry, and physics; more curricula emphasize life and/or physical sciences than earth sciences. We assume that the scientific, mathematical, or technological accuracy of these curricula is sound because our informal inspection of the materials bore this out; and because the developer teams included scientists, mathematicians, and engineers. In selecting curricula, we disregarded traditional grade-topic correlations. For example, if a product designed for high school students had good workplace connections but addressed general mathematics, it still was reviewed even though many high school students study more advanced mathematics topics. In general, however, most of the products reviewed here address grade-relevant mathematics and science topics (i.e., those taken by the majority of students in the targeted grades).

This guide also gives some attention to the applications of technology education in workplace contexts (see, for example, our reviews of the *Integrated Mathematics, Science, and Technology Project (IMaST)*; *Materials World Modules*; and *SciTeKS*). By "technology education," we mean the emerging school subject that includes such topics as the design processes used by engineers (Raizen et al., 1995). We also have included curricula that explain the design and use of technological devices (*PHYS-MA-TECH*), but we consider such topics to be as much a part of science and mathematics as they are of technology education.

We include an equal number of curricula for mathematics and science; only a few give substantial attention to technology education. Given this lack, we frequently omit the latter term, using instead the phrase "mathematics and science" to describe the curriculum's content. The order in which the terms "mathematics" and "science" are used in the text has no meaning unless indicated otherwise; generally we use the alphabetical ordering of "mathematics" followed by "science."

A Way to Meet the Goals of Science, Mathematics, and Technology Education

Engaging Students Through Real-World Curricula. Science educators have argued for decades that instruction should teach not only the *concepts* specified by the various scientific disciplines but also their *applications*. This viewpoint has become widely accepted in the science education community in recent years and has been incorporated in national curriculum standards. More recently, a similar view has been accepted by the mathematics education community.

In recent years, many curriculum materials have incorporated real-world contexts that seek to make mathematics and science more engaging to students by making the topics more relevant to their daily lives. Examples include teaching the chemistry involved in cooking, the physics behind children's toys, or the mathematics of quilt patterns. Providing these contexts certainly can help students *understand* mathematics and science concepts better than they would if they were grappling only with theoretical and abstract terms. How often these real-world contexts better *engage* students is a little more questionable. Although the contexts provided may be familiar to students, they are not necessarily of interest. Sometimes, too, the real-world contexts seem more contrived than authentic.

Explaining workplace uses of science, mathematics, and technology is an obvious but often unexplored way of making subject matter more relevant and useful to students' lives (Hurd, 1998; Richmond, 1998). What could be more real world than workplace contexts? And perhaps conveying the usefulness of school knowledge through jobs or careers that students might wish to pursue will engage them more than do some of the commonly presented "real-world" contexts. In this regard, MSEB (1998, p. 10) notes: ". . . although some students are aware that certain mathematics courses are necessary in order to gain entry into particular career paths, many students are unaware of how particular topics or problem-solving approaches will have relevance in *any* workplace [emphasis added]."

More Comprehensive Understanding Through Curriculum Integration. Another widely held, but seldom implemented, goal of science and mathematics education is to integrate knowledge to understand whole phenomena rather than isolated aspects. The natural things that occur around us are whole; the fields of study used to investigate them are human inventions and conventions. As more areas of specialization—and courses—are created to study the world, it becomes increasingly difficult for students to perceive the relationships among them. We argue here that a curriculum relating to workplace contexts helps many students make better sense of the world than would a traditional, exclusively theory-based approach.

All the reviewed curricula connect, or integrate, science and mathematics with workplace contexts. A few curricula also integrate school subjects: *IMaST* integrates mathematics, science, and technology; *PHYS-MA-TECH* combines physics, mathematics, and technology; and *Real World Mathematics Through Science, FUTURES*, and *Interactions* integrate mathematics and science.

A Way to Meet the Goals of School-to-Work, Tech Prep, Academic-Vocational Integration, and Similar Programs[1]

Need for Academic-Vocational Curriculum Integration. In the past, schools often had two major courses of study: an academic program for the college-bound students and a vocational program for the non-college-bound. The latter were composed of courses such as industrial arts, drafting, home economics, and the like. These courses are still prevalent, but their content and instructional approaches are evolving to produce graduates who can maintain the nation's economic competitiveness in the global marketplace.

When manufacturing was a principle component of U.S. industry, companies needed masses of workers who either were craftsmen or able to do repetitive tasks that did not require much use of mathematics or science. These occupations today have largely migrated to developing nations, and the U.S. economy today is based on service and information industries. Such industries require an entirely different set of knowledge and skills, including an understanding of mathematics and science, problem-solving ability, independent initiative combined with the ability to work collaboratively, communication skills, and so on. As a result, the private sector is calling for major changes in school mathematics and science to make it better reflect the realities of today's workplace. For example, a coalition of 13 business organizations managed by the National Alliance of Businesses just released *The Formula for Success: A Business Leader's Guide to Supporting Math and Science Achievement* (NAB, 1998). Business leaders and experts in mathematics and science education are investing their time to meet and discuss these issues, and both businesses and government are committing resources to address them (Institute on Education and the Economy, 1998; MSEB, 1995).

Traditional vocational programs are under pressure from business leaders, professional organizations, and policymakers to become as content rigorous as academic programs (AFT, 1996; Bottoms and Sharpe, 1996; NBPTS, 1997). In response, teachers of vocational courses such as metal shop, automotive repair, and home economics are striving to include the academic mathematics and science concepts that underpin their activities. A prevalent label used in the last few years to name this movement is "integrating academic and vocational education." Thus, using curricula that connect mathematics and science to workplace contexts addresses those needs of the vocational education

---

[1]We hope that educators who work with these programs will forgive some oversimplifications made here in order to keep our explanations brief. Additionally, throughout the book, we occasionally use the term "applied" as a general label to refer to all of these programs; some educators in these programs would differ with this descriptor, but we hope they will appreciate our need to use it as a convenience.

---

community arising from the changing requirements of the businesses and industries to which their programs are connected.

Goals of School-to-Work, Tech Prep, and Similar Programs. While vocational programs are still very common, some proponents of reform in applied courses of study are creating very different approaches such as school-to-work, tech prep, occupational clusters, and career academies. The features of these programs vary, and there is considerable overlap in the definitions used to describe them. Grubb (1995a and b) presents a comprehensive explanation and contrast of these approaches; Olson (1997) and Ryan and Imel (1996) provide good overviews of school-to-work programs, one of the more widespread trends since Congress passed the School-to-Work Opportunities Act in 1994. Tech prep programs typically are "2 + 2" courses of study, explicitly articulating the last two years of high school with two years at a community college, whereas the other programs usually are confined to high school. What all the programs share is a commitment to transforming the school curriculum to reflect workplace contexts, in part by either affording students opportunities for experiences "on location" or creating classroom activities that simulate workplaces as authentically as possible. Like vocational programs, these curricula should incorporate the academic mathematics and science that form the basis of workplace activities and thereby better equip workers to adapt procedures in the face of new circumstances.

Meeting National Curriculum and Workplace Performance Standards

The National Mathematics and Science Curriculum Standards. The curriculum standards documents issued in recent years do not specifically call for connecting school learning to workplace contexts. Undoubtedly, however, making such connections can fulfill the standards' more general learning aims. All national curriculum standards in relevant academic subjects recommend "real-world" content—that is, illustrating the applications of concepts rather than just presenting theory. They also advocate hands-on activities. Further, the following statements of the standards' developers reflect strong recognition of the fact that school curricula must change to meet changing workplace demands for mathematics and science knowledge.

> Traditional notions of basic mathematical competence have been outstripped by ever-higher expectations of the skills and knowledge of new workers; new methods of production demand a technologically competent work force. . . . Although mathematics is not taught in schools solely so students can get jobs, we are convinced that in-school experiences should reflect to some extent those of today's workplace (NCTM, 1989, pp. 3-4). Scientific literacy is of increasing importance in the workplace. More and more jobs demand advanced skills, requiring that people be able to learn, reason, think creatively, make decisions, and solve problems. . . . A goal that underlies the National Science Education Standards is to educate students who are able to increase their economic productivity through the use of the knowledge, understanding, and skills of the scientific literate person in their careers (NRC, 1996, pp. 1, 13).

Chapter 3 discusses the extent to which the reviewed curricula are consistent with the national mathematics and science standards. A few of the curricula reviewed in this guide refer additionally or alternatively to the science or mathematics standards of particular states.

Workplace Performance Standards. Educators need to be aware of two other kinds of standards that bear on how school curricula should connect to workplace contexts. At the U.S. Department of Labor, in collaboration with the U.S. Department of Education, the Secretary's Commission on Achieving Necessary Skills (SCANS) in 1991 released *What Work Requires of Schools: A SCANS Report for America 2000*. The report lays out the kinds of skills all employees will need in contemporary workplaces: obtaining information, understanding and using systems, selecting and using technology, developing interpersonal skills (working with others), and organizing and allocating resources. Several of the curricula reviewed in this guide specifically indicate how they address these general workplace skills in the context of science and mathematics instruction.

Building on SCANS, the Department of Education funded efforts by groups of particular industries to develop voluntary industry skill standards for agricultural biotechnology technicians, automotive technicians, grocery workers, and over a dozen others. Unfortunately, the development of these skill standards occurred independently of the development of the national academic content standards for schools (Bailey, 1997, 1998). This may partly explain why the industry skills standards concentrate on descriptions of job functions but generally fail to outline the mathematics or science these workers should know. One notable exception is the chemical technician standards developed by the American Chemical Society (Hofstader and Chapman, 1997) which do explicitly and extensively detail the chemical knowledge and processes that technicians must know and perform. If all skill standards had been similarly prepared, teachers would have been able to use these documents as another tool to identify and establish links between school curriculum and various kinds of workplaces.

Addressing Global Curriculum Trends

To the extent that connecting mathematics and science to workplace contexts takes hold in the United States, the nation will be addressing an international trend. From case studies of science and mathematics curricula conducted by researchers in 13 countries, Black and Atkin (1996) found that the clearest discernible international curriculum trend was an effort to make school science and mathematics education more practical, with connections to students' everyday lives. In this regard, the connection of workplace contexts to academic subject matter is being addressed around the world, and many countries are consequently struggling with how to better connect the school curriculum to the workplace. Some countries have long-standing traditions of devoting substantial resources to workplace-oriented programs but see a need to revamp them to adjust to changes in national and global economies. Other countries have not previously devoted much effort on the matter and now are worried that their school curricula are so out of step with workplace needs that they must devise substantial new initiatives.

Thus, insights from abroad could be illuminating to any U.S. state or district, regardless of where it is in its thinking on how to make its school curricula connect to workplace contexts (Gaskell and

Hepburn, 1997; Jones, 1997; McFarland and Vickers, 1994; Stern, Bailey, and Merritt, 1997; Stern and Wagner, 1999; Welzel, 1995).

Meeting the Needs of All Students

Connecting science and mathematics to workplace contexts is consistent with what research has revealed about how students learn. Further, educators need to provide all students—including the college-bound—with knowledge of workplace contexts, because every student will sooner or later enter the world of work.

Workplace Connections Foster Student Learning. MSEB (1998, p. 11) notes that: "The power of using workplace problems to teach mathematics lies not so much in motivation, for no context will motivate all students. The real power is in connecting to students' thinking." Raizen (1994, 1995), Harwell and Blank (1997), and many others have written extensively on the research base for linking learning and work. Knowledge is best gained through experience, not through theory and memorization. Students should not just *know* science and mathematics; they should be able to *do* science and mathematics. While school science and mathematics activities typically lean toward prescribed laboratories and exercises, workplace problems usually are open-ended investigations with multiple solution paths; these are experiences that not only reflect the way the real world works, but also that better reflect the type of learning called for—not coincidentally—by the national curriculum standards.

***All* Students Need to Understand Workplaces.** The workplace has changed dramatically, and traditional mathematics and science instruction will increasingly fail to prepare students for the workplace, whether they enter it after high school, college, or graduate school. It is commonly accepted that students who will go directly into the workforce upon graduation from high school could benefit from a school curriculum that makes connections to workplace contexts. However, there is hesitation to offer such curricula to college-bound students, despite strong arguments for doing so.

For example, in the course of the interviews undertaken for this book, we spoke to the vice president for research of a prominent chemical manufacturing firm. This executive complained that his company was having to invest heavily in training *doctoral* graduates in chemistry because they do not have the knowledge or skills to perform their work effectively. They have almost no experience in thinking about applications of the sophisticated chemistry they have learned. Moreover, their academic research emphasized solitary, discipline-specific work in stark contrast to the collaborative, integrated work that is the mainstay of corporate research.

Even though a solely academic program can fail to fully prepare even some of the best mathematics and science students for their eventual occupation, some high school instructors are reluctant to provide college-bound students with a curriculum that makes connections to workplaces. Vickers and Steinberg (1998, p. 3) note the following: "One major barrier is the misperception—widely shared among many educators—that school-to-work programs are the latest attempt to provide an appropriate (if lesser) education for the 'non-college bound.'" In fact, Vickers and Steinberg (1998) report thatresearch by Jobs for the Future on 10 such programs found that they often accomplished the following:

- a higher college-going rate among their graduates than that of the district as a whole, and

- an increased number of students taking demanding science and mathematics courses while in school.

Bailey and Merritt (1997a and b) discuss similar findings from other research and provide examples of applied programs that teach academic skills and prepare students for college. In this regard, Vickers and Steinberg note:

> The evidence suggests that students are more willing and able to grapple with complex material when they are given the opportunity to construct and frame the knowledge as it connects to tangible activities and phenomena in the real world. Certainly some students might still be better at understanding difficult science texts or learning the terminology or formulas. But one of the lessons from successful school-to-work programs is that given work-related contexts for their learning, a much broader range of students seem able to participate successfully in science courses and conceive of themselves as capable of entering college programs and careers in technical and scientific areas (Vickers and Steinberg, 1998, p. 4).

Most of the curricula reviewed in this guide cannot claim to support such dramatic changes because they are not designed to be used in school-to-work programs. Nevertheless, they are a significant departure from traditional curricula and can provide teachers with innovative ideas for beginning or strengthening the connections between school science and mathematics and workplace contexts.

The Professional Rewards of Making Connections

While the reviewed curricula may help instructors move toward curriculum integration, dramatic change is more likely if teachers in different programs collaborate to share their complementary expertise. Academic and applied instructors have much to offer each other, but may not realize it. Many academic instructors have little familiarity with specific applications of mathematics and science in occupations because their own education did not include such connections. For their part, many teachers in applied programs have not had the opportunity in their preparation to learn the mathematical and scientific principles that underlie the tools and procedures used in workplace-oriented curricula. Thus, although the academic and applied education communities share an agenda to make the school curriculum more relevant to students' lives, they seldom communicate sufficiently to recognize this common ground or identify the relative strengths they could contribute to each others' efforts. We grant that there can be practical barriers to overcome; for one thing, academic and vocational teachers might not even be in the same school building. But these barriers should be overcome as these two communities begin to approach each other with respect for what the other knows, not criticism for what they do not know. Moreover, besides providing needed knowledge, collaboration can itself be a reward by breaking through the isolation felt by many U.S. teachers.

Of late, some professional organizations have fostered small but healthy attempts at cross-field collaboration. For example, the National Council of Teachers of Mathematics and the American Vocational Association established a joint committee in 1995 to explore collaboration. Also, as previously noted, the Mathematical Sciences Education Board recently published *High School Mathematics at Work* (1998). The Board Certification Standards for Vocational Education require that applied program teachers infuse academic content into their curriculum, in part by collaborating with academic teachers (NBPTS, 1997, pp. 24, 27). Perhaps in the near future, the next versions of academic content standards will require teachers to become familiar with some major applications of mathematics and science by collaborating with instructors in applied programs.

Six Ways That 2 Curriculum Materials Can Connect to Workplace Contexts

The curriculum materials reviewed in this guide connect to workplace contexts in a wide variety of ways; all of them are useful, with some connections being more conceptually rich (or stronger) than others. Table 2.1 describes the following six types of connections, which can be grouped by their relative strengths. The two strongest connections are:

- providing students with workplace experiences, and

- simulating workplace activities in the classroom.

Few nationally useful curricula go this far in connecting to workplaces. Two other strong ways of connecting are:

- adding mathematics, science, or topics found in the workplace to the school curriculum; and

- using workplace examples to explain subject matter.

The latter is the most common kind of connection found among the reviewed curricula. The last two ways of connecting are:

- illustrating how mathematics, science, or technology is used in different occupations; and

- obtaining information from workplaces.

These kinds of connections are important and useful, but not as conceptually rich or as difficult to develop or implement as the previous four types of connections. Table 2.2 shows the most prominent ways in which each of the guide's 23 reviewed curricula connect to workplace contexts. The remainder of this chapter describes these connections.

Table 2.1

Six Ways That Curriculum Materials Can Connect to Workplace Contexts

Type of Connection	Description
Providing students with workplace experiences	Students go to workplaces for structured learning experiences that are articulated with their classroom learning.
Simulating workplace activities in the classroom	Students simulate workplace activities in the classroom through hands-on investigations or procedures, or by writing business communications.
Adding workplace math, science, or technology topics to the school curriculum	The curriculum includes topics used in business and industry but not found in typical school courses.
Using workplace examples to illustrate math, science, and technology	The curriculum uses workplace contexts for student problems or describes workplace scenarios that illustrate the application of math, science, or technology concepts. The curriculum primarily includes paper-and-pencil problems or exercises.
Illustrating the math, science, and technology used in occupations	The curriculum includes paragraph-length (or longer) descriptions of how people specifically make use of mathematics, science, or technology in their work.
Obtaining information from workplaces	The curriculum encourages teachers to invite workers to the classroom or to have students obtain information by contacting businesses through letters, calls, or visits.

Table 2.2

Types of Workplace Connections Featured in Reviewed Curricula: Mathematics

Mathematics Curriculum	Provides workplace experiences	Simulates workplace activities	Adds workplace math/science/technology topics to curriculum	Uses workplace examples to illustrate math/science & technology	Illustrates the math/science & technology used in occupations	Obtains information from workplaces
CORD Algebra, Geometry		✓			✓	
Excursions in Real-World				✓		
FUTURES		✓		✓	✓	✓
High School Math at Work			✓	✓		
Interactions		✓		✓	✓	✓
Math for Bus./Ind.			✓	✓		
Math for Technology		✓		✓		
Mathemedia				✓		
MathNet		✓		✓		
Math Through Science			✓	✓	✓	
She Does Math				✓	✓	
Tools for Agricultural Math				✓		

Note: A checkmark indicates that the type of workplace connection is a noteworthy feature of the curriculum: the connection was prevalent in the product, or, alternatively, the connection might be infrequent but extensively elaborated in each instance. The absence of a checkmark conveys that the connection was absent, rarely present, or present frequently but very briefly in each instance.

Table 2.2 (continued)

Types of Workplace Connections Featured in Reviewed Curricula: Science and Integrated

Science Curriculum	Provides workplace experiences	Simulates workplace activities	Adds workplace math/science/technology topics to curriculum	Uses workplace examples to illustrate math/science & technology	Illustrates the math/science & technology used in occupations	Obtains information from workplaces
CORD Biology/Chemistry				✓	✓	✓
ChemCom			✓		✓	
Event-Based Science		✓	✓			
IMaST		✓	✓		✓	
Materials World Modules		✓	✓			
Offshore Oil Drilling			✓		✓	
PHYS-MA-TECH		✓				
Practical Exercises				✓	✓	
CORD Principles of Tech.				✓		
SciTeKS		✓			✓	
Working to Learn	✓	✓				

Note: A checkmark indicates that the type of workplace connection is a noteworthy feature of the curriculum: the connection was prevalent in the product, or, alternatively, the connection might be infrequent but extensively elaborated in each instance. The absence of a checkmark conveys that the connection was absent, rarely present, or present frequently but very briefly in each instance.

Providing Students With Workplace Experiences

Only one of the curricula reviewed gives students opportunities to learn at workplaces. Each Working to Learn unit provides students with three "Common Workplace Experiences," which are either full- or half-day sessions. These on-site experiences are located in three industries/environments found in most U.S. communities, thus permitting local implementation across the country: hospitals, heating and air conditioning companies, and bodies of water. Underlying these Workplace Experiences is a thorough and thoughtful instructional design, which raises them far above the level of simple field trips with vaguely defined learning purposes and activities that are all too often only weakly connected to classroom instruction. The Working to Learn Workplace Experiences include:

- advice for teachers on recruiting suitable workplace instructors,
- advice on collaborating with workplace instructors,
- classroom instruction that explicitly connects with students' workplace experiences,
- worksheets for students to complete during the workplace experiences, and
- both general guidance and explicit directions for workplace instructors.

Figure 2.1 illustrates the last point, exemplifying the kind of information that Working to Learn provides to prepare workplace instructors for a visit by listing and explaining:

- general expectations students bring to the workplace,
- specific learning objectives for the visit,
- knowledge students will already have learned in class before visiting as well as what they will learn in class after the visit,
- equipment and materials the workplace instructor will need, and
- an overview of the learning activities the workplace instructor should carry out.

Further illustrations of the approach taken, and guidance provided, by Working to Learn are shown in the sample pages accompanying our review in chapter 5. These contain the specific directions the workplace instructor receives for conducting each learning activity during the Workplace Experience (pp. 234-236). Part of the worksheet students complete during the workplace activities is shown on p. 237; page 233 shows, in part, the classroom learning that would prepare students for the Workplace Experience.

We certainly found curricula other than Working to Learn that incorporate student experiences in the workplace. The school-to-work, tech prep, and other applied curriculum programs in the United States have, during this decade, developed hundreds—many of them, thousands—of curriculum materials providing students with workplace experiences. As noted in chapter 1, however, we did not include these materials in this guide because they (1) are typically linked to particularly local industries or businesses that are not accessible for most teachers around the country, and/or (2) do not include sufficient implementation instructions for teachers other than the developers to readily use them. In contrast, Working to Learn ably surmounts both of these limitations.

Figure 2.1 – Providing Students With Workplace Experiences: Example From Working to Learn Cardiovascular Unit

COMMON WORKPLACE EXPERIENCE

2

HEMATOLOGY LABORATORY SUPERVISOR GUIDELINES

The students who will visit your department are studying the cardiovascular system. While the students are in your department, they should gain direct experiences that will help them understand what their blood is composed of, what the cells in the blood do, what tests are performed on blood samples, and how blood disorders are diagnosed. Because these are such large topics, consider focusing on the anemias rather than discussing blood disorders "in general." The students are being asked to understand the logic of diagnosis, rather than "cover" a wide range of different blood disorders in a superficial way. As you work with the students, try to illustrate what you are teaching them by using examples based on the anemias.

Many of the students you will meet are involved in internships in your hospital. You may want to find out where these students are working, so that you can call on them to contribute their knowledge during this session.

WHAT STUDENTS WANT FROM YOU

Research conducted during the development of this curriculum focused on what students thought of work-based learning and what they valued most about their workplace visits.*

- Students were really positive about learning at work: to them, work was "real," in contrast with school; the learning exercises in school often seemed contrived.

- Students loved being with "really smart, friendly people in workplaces, people who are so enthusiastic about what they do that you want to learn from them."

---

* Felicia Hayes, a graduate student at the University of Massachusetts, conducted ethnographic interviews with students and offered these insights into their thinking.

WORKING TO LEARN   155

Figure 2.1 – Continued

- Some students were surprised when they found that what they were doing in the workplace corresponded with what they were doing at school—they thought this was just an coincidence, rather than something planned. Talk with students about *why* their workplace experiences match their classroom lessons on the cardiovascular system.

- Students worried when they observed something, or were told to do something, but didn't really understand what was going on. They were quite anxious when they felt their questions were not welcomed. Encourage students to ask questions. Allow time to discuss their concerns, unsolved puzzles, and requests for more information.

OBJECTIVES

The hospital experience should help the students to:

- Learn what kind of work is done in the hematology laboratory, who does the work, and why it is important;

- Learn to identify the key components of the blood by examining slides of appropriately stained blood smears;

- Become aware of the proper safety and collection procedures used in handling blood;

- Observe while a hematocrit test is performed on a blood sample;

- Take a tour in which you show them how blood specimens are collected, visit the specimen drop-off area and the laboratory, and find out how data on each blood sample are entered into the computer;

- Become familiar with the procedures the department follows in collecting blood samples and conducting a complete blood count;

- Be able to describe and recognize some of the general, observable symptoms associated with anemia; and

- Learn about the main types of anemia, and what tests are used to identify these.

CLASSROOM LEARNING

Before their visit to the blood clinic, the students have:

- Learned how the circulatory system works and "followed a drop of blood" throughout the body;

- Explored the role of the red blood cells in oxygen and carbon dioxide transportation; and

- Learned that the blood also transports nutrients, wastes, and heat throughout the body.

The students should know the following terms: plasma, platelet, red blood cell, white blood cell.

Figure 2.1 – Continued

When the students return to class after their visit to the hematology laboratory they will:

- Use a hemocytometer and carry out a red blood cell count;

- Examine blood smears on microscope slides;

- Discuss how a individual's vital signs change when he or she exercises, and interpret these changes in terms of what the blood is required to do;

- Read about how blood is formed and how dietary deficiencies and bone marrow disorders can lead to blood diseases;

- Learn to use data such as vital signs and blood counts to diagnose leukemia and different forms of anemia; and

- Return to the hospital to visit the EKG clinic.

MATERIALS

You will need to use the following materials when you meet with the students, so please try to assemble them in advance. (If your hospital has a school-to-work coordinator, you might ask for his or her help in getting materials together.)

1. Collect the handouts your hospital uses to explain anemia and leukemia to patients (make sure you have enough copies to distribute to each student).

2. Gather together some slides—use either microscope slides, or transparencies and a projector—to show:

    - a blood smear, in which all the elements of the blood can be identified;

    - a slide (or slides) showing different kinds of white blood cells; and

    - a slide (or slides) showing the difference between normal and sickle cell erythrocytes.

3. Be prepared to demonstrate a hematocrit test. If your laboratory no longer uses a spun-down 'crit, you will probably find the necessary equipment in the donor center or in an operating room. Have two samples of blood on hand (Tube A = normal and Tube B = anemic), a centrifuge, and several spare hematocrit tubes so that you can pass them around the group. (Dilute a sample of normal blood with plasma if you have no anemic blood on hand.)

    Quite possibly, your hospital now uses fully automatic hematology machines, therefore the centrifuge is not so common. From a teaching perspective, however, a spun-down sample is easier to interpret and is more visually compelling than a printout from a machine. If possible, try to obtain a centrifuge for this student visit.

Figure 2.1 – Continued

4. Make sure you have enough workplace sheets and clipboards so that each student has a set. You will also need colored pencils (the school should supply these).

5. Assemble at least two sets of the equipment used for preparing samples for a complete blood count—that is, clean specimen containers, complete blood count labels, #20 gauge needles, #22 gauge needles, lavender topped tubes, and several copies of an (anonymous) sample printout from a complete blood count examination.

STRUCTURE OF THE VISIT

Students will carry clipboards with a series of questions that they need to answer during the day (see workplace sheet Student Questions).

To meet the objectives for this visit and maximize the students' learning, the day should be divided into three sessions:

- Presentation and discussion
- Laboratory tour (reorganize the class into small groups, if necessary)
- Final wrap-up and discussion

Allow at least 1 1/2 hours for the presentation and discussion, 1 hour for the laboratory tour, and about 45 minutes for the final wrap-up and discussion. Encourage students to ask questions at every stage of their visit. The school-to-work coordinator or the classroom teacher should work with you to decide on arrangements for assembling the students at the beginning of the day, having lunch, and signing off at the end of the day.

Suggested student activities for each session of the visit are described below. Review the workplace sheets before planning what you will do with the students. The activities are offered as guidelines, rather than as prescriptions. However, if you make changes, you will still need to make sure that the students can complete their workplace sheets within the time constraints.

ACTIVITIES

Be sure to schedule a conference room, or other meeting area, for both the presentation and discussion and the final wrap-up sessions. Arrange a tour around the hospital, so that the students will see how blood specimens are collected, how and where the laboratory tests are conducted, and how the data on each sample are entered into the computer.

Simulating Workplace Activities in the Classroom

In terms of making workplace connections, the next best thing a curriculum can do short of having students go to an actual workplace is to have students simulate actual workplace activities in the classroom.

The reviewed products falling within this category have students simulate workplace activities in three ways: (1) by conducting science or mathematics activities that workers perform; (2) by using engineering design principles; or (3) by practicing general workplace skills in science or mathematics contexts (e.g., business of mathematical information). (Note that, although solving paper-and-pencil problems is a common and important workplace activity, we assign this to another category—using workplace examples to illustrate math and science—in this typology of connections.) Several of the reviewed curricula use at least one of these simulation methods. Science Technology: Knowledge and Skills (SciTeKS) is the product that most extensively connects to the workplace in these ways; it makes use of all three simulation modes.

Conducting Scientific or Mathematical Workplace Activities. SciTeKS greatly relies on this simulation approach. Through multimedia, it provides simulations of workplace activities for the student featuring, on video, a step-by-step tour of the technical processes used in industries; and, on CD-ROM, interactive simulations of industrial processes. Also, SciTeKS laboratories require students to model industrial laboratory skills (see figure 2.2). MathNet has students perform such activities as building models of bridges to test the strength of their structural design and diagnosing electronics problems in automobiles (see sample pages included with our review, pp. 116, 119). Mathematics for Technology laboratories include workplace-relevant activities such as testing the structural strength of different geometrical designs, analyzing staircase specifications in different types of buildings, and using precision tools to make engineering measurements. PHYS-MA-TECH labs help students understand the mathematics and physics used in the design and operation of 45 technological devices such as burglar alarms, thermostats, lasers, bar codes, and centrifuges.

Two middle school curricula also have students simulate workplace activities, although the level of complexity is simplified to accommodate the younger students' knowledge and abilities. In each Event-Based Science module, students are assigned the roles and activities of the various professionals involved in the module's topic. In the "Earthquake!" module, for example, students become familiar with the activities of a geologist, chief of transportation, director of utilities, city planner, architect, and civil engineer (see sample page included with our review, p. 164). Similarly, in the Integrated Mathematics, Science, and Technology Project (IMaST), students carry out the activities used in various occupations (see, for example, the agricultural procedures included with our review, p. 173).

Using Engineering Design Principles. Disturbingly, but perhaps not surprisingly, typical science curricula ignore engineering. When referring to the kinds of work that use science, the school curriculum focuses on scientists and rarely references the millions of engineers in industry and government. Perhaps a main cause of this gaping omission is that science teachers typically are not exposed to engineering in their own education, since the higher education pathways for science and engineering majors are mostly separate. Consequently, science educators emphasize with their

Figure 2.2 – Simulations—Conducting Scientific/Mathematical Workplace Activities: Example From SciTeKS Polymer Research and Development Unit

---

Important Concepts, Processes and Skills For This Module

Science Concepts
When you finish this module, you should be able to *define and give examples of:*
- Polymer
- Polymer properties (density, viscosity, tensile strength, resistance to impact, temperature sensitivity, permeability)
- Relationship between polymer properties and uses
- Relationship between structure of polymers and their uses
- Common tests for polymer properties
- Chemical structure

Science Processes
When you finish this module, you should be able to:
- *Define* problems to be investigated
- *Generate* questions and hypotheses
- *Test* explanations
- *Use* models
- *Construct* a valid experimental test
- *Gather* and *record* data
- *Organize* data into charts and graphs
- *Analyze* data using graphs
- *Interpret* data
- *Arrive* at conclusions based on data
- *Communicate* results
- *Revise* testing procedures

 Multimedia Links

You will be able to practice a number of the tests and skills listed here through multimedia simulations. You will also work on developing these skills through your labwork and your research.

While you are building your knowledge of the polymer research and development process throughout the course of the module, you will find it useful to revisit the encyclopedia periodically to refresh your understanding of certain key terms and tests.

Laboratory Skills
When you finish this module, you should be able to:
- *Calibrate* and use a balance
- *Follow and devise* directions for an experimental test
- *Measure* viscosity, permeability, tensile strength, stress/strain, impact resistance, temperature sensitivity
- *Calibrate* an instrument for polymer testing
- *Follow* appropriate safety procedures
- *Prepare* samples
- *Practice* proper disposal procedures

Workplace Skills
When you finish this module, you should be able to:
- *Read and understand* a standard operating procedure
- *Follow* a standard operating procedure
- *Access* computers as necessary (including using the Internet)
- *Interpret* a flow diagram
- *Troubleshoot* testing problems
- *Keep* accurate records
- *Work cooperatively* with team members
- *Work* to meet customer needs
- *Communicate findings* to co-workers

students the steps of the scientific method—identify a problem, develop a hypothesis, test the hypothesis, and make conclusions—but do not mention the engineering design approaches that might more appropriately be brought to bear on many problems.

Figure 2.3 illustrates an engineering design approach used by Materials World Modules—also featured, to a lesser extent, in SciTeKS and ImaST—state the problem and design goals, write a design brief, build the design, test the design, evaluate the design, redesign, and implement the design. The first available module of World in Motion (see appendix A), developed by the Society of Automotive Engineers, engages middle-grade students in designing toys both to facilitate an understanding of the mathematics and science of gears, mechanical advantage, torque, etc.; and to provide experience with the engineering design process.

Practicing General Workplace Skills in a Science or Mathematics Context. The 1991–standards document, *What Work Requires of Schools: A SCANS Report for America 2000* (described further in chapter 1), sets forth (among others) a key worker literacy goal: the ability to communicate business information effectively, both in terms of reading and writing. Innumerable stories in the mass media and business periodicals decry the inability of new workers to communicate satisfactorily. Traditional mathematics and science curricula already help address this dilemma whenever they require students to document explanations of their solutions to extended problems, write laboratory reports, etc. These approaches do not, however, familiarize students with business communication of technical information.

In contrast, FUTURES, especially its new school-to-career edition, provides many opportunities to read and write mathematical or scientific information in the form of business communications (see sample page included with our review, p. 77). Each chapter of CORD's (Consortium for Occupational Research and Development) Algebra 1 and Geometry textbooks have one or two "Workplace Communications" sections, in which students are asked to read (most often) and/or write. An example with our review has students read and write a brief proposal (bid) to provide products (see p. 56). Each SciTeKS module has students perform scientific versions of general workplace skills such as establishing a time line, developing and writing a standard operating procedure, interpreting a process diagram, and troubleshooting a system. These activities are listed under "Workplace Skills" in the introduction to each SciTeKS module (see figure 2.2).

Adding Workplace Math and Science Topics to the School Curriculum

A few of the reviewed curricula include some mathematics or science that is used in business and industries but not found in typical school science and mathematics courses. For example, organic chemistry and materials chemistry are very large and growing components of U.S. industry—and, indeed, of the world we encounter in our daily lives—yet traditional U.S. chemistry texts give very little attention to organic chemistry and even less to materials science. Other countries' high school curricula give substantial attention to organic chemistry (Britton and Raizen, 1996.) Curricula that solidly address these topics are helping to prepare more scientifically literate students, graduates who

Figure 2.3 – Simulations—Using Engineering Design Principles: Example From Materials World Modules, Biodegradable Materials Module

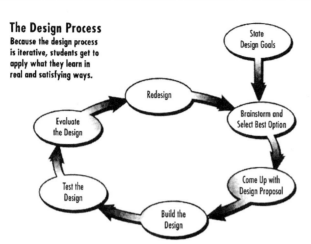

The Design Process
Because the design process is iterative, students get to apply what they learn in real and satisfying ways.

may produce designs that just meet the goals but offer other benefits such as incorporating low-cost materials or being easy to construct. Emphasize that all designs that meet the performance goals are successful. Each group of students can then present the particular benefits of their design.

Learning from the Design Process
In working on the Design Projects, students should not just focus on producing a successful design. They should also strive to understand how and why their design meets the stated goals and to show the rest of the class why their particular design is a good one. You can help students learn

from the Design Projects by reinforcing these objectives.

There are several other ways you can promote learning as students engage in the design process. First, you may wish to have students focus on experimentation when they work on the initial design and then have only the redesigned product subject to the formal design challenge or contest. This frees students to explore, because they won't be penalized if their initial design doesn't perform well. Second, encourage students to share ideas. Give students an opportunity to communicate the results from their initial designs before final designs are built. This lets

students reflect on other groups' designs as well as their own. Students may draw on another group's idea to come up with a modification of their first design. The more ideas students are exposed to, the more new ideas they will discover.

Designing for the Real World
Real-world designs are often a compromise of performance and cost, wrapped in a package that will appeal to the consumer. When students work on the Design Projects, they can incorporate such design constraints as cost, ease of construction, durability, environmental impact, and customer appeal. For their final report or presentation, they can prepare advertising campaigns or marketing plans for their products, or suggest new markets and new applications for the materials that they designed. Margin notes in the Teacher's Edition (often labeled Portfolio Projects) give suggestions on how to incorporate such real-world issues into the Design Projects.

127

will better understand the world around them and be familiar with many more chemical workplaces than students who take traditional high school chemistry.

Unusual Science Topics. Chemistry in the Community (ChemCom) devotes significant attention to organic chemistry in its units on "Petroleum" and "Understanding Food" (see the table of contents included with our review on p. 155 for more detailed topics). ChemCom also emphasizes another aspect of chemistry that traditional texts in the U.S. all but ignore, the chemical industry; some other countries build this into the chemistry curriculum (Britton and Raizen, 1996). Industrial chemistry is the subject of one of ChemCom's eight units. Additionally, it incorporates industrial chemistry in its other chapters as well (see sample page included with our review, p. 156).

Some other countries expect their high school graduates to know how their nations commercially produce chemicals that are major parts of their national commerce. Traditional U.S. chemistry textbooks seldom even consider such rigorous but practical topics because they are organized around a theoretical framework, even though many more industrial chemists are employed in this country than academic chemists. Addressing this gap, Materials World Modules educates students about another aspect of chemistry and other sciences that is prevalent in industry and our lives: modern materials such as biodegradable materials, biosensors, ceramics, composites, concrete, and polymers.

Chemistry for the Technologies (see appendix A) was developed by the state of South Carolina after it found no commercially available teaching resources focused on preparing students for occupations that require a knowledge of the technological aspects of chemistry—e.g., laboratory technicians in government or industry; process operators in chemical, textile, or paper plants; medical technologists; and forensic chemistry technicians. The curriculum's 14 chapters are scientifically challenging but, at the same time, are focused on industry-relevant topics such as viscosity of motor oils, recycling copper, esters, gas chromatography, and production of plastics and polymers. Like many industries, the curriculum emphasizes accurate and precise measurement, and an understanding of statistics.

Primarily through illustration of the science used in various occupations, Offshore Oil Drilling gives detailed explanations of the process and technology of how the industry drills for oil, something unlikely to be found in traditional science textbooks. About one-third of IMaST is devoted to technology, with modules covering such rarely addressed topics as "Developing and Using a Prosthetic Hand," "Understanding Technology Processes," "Design of Fluid and Electrical Systems," and "Investigating Types of Materials."

Unusual Mathematics Topics. Four of the reviewed mathematics curricula include math seldom found in traditional courses for grades 6-12. While Mathematics Applications for Business and Industry mostly covers topics commonly found in school mathematics, it also devotes one of its nine chapters to "Statistical Process and Control." Figure 2.4 gives an example from this chapter, wherein manufacturing industries use mathematics to ensure quality control of the amounts of products they deliver. The curriculum enhances the authenticity of its workplace connections by introducing terminology commonly used in such industrial processes.

Most of the mathematics in the 14 extended problems in High School Mathematics at Work would be familiar to secondary mathematics teachers; some problems, however, feature less typical mathematics. Students use elegant yet sophisticated graphical analysis for optimization problems like

Figure 2.4 – Adding Workplace Math/Science Topics to the School Curriculum: Example From Mathematics Applications for Business and Industry Statistical Process and Control

> **Scenario 2: Soda Bottling**
> *Topics: process, product, variation, capability*
>
> A machine at a bottling plant fills aluminum cans with soda. The cans of soda are advertised as containing 12 ounces each.

1. What inputs do you think are used in the process of filling soda cans?

2. What is the output of the filling process?

3. When you buy a can of soda do you expect there to be exactly 12 ounces of soda in the can? Explain why or why not.

4. Do you think that all the cans filled during this process will contain exactly the same amount of soda? Explain why or why not.

No two cans of soda can ever have exactly the same amount of soda in them. There may be a large difference or a difference so small that it can not even be measured.

> The fact that individual measurements will have differences is called **variability**.

6-2

Figure 2.4 – Continued

There are many factors that contribute to variation in a process - the employees, the machines and materials used, and the measurements that are taken- these are all factors that affect the performance of a process. The factors that contribute to variation in a process are classified as either chance causes or assignable causes. Chance causes of variation in the soda filling process could be the quality of the machine being used, or the ability of the employees operating the machine. Assignable causes are when a part of the machine has broken or when the machine is out of adjustment.

> **Chance causes** are natural variations that are expected in any process. They occur in a random manner. **Assignable causes** of variability are variations that are due to unexpected occurrences in a process. They are unpredictable and occur non-randomly.

To produce products that are consistently within an expected range, manufacturers want to eliminate all causes of assignable variation.

> A stable process has only chance causes of variation. A stable process is called **in control**. An unstable process has assignable causes of variation. This type of process is called **out of control.**

If the filling process is out of control the cans may be over-filled or under-filled. The quality control inspectors at the plant must examine the product periodically to determine if the process is operating as specified.

Suppose that four cans of soda are sampled from the production line each hour and the volume of soda in each can is measured. Some sample values are listed below.

Measurements in fluid ounces

Sample number	Can 1	Can 2	Can 3	Can 4
1	12.12	12.15	12.08	11.97
2	12.10	12.13	12.12	12.10
3	12.03	12.25	12.09	12.06
4	12.09	12.06	12.19	12.10
5	12.16	11.99	12.08	12.17
6	12.08	12.11	12.17	12.08
7	12.12	12.09	11.97	12.11
8	12.13	12.13	12.12	12.04
9	12.13	12.19	12.10	12.07
10	12.09	12.13	12.01	11.99

6-3

Figure 2.4 – Continued

You can see that the amount of soda in the cans varies. How much variation are we willing to accept?

> The **capability** of a process is a measure of the amount of variation that we are willing to accept as normal. Capability is the ability of the process to produce a product that meets specifications.

5.   Draw a histogram of all the sample values. Does it look approximately normal?

6.   Use the statistical functions on your calculator to calculate the mean and standard deviation of the sample volumes.

7.   Because finding the mean and standard deviation this way is very time consuming, even with a calculator, technicians in factories use a simpler method.

     a.   Begin by calculating the mean and range of each sample.

Sample number	Can 1	Can 2	Can 3	Can 4	$\bar{x}$	R
1	12.12	12.15	12.08	11.97		
2	12.10	12.13	12.12	12.10		
3	12.03	12.25	12.09	12.06		
4	12.09	12.06	12.19	12.10		
5	12.16	11.99	12.08	12.17		
6	12.08	12.11	12.17	12.08		
7	12.12	12.09	11.97	12.11		
8	12.13	12.13	12.12	12.04		
9	12.13	12.19	12.10	12.07		
10	12.09	12.13	12.01	11.99		

6-4

determining the efficiency of ambulance runs, the ideal placement and response rules for multiple elevators in an office building, and best timing sequence for traffic signals on a major thoroughfare.

Two modules of the 10 in Real-World Mathematics Through Science address mathematics one would be unlikely to find in typical middle school mathematics courses. The "Secret Codes" module devotes its several weeks of instruction to the mathematics of cryptology (see this module's table of contents with our review on p. 123). Admittedly, not too many students will later be employed as spies, but studying the mathematical principles underlying code work is very interesting. Students are similarly exposed to some of the mathematics and science used in law enforcement in the module "Classifying Fingerprints."

The developers of ThinkSmart (see appendix A) have, after studying many industries, identified the 70 mathematics concepts they claim are used in solving 90 percent of workplace problems. Although most of these concepts only depend upon arithmetic and other simple mathematics operations, some of these industrial mathematics procedures are rarely found in the school mathematics curriculum. For example, an entire videotape and accompanying lesson are spent on five optimization techniques used to determine the best route for fire trucks in traveling between two points in an urban setting.

Using Workplace Examples to Illustrate Math and Science

The curricula in this category illustrate workplace connections to science or mathematics topics in two ways: (1) by using workplace contexts for student problems and/or (2) by describing workplace scenarios that illustrate the application of science or mathematics concepts.

CORD's Applications in Biology/Chemistry and Principles of Technology curricula use workplace scenarios to illustrate applications of concepts. Figure 2.5 is an introductory page of the Principles of Technology unit on "Waves and Vibrations." It details how an understanding of vibrations and waves is important to the operation of ships, and thereby helps motivate students to learn the material to come. Similarly, in a workplace scenario called "Cool Rescue" (see the sample page included with our review, p. 146), Applications of Biology/Chemistry describes the actions paramedics would take to treat a patient, and thus provides a workplace application of many concepts students have studied: respiration, evaporation, humidity, thermal insulation, homeostasis, metabolism, and circulation.

The most common connection mechanism used by the reviewed curricula is, by far, to put scientific or mathematics problems in the context of workplaces. They use a variety of specific approaches to do this, as demonstrated on the sample pages included with our reviews of all the mathematics curricula and the following science curricula: Applications in Biology/Chemistry, Practical Exercises in Applying Knowledge, and Principles of Technology. As but one example, an extended problem in Excursions in Real-World Mathematics requires students to determine how much pesticide to use on a field of specific but irregular dimensions; students are then asked to determine the concentration of pesticide required (see Figure 2.6).

Given the plethora of uses of this type of connection, it is helpful to further categorize them in terms of the relative strength of their workplace connections (see table 2.3). One way to appraise the strength of workplace connections is to determine whether the overall organization of the curriculum

Figure 2.5 – Using Workplace Examples to Illustrate Math/ Science: Example from Principles of Technology, Waves and Vibrations

A TECHNICIAN TALKS ABOUT WAVES AND VIBRATIONS...

I'm a technician on an ocean-going ship. My job is to maintain the ship's engine-room equipment. My ship is powered by large, gas-turbine engines. The gas-turbine engines are sort of like jet engines. They have huge, rotating fans with many blades. These fans are very sensitive to vibrations. Vibrations can affect alignment because there's only a small clearance between the blades and the housing.

Vibrations always create problems on an ocean-going ship. The effect of waves on the hull of the ship and the vibrations caused by propeller movement in the water are felt throughout the ship. As a result, the whole structure throbs with vibrations. The gas turbines can't tolerate these vibrations. That's because vibrations can cause misalignment and damage to the turbines.

The solution to controlling damaging vibrations is to isolate them from the gas-turbine power units. To do this, we mount the gas-turbine power units on rigid frames. We secure the frames to the deck with "absorbing pads." These rubber/composition pads are similar to motor mounts on an automobile. The pads absorb—or "damp out"—the vibrations. The pads "block" the vibrations from entering the frame of the gas turbine. These pads are checked often. And pads are changed whenever they start to show some wear.

Other parts of the ship also have equipment that requires damping devices. The metal lathe, milling machine, grinder and other on-board machine-room equipment are mounted on absorbing pads—like the gas turbines—to isolate unwanted vibrations.

Vibrations can destroy solder joints and cause open circuits in electronic equipment. This would be very bad for navigational devices—like the compass and radar units that we need to operate in bad weather and darkness. So damping pads or shock absorbers are built into the equipment, or they are added when the equipment is mounted on the ship. All sensitive electronic equipment on board is classified as "industrial grade, shockproof."

There are many other kinds of equipment on the ship. Some of them rotate when they operate. Vibrations can cause a short service

life on ball bearings in this equipment. Maintaining the engine-room equipment is important work on this ship. And knowing about waves and vibrations helps me do my job better.

HOW DO WAVES AND VIBRATIONS AFFECT OUR LIVES?

It's a quiet day in southern California. But along a crack in the earth called the "San Andreas Fault," there's a lot going on. Below ground level, huge slabs of rock have been subjected to large forces for a long period of time. Now they suddenly slip past one another, releasing large amounts of energy. The earth's crust moves with a jolt, sending a "ground wave" traveling through the earth's crust. Thousands of miles away, a team of scientists and technicians observe the effect of the ground wave on their seismograph. A seismograph is a recording device that traces out curves. The "swing" of the curves indicates the strength of ground waves. (See Figure 9-1.)

Fig. 9-1 Technicians study the response of a seismograph to ground waves.

What the technicians and scientists are witnessing is an earthquake. The huge ground wave (earthquake) can destroy or damage buildings, cause landslides—or even create tidal waves in oceans. Detection and analysis of the ground wave on a seismograph tell scientists a lot about the location and strength of the earthquake.

Earthquakes and ground waves are not the only types of waves and vibrations that affect our lives. Operating powerful compressors in the basement of a research lab may cause unwanted vibrations in a laser lab on the first

Figure 2.6 – Using Workplace Examples to Illustrate Math/Science: Example From Excursions in Real-World Mathematics

Mixing Herbicide for Field Application

In order to eliminate unwanted plants, gardeners, farmers, homeowners, and many others use chemicals called herbicides. For example, many people choose to remove dandelions and clover in their lawns using herbicides. Farmers use herbicides in fields to ensure that the food or seed product they intend to grow is protected from invasion by undesirable weeds.

1. Suppose Ron wants to spray an eight foot by one hundred foot strip of a field with a certain 75 WDG herbicide. A 75 WDG herbicide is comprised of 75% active ingredients and 25% inert ingredients. The active ingredients eliminate unwanted plants. The inert ingredients prevent the dry herbicide from packing and hardening. A WDG herbicide is purchased in granular form and needs to be mixed with water before application. A WDG (water displaceable granules) herbicide is not absorbed into the water like sugar, but rather floats in the water like flour.

The instructions accompanying this herbicide state that the desired application amount for your field is 0.031 pounds of active ingredient per acre $\left(\dfrac{\text{lb ai}}{\text{acre}} \right)$. (Note: the abbreviation for active ingredient is, for example, "g ai" meaning grams active ingredient.) The documentation accompanying your spraying equipment recommends that when using 75 WDG you need 20 gallons of water to spray an entire acre. How much active ingredient is needed to spray the field strip? How much of the dry herbicide (75 WDG) is needed? How much water is needed?

2. The field sketched below was measured using a wheel measuring tool (with a counter like a speedometer) precise to the foot. (Note: the sketch is not to scale.) The field (not including the area surrounding the house) must be sprayed with a solution of 50 gallons of water and 2.5 grams of a 35 WDG herbicide. How much active ingredient is being applied? What is the application concentration per acre? How many gallons per acre should you use? Are your results reasonable?

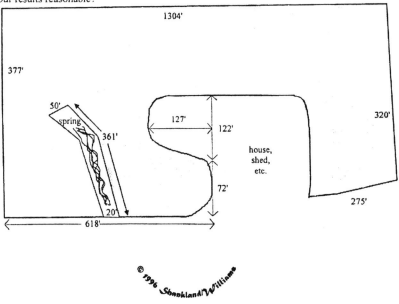

makes use of workplace contexts or uses a traditional mathematics and science topic organization. Thus, for example, chapter titles in CORD's Algebra 1 include "Integers and Vectors" and "Quadratic Functions," whereas the problems of Excursions in Real-World Mathematics have titles like "Navigating in a Fog" and "Machining Parts of Airplanes." Curricula such as the latter are generally, but not necessarily always, more strongly connected to workplace contexts than the former.

In appraising the strength of the curriculum's workplace connections, it is also helpful to look at the extent and ways in which the curriculum uses workplace contexts. Are workplace contexts the main vehicle for explaining subject matter concepts; or is the treatment traditional, with workplace

Table 2.3

**Relative Strength of Workplace Connections
in Curricula Using Workplace Examples**

Curricula with extensive connections (all curricula are mathematics)	Curricula with less extensive connections (mathematics, followed by science)
Excursions in Real-World Mathematics	CORD Algebra 1, Geometry
FUTURES	MathNet
High School Mathematics at Work	Agriculture-Based Math
Interactions	CORD Biology/Chemistry
Math for Business and Industry	Practical Exercises in Applying Knowledge
Mathematics for Technology	CORD Principles of Technology
Mathemedia	
Real-World Mathematics Through Science	
She Does Math!	

contexts used in a secondary role—for example, to illustrate applications of the topics? Mathemedia, for instance, uses an overall organization involving mathematics topics such as "Fractions" and "Area and Volume"; but almost every page uses workplace contexts to explain the mathematics, as shown in figure 2.7.

Illustrating the Math and Science Used in Occupations

Traditional mathematics and science textbooks have increasingly been including information about careers that use mathematics, science, or technology. While there may be quite a bit of this information spread throughout the text, each instance is usually brief, more often than not limited to name of the job, education required, and perhaps a few sentences describing job activities. Some career information is limited to photographs of people doing their jobs, with a short caption naming the occupation or describing the activity. Such kinds of surface information are included in many of the curricula cited in table 2.1 as using this type of connection.

Figure 2.7 – Using Workplace Examples to Illustrate Math/Science: Example From Mathemedia

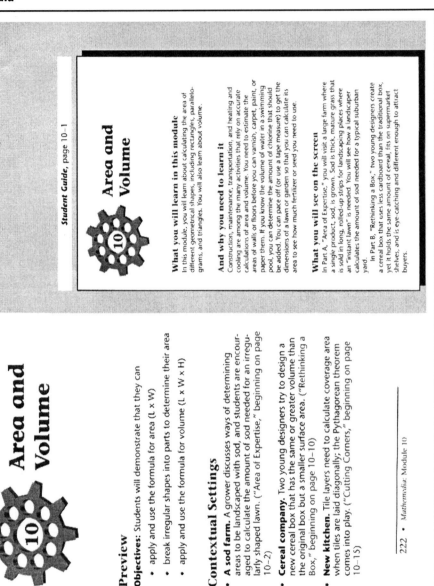

Area and Volume

Preview

Objectives: Students will demonstrate that they can

- apply and use the formula for area (L x W)
- break irregular shapes into parts to determine their area
- apply and use the formula for volume (L x W x H)

Contextual Settings

- **A sod farm.** A grower discusses ways of determining areas to be landscaped with sod, and students are encouraged to calculate the amount of sod needed for an irregularly shaped lawn. ("Area of Expertise," beginning on page 10–2)

- **Cereal company.** Two young designers try to design a new cereal box that has the same or greater volume than the original box but a smaller surface area. ("Rethinking a Box," beginning on page 10–10)

- **New kitchen.** Tile layers need to calculate coverage area when tiles are laid diagonally; the Pythagorean theorem comes into play. ("Cutting Corners," beginning on page 10–15)

222 • *Mathemedia:* Module 10

Student Guide, page 10–1

Area and Volume

What you will learn in this module

In this module, you will learn about calculating the area of different geometrical shapes, including rectangles, parallelograms, and triangles. You will also learn about volume.

And why you need to learn it

Construction, maintenance, transportation, and heating and cooling are among the many activities that rely on accurate calculations of area and volume. You need to estimate the areas of walls or floors before you can varnish, carpet, paint, or paper them. If you know the volume of water in a swimming pool, you can determine the amount of chlorine that should be added. You can pace off (or use a tape measure) to get the dimensions of a lawn or garden so that you can calculate its area to see how much fertilizer or seed you need to use.

What you will see on the screen

In Part A, "Area of Expertise," you will visit a large farm where a single product, sod, is grown. Sod is thick, mature grass that is sold in long, rolled-up strips for landscaping places where an "instant lawn" is needed. You will see how a landscaper calculates the amount of sod needed for a typical suburban yard.

In Part B, "Rethinking a Box," two young designers create a cereal box that uses less cardboard than the traditional box, yet it holds the same amount of cereal, fits on supermarket shelves, and is eye-catching and different enough to attract buyers.

However, most of the noted curricula additionally include descriptions about how various professionals make use of mathematics, science, or technology in their work. The supplementary resource She Does Math! is entirely devoted to this purpose. Each of the 33 authors describes her education and career history on about a page, and then presents several pages containing mathematics problems she encounters in her work, as illustrated in the sample pages with our review (pp. 130-133). The two video series FUTURES and Interactions spend much of their time showing how various professionals use mathematics or science in their work (see the synopsis of a FUTURES episode on p. 74 of our review). The fact that both series name their episodes according to the professions highlighted indicates their attention to this type of connection.

ChemCom has 20 "Chemistry at Work" pages in which profiles of chemists include details about the science used in their work. In figure 2.8, the ChemCom profile of a metallurgist presents the specifics of the chemistry she uses in extracting gold. Applications in Biology/Chemistry has about 10 similar profiles in each of its units (see sample page included with our review, p. 147). The 10 Real-World Mathematics Through Science modules contain one or two "Career Links" in each, which, in about one page, describe the mathematics or science used by various professionals (see sample page included with our review, p. 126). Describing the science used in jobs is a central characteristic of the 60 activities that comprise Practical Exercises in Applying Knowledge (see sample page included with our review, p. 204), but each treatment is substantially briefer than those found in the curricula described above. The mathematics, science, or technology used by professionals is briefly described in IMaST's many "Career Connections" (see sample pages included with our review, pp. 176-177). CORD's Algebra 1 and Geometry illustrate how mathematics is used in occupations, but takes something of a different tack. The table of contents for every chapter lists about 25 to 40 occupations and identifies those pages of the text that contain information relevant to them (see p. 54). And finally, the short, single unit Offshore Oil Drilling is included in this guide in part because it gives profiles of occupations in the oil industry such as drilling engineer, environmental/civil engineer, and mud extraction engineer (see sample page included with our review, p. 191). While the oil industry is a significant U.S. employer, few traditional curricula mention these occupations.

The curricula discussed thus far incorporate this information as a separately identifiable element, generally as some sort of career profile feature. In contrast, the entirety of each unit of SciTeKS and Working to Learn familiarizes students with the science used by wastewater treatment technicians, nurses, and so on.

Obtaining Information From Workplaces

Several products include various suggestions of businesses or professionals who can provide data or other information on the topics under study. These curricula encourage teachers to invite workers to the classroom or have students write letters to, visit, or call businesses. More than any other curriculum reviewed, CORD's Applications in Biology/Chemistry includes activities that involve contacting workplaces: about 25 sets of extension activities, to be conducted over the course of a school year, often require students to obtain information or data from area workplaces. An example of these activities, taken from the curriculum's Animal Processes unit, is shown in figure 2.9.

Figure 2.8 – Illustrating the Math/Science Used in Occupations: Example from ChemCom

CHEMISTRY AT WORK

All That's Gold Doesn't Glitter . . . Or Does It?

Did you ever wonder where the metal comes from that makes up a high school gold ring—or who was responsible for finding the material in the first place? **Sandy Haslem** might have helped. She's a metallurgist with Barrick Goldstrike, a mining company in Elko, Nevada, that finds and recovers gold.

It's not an easy job. The concentration of gold in the earth's crust is only about 15 parts per billion (ppb). But by using a knowledge of chemistry and highly efficient recovery methods, Sandy and her coworkers can extract gold from material that contains as little as 0.47 grams of gold per metric ton (1,000 kg)!

One method of gold recovery is "heap leaching." Material thought to contain gold is stacked on an impermeable pad, and a dilute basic solution containing cyanide ions (CN^-) is dripped down through the heap. A gold cyanide complex, $[Au(CN)_2]^-$, forms with any gold atoms that it contacts:

$$4\,Au + 8\,CN^- + 2\,H_2O + O_2 \rightarrow 4\,[Au(CN)_2]^- + 4\,OH^-$$

Later, the gold is recovered through a process called electrowinning, which uses an electrical current to transfer the gold onto steel wool. Finally, technicians heat the gold-plated steel wool to liquify the gold, and pour the liquid gold into bar molds.

Sandy supervises lab employees who research and develop safe and economical methods for recovering gold. Sandy and her team also monitor a mine's processing operations and make sure that the environment isn't degraded as a result of those operations.

Some Questions To Ponder . . .

Your class ring is not 100% pure gold. Pure gold is very soft, so it is mixed with other metals (copper, silver, nickel, or zinc) to increase its hardness and durability. The more of the other metal added, the lower the karat value. Pure gold is 24 karat. Your ring is probably 12 karat, or about 50% gold.

Because of the specialized processes it uses, Sandy's company is able to profitably recover gold from fairly low-grade ore—that is, ore containing extremely small traces of gold. A more common ore grade for the gold mining industry is 1.6 grams of gold per metric ton of ore.

1. If a class ring has a mass of 11 g, how many metric tons of ore were processed in order to produce the gold to make the ring?

2. What is the value of the gold in the class ring, if the market value for gold is $14 per gram? (You may want to try using today's actual price for gold, available in the business section of many newspapers).

3. Gold miners in the last century looked for gold nuggets. What property of gold allowed them to be able to find it in this form?

Photograph courtesy of Barrick Goldstrike

141

taken from the curriculum's Animal Processes unit, is shown in figure 2.9.

FUTURES also looks to the workplace as a source of information. For example, the Teacher's Guide to the "Personal Communication" videotape makes specific suggestions for bringing an engineer from a mobile phone company into the class, and for having students visit an electronics store and a telephone switching station (see sample page included with our review, p. 75). Similarly, the "Math at Home" activity in the Teacher's Guide for the "Fashion Industry" videotape of Interactions asks students to visit clothing and fabric stores to determine and compare the prices of buying ready-made clothes versus making their own (see sample page included with our review, p. 89).

In all of these curricula, the connections are incorporated as optional activities (whether explicitly labeled as such or not): that is, students will be able to understand a majority of the curriculum's content without making these workplace contacts. However, even if teachers and students decide not to exercise these options, just reading the suggestions can still help teachers and students realize which businesses and professions are connected to particular topics in mathematics, science, or technology, and also, perhaps, how they are connected.

Activities by Occupational Area

General

Occupational Hazard—Temperature

- Make a list of occupations in which people have to cope with temperature extremes. What precautions are routinely taken by these workers to prevent hypothermia or hyperthermia?

Planning for a Race

- People who coordinate and plan popular racing events such as running marathons and cycle races have to consider the effects of heat and/or cold.

- Contact the sponsors of such a race or other sporting event in your region or town and find out what measures are taken to prevent hypothermia or hyperthermia during popular races.

Agriscience

Protecting Livestock from Heat and Cold

- Choose an animal that commonly experiences summer heat or winter cold on a farm or ranch. Use a livestock handbook or animal husbandry manual to find out what

Applications in Biology / Chemistry

Figure 2.9 – Continued

precautions must be taken to make sure the animal does not become overexposed.

Health Occupations

Temperature Fluctuations

- Contact a nurse or a paramedic and find out how the body's normal mechanisms for temperature control can be disrupted when a person goes into shock after an injury or emotional trauma. Find out how shock is treated.

- Write a brief report in your *ABC* notebook about the effect of shock on body-temperature control.

- Find out how oral, rectal, axillary, and tympanic (eardrum) temperatures are measured. How are these recorded in patient charts, and what temperature is considered normal for each site?

Family and Consumer Science

Microfiber

- Write to a representative of the textile industry for information on a new cloth called microfiber. Give a presentation to the class that includes:

  - what its characteristics are,

  - how it helps the wearer retain or get rid of body heat, and

  - why it functions the way it does.

Clothing to Fight Fires In

- Interview a firefighter and explore the protective clothing designed for firefighters in urban blazes and in forest fires. How do the various features help maintain homeostasis?

How Materials **3** Were Selected and Reviewed

This chapter explains the criteria we developed for determining whether materials should be included in this guide; it also presents a general overview of the materials contained in this book and explains the information provided in the individual product reviews included in chapters 4 and 5.

Selection Criteria

Curriculum materials had to have all of the following three characteristics to be included in this guide:

1. They had to connect science, mathematics, and/or technology topics to workplace contexts.

2. They had to be sufficiently developed and detailed so that readers could understand how to use them.

3. They had to be intended for grades 6-12.

These criteria provided us with sufficient flexibility to include draft materials (provided they were sufficiently advanced, in accordance with criterion 2); but precluded the inclusion of long-term project materials—which, although they can be excellent instructional activities, are by nature vaguely defined. Regarding criterion 3, tech prep curricula only were included if they had high school components.

Pedagogical characteristics were considered as a criterion for selections, but we did not wish to screen from this guide interesting materials covering what is to millions of teachers a new area—instruction that explicitly makes connections to the workplace. Therefore, a few curricula with interesting workplace connections are included even though some of their pedagogical characteristics are weak. However, our reviews include information on assessment, instructional activities, materials required, etc., so readers can make their own determination of whether the pedagogical features of the curricula suit their instructional purposes.

The porfolio does not include titles such as "applied math," "consumer math" or "mathematics for building construction." While dozens—if not hundreds—of such books are available, they mostly connect with workplaces only by delimiting the mathematics they cover to that used in particular workplaces, not by using an instructional approach that specifically links mathematics to workplace contexts. Further, the pedagogical approach used in many of these books relies heavily on exposition accompanied by drill-and-practice exercises, an approach that is inconsistent with the National Council of Teachers of Mathematics (NCTM) standards.

The portfolio of 23 reviewed curricula attempts to balance the content areas addressed by the guide. There are about the same numbers of mathematics and science products reviewed; further, we have tried to identify products for specific math and science fields (algebra, geometry, biology, chemistry, earth sciences, and physics). Appendix A briefly describes additional curricula that mostly met the eligibility criteria but could not be included in chapters 4 and 5 due to space limitations. Generally, the reviewed curricula have stronger workplace connections than those in Appendix A. However, achieving a balance among subjects sometimes resulted in placing a product in the appendix even though its workplace connections were comparable in strength to those in chapters 4 and 5.

Characteristics of Reviewed Materials

Table 3.1 provides the titles, dates of publication, developers, funders/contributors, and grade ranges—HS (high school), MS (middle school), or both—of the curriculum materials reviewed in this guide. Notice the following patterns:

- Most of these products will be new to readers, in part because they are very recent: 16 of the 23 were published since 1996, and 13 since 1998.

- A few of the materials were developed by companies, individual authors, or professional societies; most were created under the leadership of university, college, or community college faculty, sometimes in collaboration with high school teachers and/or people working in the various industries or occupations addressed.

- The most common source of external funding support was one of two programs of the National Science Foundation: Instructional Materials Development (IMD) or Advanced Technological Education (ATE). A few received support from other federal agencies (the National Aeronautics and Space Administration, U.S. Department of Education, U.S. Department of Energy); state governments; private corporations; or foundations. Some of these were secondary funding sources that are listed in the individual reviews but not in table 3.1.

- While fewer of the products are designed for middle school students (8 of 23) than for high school students, middle grade teachers may benefit from obtaining some of the high school products as reference materials to augment their courses with connections to workplaces.

Table 3.1

General Characteristics of Reviewed Mathematics Curricula

Date	Curriculum Name	Developer(s)	Main Funder(s)	Grade
1998	CORD Algebra 1, Geometry	CORD	CORD	HS
1999	Excursions in Real-World Mathematics	Mt. Hood Community College	NSF-ATE	Both
1990, 1992	FUTURES with Jaime Escalante	FASE	Companies, federal agencies	Both
1998	High School Mathematics at Work	MSEB	The Pew Charitable Trusts	HS
1994-96	Interactions	FASE	Industries, NSF-IMD	MS
1998	Mathematical Applications for Business and Industry	Adirondack Community College	NSF-ATE	HS
1996-97	Mathematics for Technology	Wentworth Institute of Technology	NSF-ATE	HS
1995	Mathemedia	AIT	AIT	Both
1998	MathNet	University of Wisconsin-Madison	U.S. Department of Education	HS
1994-98	Real-World Mathematics Through Science	Washington MESA	Discuren Foundation, NSF-IMD	MS
1995	She Does Math!	33 Authors	—	HS
1999	Agriculture-Based Mathematics	Washington State University	NSF-ATE	HS

Table 3.1 (continued)

General Characteristics of Reviewed Curricula in Science or Integrated Subjects

Date	Curriculum Name	Developer(s)	Main Funder(s)	Grade
1999	Applications in Biology/Chemistry	CORD	CORD	HS
1998	ChemCom	ACS	NSF-IMD	HS
1996-98	Event-Based Science	Montgomery County, Maryland, schools	News media companies	MS
1998	Integrated Mathematics, Science, and Technology Project (IMaST)	Illinois State University	NSF-IMD, Illinois	MS
1997-98	Materials World Modules	Northwestern University	NSF-IMD	HS
1995	Offshore Oil Drilling	California SS&C Project	American Petroleum Institute, NSF-IMD	HS
1992	PHYS-MA-TECH	Northern Illinois State University, high schools	Industries, NSF-ATE, Illinois	HS
1995	Practical Exercises in Applying Knowledge	COIN Educational Products, Oklahoma Department of Vocational Education, CIMC	COIN, CIMC	HS
1990-1994	Principles of Technology	CORD	CORD	HS
1999	Science, Technology, Knowledge, and Skills (SciTeKS)	ACS	NSF-ATE	HS
1996	Working to Learn	TERC	The Pew Charitable Trusts	HS

The purposes, sizes, media, components, and costs of the reviewed curricula vary considerably.

- Each review stipulates whether the curriculum is intended to be used as a semester- or year-long course, or as a supplement; the guide contains more of the latter than the former. Two of the curriculum materials are intended as resource books rather than as curricula to be implemented: Real-World Mathematics and She Does Math!. The supplemental curricula often come as separately sold units.

- Most products are very substantial, comprised of hundreds of pages or many videotapes. Most supplementary curricula also have multiple units. The smallest product is Offshore Oil Drilling, which is a single module for supplementary use over several weeks. The largest product is Principles of Technology, which has enough material for two school years. The size of the product typically is proportional to its intended role in the curriculum.

- Most of the products are primarily print-based. Three math curricula are video-based (FUTURES, Interactions, and Mathemedia), but have accompanying print material for student work. Several primarily print-based products also include supporting videotapes. SciTeKS makes extensive use of print, video, and CD-ROM.

- The printed products are packaged in many ways: large hard-cover textbooks, spiral-bound books, three-ring binders, small softcover books, and more. Some materials—particularly those in draft form or those that are not commercially published—are only comprised of text with color graphics, diagrams, or photographs of limited visual quality.

- The cost of the reviewed products ranges from free to hundreds of dollars; in fact, it varies so widely that stating an average cost would not be at all informative.

Consistency With National Curriculum Standards

Since their development, the national curriculum standards in mathematics (by NCTM, 1989) and in science (by the National Research Council [NRC], 1996, and the science benchmarks from Project 2061 of the American Association for the Advancement of Science, 1993), have gained increasing credibility, prominence, and importance. Many states and districts are revising their curriculum frameworks to make them consistent with the national standards, and the policies of these jurisdictions for adopting curriculum materials call for them to be aligned with appropriate standards. This section discusses the consistency of the reviewed curricula with the NCTM and NRC standards. As discussed in chapter 1, some products also reference state curriculum standards, draft national standards in technology education from the International Technology Education Association (ITEA), industry skills standards, and general workplace skills standards (SCANS, 1991).

About a quarter of the reviewed curricula provide checklists or discussions that indicate, to varying degrees of specificity, which of the standards' topics they address. Another quarter make some mention of standards alignment, limited to a sentence or a few sentences like "the product is consistent with the national standards." But what does addressing, or being "consistent with" or "aligned with," national standards specifically mean? The only way to really determine this meaning is to inspect the product quite thoroughly, from a position of familiarity with the standards documents. Several professional organizations have developed elaborate instruments (questions, checklists) and procedures for analyzing the correspondence of curriculum materials' topics to those of the national curriculum standards. Such an analysis was beyond the scope of this guide.

Instead, we informally inspected the mathematics or science topics found in the 50 percent of the curricula whose authors provided information about their consistency with standards. We sometimes found this claim of alignment to be rather loose. Some developers seem to have based their statements of consistency on the fact that the topics in their curriculum are also found in the standards, at the grade range addressed by their product. This is not very meaningful, particularly because the standards—much like many textbooks—include far more topics than any teacher or student could cover in a given course. Therefore, one is bound to find most topics included in the standards.

We could, on the other hand, gauge whether the curriculum materials used pedagogical approaches articulated in the standards documents. For example, do the curricula encourage hands-on student inquiry and written communication by, respectively, incorporating appropriately designed investigations and questions that require students to generate extended responses? We paid considerable attention to these and other pedagogical characteristics of the reviewed curricula and found that most of them have some desirable approaches. For the specifics of this finding, see the "Instructional Approach" (especially) and "Curriculum Components" portions of our reviews in chapters 4 and 5. Merely relying on an inspection of the samples pages from the curriculum could lead to an incorrect conclusion. Because the space for sample pages was limited, the first criterion for selecting them was to choose ones that illustrate workplace connections, so these pages may or may not also illustrate the curriculum's range of pedagogical features.

About 50 percent of the curricula reviewed in this guide provide no information at all about the extent to which they fulfill the intent of the national curriculum standards. Does this mean that anyone interested in quality curriculum materials should automatically avoid these curricula? The answer is no, for the following four reasons. First, a few of them were written before the national standards were in place. Second, some curricula are in draft form; the final versions could well contain a discussion of their attention to curriculum standards. Third, one product (She Does Math!), while containing excellent workplace-connected problems, is a resource book rather than a curriculum fully developed for classroom implementation: such a book should not be expected to address the standards explicitly.

Finally, the absence of a discussion of conformity with national standards does not necessarily indicate an inferior curricular product. Many products on the market claim alignment with the standards when their only consistency is in terms of topic selection, while their pedagogical approaches actually conflict with those envisioned by the standards. It is quite possible at this time for a curriculum that provides no information about alignment to be just as—or even more—consistent with national standards as one that does make such claims. This circumstance will likely become less common as time passes, and professionals increasingly expect products to provide more extensive and explicit discussion of their consistency with the content and pedagogical specifications of national curriculum standards.

Information Included in the Reviews

The following pages are formatted like the reviews found in chapters 4 and 5 and explain exactly what we were trying to address in each section of our reviews. Within this format, we have used various devices to highlight and help in locating key information. Thus, the most prominent headings on the review pages are those we deemed most important to you, the reader: "Content Overview" and "Workplace Connections."

S M T   Grades 6-12

Developer

Distributor

Each review indicates intended grade levels and whether the curriculum material is intended for science (S), mathematics (M), technology (T), or some combination of these.

Funders/Contributors

What Does Each Review Contain?

This overview description cites the most important characteristics of the materials to convey to the reader, giving particular attention to the nature or strength of its workplace connections. This is not a comprehensive synopsis, but rather highlights key aspects of the product.

The main components of the product (e.g., teacher and student editions, videos) are listed, together with their prices (excluding shipping and handling). Readers must contact distributor to inquire about prices for multiple copies.

Content Overview

How the topics relate to those found in typical science, mathematics, and technology courses. The main subject areas addressed—with typical course titles, if appropriate—are listed, and the range of detailed topics covered is described. Module titles are provided for curricula that sell these modules separately.

Target Audience

The developer's/distributor's description of the kinds of teachers and students who comprise the intended audience for this curriculum.

Duration

The amount of classroom time, in days, weeks, months, or years, required by this curriculum.

Workplace Connections

A discussion of the ways in which—and the extent to which—the curriculum connects mathematics and/or science to workplace contexts. (See chapter 2 for a discussion of these various ways.)

Instructional Approach

A synopsis of the nature and extent of the pedagogical practices built into the curriculum. This summarizes what teachers and students would typically do in the course of using the curriculum, e.g.: whether small group work is merely suggested or an extensive design feature accompanied by implementation suggestions; how often hands-on activities are required; whether laboratory work is mostly prescribed for students or substantially open for them to design; and whether students exercises and problems are structured or open-ended.

Curriculum Components

A description of the main components of the curriculum (e.g., teacher's guide, student text, videotapes, etc.).

Materials

Materials or supplies, if any, needed to use this curriculum but not provided by the distributor as part of the product. Information about the extent and frequency of materials use is provided; as is information about its availability, including whether general or specialized vendors are required, and if the curriculum materials provide lists of required materials and how to obtain them.

Assessments

Whether and how the curriculum includes means of assessing student work. The use and nature of these assessments (e.g., multiple choice, open-ended, performance tasks, etc.) are described, along with any information or suggestions provided to teachers about implementing the assessments, e.g., whether the curriculum provides sample student answers to open-ended problems or scoring rubrics for teachers to use in appraising extended tasks.

Special Preparations

Indicates whether the curriculum is so different from typical courses that teachers would need to invest substantial preparation time before they use it. This could include consulting or collaborating with other subject area teachers, or learning to use complicated or unfamiliar equipment. Only included in reviews when applicable.

Teacher Resources

Training or additional materials available from the developer or distributor to help teachers use this curriculum. Only included in reviews when applicable.

Other Languages

Languages, other than English, in which the materials are available. Only included in reviews when applicable.

Standards

The self-described alignment of the materials to the curriculum or industry standards listed below.

NCTM standards	Industry standards documents
NRC standards	State curriculum specifications
AAAS Benchmarks	SCANS
for Scientific Literacy	ITEA technology education
	standards

Sample Pages

Between two and six sample pages that best illustrate the curriculum, particularly its connections to workplace contexts. When space permitted, the sample pages also were selected to show the nature of the mathematics and science content, and a range of the curriculum's instructional and other features.

Ordering Information

Full contact information for the developer and distributor, with the name of the key author(s) provided whenever appropriate.

Table of Contents

The text of the materials' table of contents, sometimes condensed to save space or expanded to an additional level of detail to better illustrate product features. In many cases, the contents of a representative module or unit are given in the interests of space. The number of pages for each main portion is provided rather than page numbers to indicate length as opposed to location.

Reviews of 4
Mathematics
Curricula

This chapter presents reviews of the following 12 curriculum materials for mathematics. Each review is accompanied by 2-6 sample pages from the curriculum. Table 3.1 provides an overview the materials' dates of publication, funding sources, and intended grade levels. Appendix A provides brief descriptions of a few additional mathematics curricula.

Developer
Center for Occupational Research and Development (CORD)

Distributor
South-Western Educational Publishing

Funders/ Contributors
CORD

CORD Algebra 1, Geometry

Mathematics in Context 1998

Derived from CORD Applied Math, a series of modules that are still available. These curricula emphasize connections between, and applications of, mathematics and everyday life. The use of mathematics in the workplace is highlighted through multi-step exercises covering 5 occupational areas. Algebra can be implemented in module format or as a complete course.

***Algebra 1**—Student ed.: hardcover, 800 pp., $43.95 (also available as parts A & B, 425 pp. each, $23.50 each); Teacher ed.: hardcover, 425 pp., $49.95 each for parts A & B; Videos: $53.95 each for parts A & B*

***Geometry**—Student ed.: hardcover, 752 pp., $43.95; Teacher ed.: hardcover, 849 pp., $75.95; Videos: $79.95/set*

Content Overview

Algebra, Geometry

Mathematics is presented in a way that bridges the gap between abstract concepts and real-world applications—concepts are introduced, practiced, and applied in a workplace context. Focus is on developing students' capacity for problem solving. Algebra and geometry content is consistent with that in traditional approaches.

Target Audience

Designed for broad cross-section of students to teach abstract concepts through concrete experiences.

Duration

Algebra—1 or 2 years; Geometry—1 year.

Workplace Connections

Workplace contexts are used throughout. Each book's preface outlines several examples of algebra/geometry in workplace applications. Each video explicitly relates the mathematics skills to people who use these skills in their occupations. Each chapter's preface answers the question

"Why do I need to learn this?" by citing workplace applications of the mathematics covered in the chapter. Workplace contexts are used for many of the examples, laboratory activities (Math Labs), and assessment exercises. Each chapter's practice problems (Math Applications) are set in the occupational contexts of agriculture and agribusiness, business and marketing, health occupations, family and consumer science, and industrial technology. Sprinkled throughout the textbooks are short sections (Workplace Communication) in which students are given a memo, fax, spreadsheet, e-mail, or purchase order from a workplace and asked to use the lesson's mathematics to verify or interpret information, perform calculations, or answer questions regarding the workplace situation.

Instructional Approach

A video scenario of a workplace application sets the stage for the mathematical concepts. In Algebra 1, the video segment ends by presenting a problem for class discussion. In each chapter, students read and work through problems in the text; engage in Activities (multi-step discovery experiences that often require manipulatives—Algeblocks—or standard classroom supplies such as graph paper, protractors, and rulers); participate in class discussions; study examples that are worked out step by step in the text; apply mathematical skills in cooperative group activities (Math Labs) that employ data collection and analysis; and perform problem-solving exercises covering 5 occupational areas (Math Applications). While the materials employ varied learning activities, they emphasize exposition and are written at an 8th-grade reading level.

Curriculum Components

Three components are needed to implement the curriculum: videos, student text, and annotated Teacher's Guide. The latter includes the full student text as well as margin notes, answers, planning guide, pacing chart, and professional articles. Supplemental materials that are available but not crucial to implementation include: Teacher's Resource Book (includes reteaching activities, lesson practice, enrichment activities, assessment, chapter projects, and solutions); Supplementary Worksheets ("Algebra" only); Solutions Manual ("Geometry" only); and a Test Databank (print version) and Test Database (electronic version, in PC and Macintosh formats). A promotional video is available from CORD.

Materials

Scientific and graphing calculators are used throughout. Students are strongly encouraged to use calculators for both Math Labs and Math Applications. Activities require materials such as manipulatives (Algeblocks) or standard classroom supplies such as graph paper, protractors, and rulers; materials are listed in the margins of the teacher's edition. Math Labs require some standard classroom supplies but also materials such as graduated cylinders, micrometer and Vernier calipers, large machine nuts and bolts, electronics supplies, and geometry software. Many of these supplies are readily available in classroom science labs or local stores; others must be obtained from outside vendors. Materials are listed at the beginning of each Math Lab.

Assessments

Each lesson ends with 20-30 pencil-and-paper short-answer items divided into 3 categories: (1) Think and Discuss (questions requiring writing or discussion), (2) Practice and Problem Solving (problems set in workplace or applied contexts), and (3) Mixed Review. No scoring guidelines are provided to the teacher. Supplementary materials include a multiple-choice Test Databank and Test Database.

Each chapter ends with 15-30 items. For algebra, these are in 3 categories: Skills-Based (problems devoid of context), Applications (contextual and workplace-based problems), and Math Lab (problems related to the chapter's laboratory activities). For geometry, items are of 4 types: Communication (no calculations required), Skills, Applications, and Math Lab.

Midway in the Algebra 1 textbook, 8 pages are devoted to Skills Review, which is composed of 16 sections, each corresponding to a skill to be mastered before beginning the second half of the textbook. For each skill, the text provides a brief review (in a couple of sentences) and 5-9 exercises.

Teacher Resources

Three types of professional development workshops are offered and taught by CORD-endorsed master teachers: 3- to 5-day comprehensive workshops at CORD's Roney Teaching Center in Waco, TX; customized topic workshops and teacher training developed according to teacher needs in local regions; and technical assistance and short courses available through CORD's Virtual Teaching Center (accessed through local teleconferencing). Call CORD at 1-800-231-3015 or send e-mail to training@ cord.org.

Other Languages

Some of the original Applied Math units are available in Spanish.

Standards

No information provided.

Sample Pages

Page 54 illustrates a table of contents that cross-references mathematics content with many occupational fields. Each chapter begins with text that contextualizes the mathematics that is covered in the chapter (p. 55). Page

56 illustrates a Workplace Communication. Activities are often introduced via a workplace application of mathematics (p. 57). Page 58 is an end-of-chapter Math Applications assessment set in the context of health occupations. Page 59 illustrates an entire Math Lab, a hands-on mathematics activity. (Note that pp. 54, 58-59 are from the algebra text, and pp. 55-57 are from the geometry text.)

Ordering Information

Developer: Center for Occupational Research and Development, P.O. Box 21206, Waco, TX 76702-1206; 1-800-231-3015; http://www.cord.org/

Distributor: South-Western Educational Publishing, 5101 Madison Road, Cincinnati, OH 45227; 1-800-824-5179; http://www.swep.com/math/index.html

Table of Contents

(Number of pages indicated in parentheses; T indicates a section is included only in the Teacher's Guide)

CHAPTER 7

Statistics and Probability

CHAPTER 8

Systems of Equations

AREA

OBJECTIVES

1. Understand the physical meaning of the area of a polygon and of a circle.
2. Solve problems involving the area of a square, rectangle, parallelogram, triangle, trapezoid, regular polygon, and circle.
3. Solve problems involving the circumference of a circle and the area of a sector of a circle.
4. Use geometric properties to find the probability of an event.

Builders use area formulas to design and build landscapes, pools, and decks around homes, office buildings, and schools. It is important that builders know the relationship between linear measurement and area measurement. For example, a carpenter measures the length and width of a deck in feet or meters and uses area formulas to find the number of square feet or square meters contained in the interior of the deck. The area of a square is used to determine the area of any plane figure. You will use the Area Congruence Formula and the Area Addition Formula to develop area formulas for rectangles, parallelograms triangles trapezoids, and regular polygons. Here are some of the problems you will solve.

• Finding how much carpet is needed to cover a floor
• Finding the floor space occupied by a corner cabinet
• Finding the cost of resurfacing a parking lot

Sometimes a homeowner specifies a circular shape for a garden or deck. Then the builder must know how to find the circumference and area of a circle. You will use the ratio of the circumference to the diameter of a circle and the formula for the area of a polygon to determine the area of a circle. One problem you will solve involves finding the area of a silicon wafer used to manufacture integrated circuits.

Chapter 8   Area   **8-3**

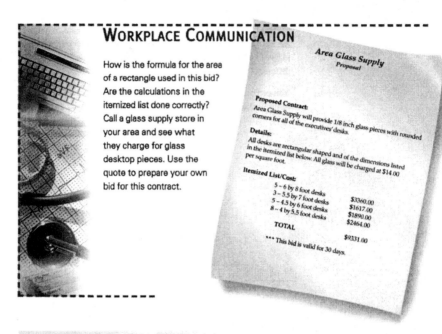

How is the formula for the area of a rectangle used in this bid? Are the calculations in the itemized list done correctly? Call a glass supply store in your area and see what they charge for glass desktop pieces. Use the quote to prepare your own bid for this contract.

Area Glass Supply
Proposal

Proposed Contract:
Area Glass Supply will provide 1/8 inch glass pieces with rounded corners for all of the executives' desks.

Details:
All desks are rectangular shaped and of the dimensions listed in the itemized list below. All glass will be charged at $14.00 per square foot.

Itemized List/Cost:

5 – 6 by 8 foot desks	$3360.00
3 – 5.5 by 7 foot desks	$1617.00
5 – 4.5 by 6 foot desks	$1890.00
8 – 4 by 5.5 foot desks	$2464.00
TOTAL	$9331.00

*** This bid is valid for 30 days.

LESSON ASSESSMENT

Think and Discuss

1 What determines the unit of measure for the area of a rectangle or square?

2 State the Area Congruence Property as a conditional. What is the converse of the conditional? Is the converse true? Explain why or why not.

3 A square is x units on a side. Each side is increased by y units. What is the increase in the area of the square? Illustrate your answer with a model.

4 A square is x units on a side. A smaller square y units on a side is removed from the lower left corner of the larger square. What is the area of the remaining figure? Illustrate your answer with a model.

8-8 Chapter 8   Area

LESSON 8.2 PARALLELOGRAMS AND TRIANGLES

Devon's company applies coatings to glass products. He needs to calculate the amount of ultraviolet reflective coating for pieces of antique glass in the shape of parallelogram *ABCD*.

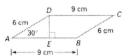

How can Devon find the area of *ABCD*?

ACTIVITY 1   **Finding the Area of a Parallelogram**

1 Draw parallelogram *ABCD* on graph paper.

2 The **base** of a parallelogram can be any of the four sides. Pick $\overline{AB}$ as the base. The **altitude** is a segment drawn perpendicular to the base from a point on the opposite side. Draw altitude $\overline{ED}$. Use the 30°–60°–90° Triangle Theorem to find *ED*.

3 Cut △*ADE* from the parallelogram and slide it to the right so that $\overline{AD}$ fits over $\overline{BC}$.

4 Classify the quadrilateral you have formed. What is the area of this quadrilateral? Why does the area of the new quadrilateral equal the area of the original parallelogram?

In Activity 1, you found the area of parallelogram *ABCD* by multiplying the length of the base by the length of the altitude.

> **Area of a Parallelogram**
> The area *A* of a parallelogram with base *b* and corresponding altitude *h* is
> $$A = bh$$

8.2 Parallelograms and Triangles **8-11**

The drip rate of a patient's IV changes depending on the position of the patient's arm. Over the course of a couple of hours, you count and record the number of drops per minute several times.

Number of Drops per Minute

10	12	10	8
11	11	10	9
11	11		

61 Draw a frequency distribution of the drip rates.

62 What are the values of the mean, mode, and median of this data?

63 What is the range of these data?

A consumer magazine performed a study on the leading brands of black tea, analyzing the caffeine content of a cup of each brand. The table lists the findings, in milligrams of caffeine per cup of brewed tea.

Brand	Caffeine (mg/cup)	Brand	Caffeine (mg/cup)
1	43	14	77
2	39	15	66
3	75	16	51
4	69	17	52
5	10	18	41
6	63	19	44
7	62	20	52
8	61	21	65
9	58	22	74
10	42	23	74
11	69	24	77
12	74	25	44
13	80		

64 Group the data by caffeine content into classes of 10 to 19, 20 to 29, and so on, and draw a histogram of the data.

65 Identify the mode and median of this data.

66 Determine the mean of the data and compare it to the mode and median you determined above.

Math Applications **7-71**

MATH LAB

Activity 1: Measuring Average Paper Thickness

Equipment Calculator
Vernier caliper
Micrometer caliper
Four large books of 500 or more numbered pages

Problem Statement

You will find the average paper thickness of four books. You will then compare your answer to the paper thickness measured with a micrometer caliper.

Procedure

a Use the vernier caliper to measure the total thickness (to the nearest thousandth of an inch) of pages 1-500 for each book. Record the thickness under these headings:

Book A   Book B   Book C   Book D

b Calculate an average paper thickness for each book by dividing the measured thickness by 250 (there are two numbered pages for each sheet of paper). Write your group's answer for the average page thickness of each book in scientific notation. Record the results for each group.

c Calculate the class average of the paper thickness for each book. Write each class-averaged paper thickness in scientific notation.

d How does the average paper thickness calculated by your group compare to the class-averaged paper thickness for each book? Which is more accurate?

e Use a micrometer caliper to measure the thickness of a single sheet of paper in each book. Record your answer in scientific notation. How does the paper thickness measured directly with the micrometer caliper compare with each paper thickness your group calculated? Which is more accurate?

Math Lab **2-33**

Developer
Mathematics Division, MHCC

Distributor
MHCC

Funders/ Contributors
National Science Foundation

Excursions in Real-World Mathematics

1999

These 89 real-world application problems were developed from interviews with people from business, industry, and faculty at Mt. Hood Community College (MHCC) and other colleges. Originally designed for entry-level community college students, the problems illustrate the use of mathematics in many professions; most are appropriate for supplementary use in high school mathematics. "Excursions" is to be used by teams of students, provides a lot of reading about workplace contexts, and involves multi-step solutions.

Web-based custom ordering; price depends upon number of problems ordered.

Content Overview

General Math, Algebra, Geometry, Statistics

The web site lists the specific mathematics topic(s)—from within the main areas of basic mathematics, beginning algebra, intermediate algebra, 2-D geometry, 3-D geometry, and statistics—addressed by each problem. Many topics are not covered in traditional algebra courses, and most are at the beginning and intermediate levels. About two-thirds of the problems involve unit conversions. The frequency of a particular topic reflects how often it was used by practitioners of mathematics.

Target Audience

"All beginning and intermediate level students, especially those in integrated math courses."

Duration

Instructional time for problems varies, but typically requires one class period.

Because all of the application problems are based on interviews with people who use mathematics in their jobs, most problems are directly connected to workplace contexts. Some problems have a real-world or academic focus rather than workplace contexts.

A wide range of workplace applications are featured, including civil engineering, publishing, construction, airplane manufacturing, forestry, electronics, surveying, and automotive repair.

Instructional Approach

Each application problem has a similar format. Students read a couple of paragraphs about the problem's context and are then given one or more mathematics problems. Students are encouraged to work in teams; many suggestions for successful teamwork are provided. Often, students report their results and solution process orally to the class, or write reports in the form of letters or memos. In a few problems, students collect their own data or use materials to build their own models. The problems can be used in guided discovery activities; introducing topics or concepts; reinforcement, contextualization, or extension of previously learned ideas; and assessment. Recommendations are provided for using each application in one or more of the following situations: in-class, begin in-class and complete at home, out-of-class, long-term project, or portfolio entry. Many problems are amenable to multiple purposes.

Curriculum Components

The instructor version addresses topics such as incorporating applications, facilitating teams, teaching problem solving, and grading. Each application situation contains three components: (1) a complete information sheet (giving information to decide when and where to assign a particular problem including: a summary of the problem, level, context, mathematical content, suggested uses, teams, technology, materials/equipment, comments, and source), (2) the problem (identical to the student version), and (3) a sample solution.

The student version of the custom-publication includes a motivational introduction and appendixes to guide the student on issues such as teams, presenting work, research, and problem-solving techniques. Each problem situation has an information sheet (this is a subset of the instructor's information sheet) and the statement of the problem.

Materials

Scientific calculators are recommended for most problems, and graphing calculators are recommended for a few. Some application problems recommend the use of spreadsheet software; a couple recommend Geometer's

Sketchpad software. For a few application problems, students use instruments such as clinometers, voltmeters, and milli-amp meters to collect data. Commonly available materials such as graph paper, rulers, measuring tape, and compasses are often required.

Assessments

Many application problems suggest whether they can be used for short in-class or take-home assessment purposes. Some general suggestions are provided on having students create portfolios of their work on in-depth projects. Grading guidelines, including several scoring rubrics, are provided.

Special Preparations

Teachers who implement these application problems as they were intended—that is, with students working in teams on multi-step problems and teachers providing guidance and facilitation—spend more time on grading. They must grade student thought processes, communication of solutions, and problem-solving approaches. Also, teachers will need planning time to create a class environment in which students can pursue their own solution processes.

Standards

This resource was created in response to the NCTM Standards and standards from the American Mathematical Association of Two-Year Colleges (AMATYC).

Sample Pages

Pages 65-67 are the complete set of materials for one application-radiation shielding-including the cover sheet, problems, and sample solutions.

Ordering Information

Developer: Regina T. Shankland, 503-667-7445, shanklar@mhcc.cc.or.us (e-mail) or Sara E. Williams, 503-667-7475, williams@mhcc.cc.or.us (e-mail), Mathematics Division, Mt. Hood Community College, 26000 SE Stark Street, Gresham, OR 97030

Distributor: Harcourt Brace Custom Publishers, Saunders College Publishing; www.saunderscollege.com/math

The problems are available at the publisher's web site for instructor perusal. An instructor can then select specific problems for the publisher to custom publish for his or her students. The students in turn purchase the selected problems, which are bound together with student notes on presentation, research techniques, teams, and problem solving. The instructor receives the same materials plus complete sample solutions for the selected problems and instructor notes on incorporating applications into the curriculum, facilitating teams, evaluation, teaching problem solving, and some sample student solutions.

Table of Contents

(Number of pages indicated in parentheses)

Table of Contents
(continued)

(Number of pages indicated in parentheses)

Radiation Shielding

Summary:	The basic concepts of radiation emission and shielding are introduced. Students investigate the geometric and algebraic relationships between the distance from a radiation source and the resultant dose rate.
Level:	Beginning algebra, three-dimensional geometry
Context:	Radiation health physics
Mathematical content:	Problem solving, area, formula evaluation, rates, geometric/algebraic modeling, solving linear equations
Suggested uses:	In-class activity, out-of-class assignment
Teams:	Optional
Technology:	Scientific calculator
Materials or equipment needed:	
Comments:	Exponential reduction is dealt with on an elementary level using repeated division. Logarithms and exponents are unnecessary. The second question is a fairly advanced topic. Depending on the sophistication and geometric experience of your students, you may want to accept any answer that refers to area. This demonstrates an understanding of the units involved, if not the three-dimensional concepts.
Source:	Robert Sant, Radiological Controls
	U.S. Navy

Radiation Shielding

Light disperses radially from a source. For example, when you turn on a light, it spreads light to all areas that have no objects shadowing or blocking the light.

Radiation follows the same principle of radial dispersion. A point source of a radioactive isotope emits a dose rate of 500 mR/hr (milliroentgen per hour) measured at a distance four feet from the source. Based on the situation, what could one say about the dose rate at ten feet? Radiation dose rates are measured in roentgens per unit of time. A roentgen is the unit of measurement showing the effect of radiation on a physical body.

The algebraic relationship shown below will allow us to compute the dose rate at various distances.

$$D_1 R_1^2 = D_2 R_2^2$$

where R_i is the distance from the source, and D_i is the dose rate at *that* distance

1. Use the formula to determine the dose rate at 10 feet for the situation described above.

2. Use geometry to explain why the distances must be squared in the given equation. Hint: The variable R is used in the formula to describe the distance from the source because it refers to a radius.

A dose rate can be reduced by placing an effective shielding between the radiation source and the recipient. For example, sunscreen or clothing is extremely effective shielding from the sun's radiation. In a nuclear reactor, lead is often used as shielding. Lead has a "tenth thickness" of 2 inches. A *tenth thickness* is the width of the shielding necessary to reduce the dose rate by a factor of ten.

3. If a blanket of lead shielding 4 inches thick is placed between the source and the recipient, what will the dose rate be at 10 feet for the situation described in problem 1?

4. Is it more effective to use shielding or distance as a way to reduce the dose you receive from a radiation source?

<u>**Sample Solution—Radiation Shielding**</u>

1. If the dose rate at 4 feet is 500 mR/hr, then the dose rate at 10 feet can be computed using the given formula.

    $D_1 R_1{}^2 = D_2 R_2{}^2$

    $(500 \text{ mR/hr}) * (4 \text{ ft})^2 = D_2 * (10 \text{ ft})^2$

    $D_2 = \dfrac{(500 \text{ mR/hr}) * (4 \text{ ft})^2}{(10 \text{ ft})^2}$

    $D_2 = 80 \text{ mR/hr}$

    So, the dose rate at 10 feet is only 80 milliroentgens per hour.

2. Because radiation spreads out from a point source, you can visualize it as a sphere. The radiation travels outward, like the surface of a balloon as it is inflated. Thus, the radiation at any distance from the point source is covering the surface area of a sphere with that radius. The formula for surface area of a sphere requires squaring the radius.

3. Since lead has a tenth thickness of 2 inches, using a blanket 4 inches thick will reduce the dose rate by a factor of ten twice. "Reducing by a factor" means dividing by that number. The dose rate at 10 feet was 80 mR/hr.

    Dose Rate at 10 feet with Shielding $= \dfrac{1}{10} * \dfrac{1}{10}(80 \text{ mR/hr})$

    Dose Rate at 10 feet with Shielding $= 0.8$ mR/hr

    The dose rate at 10 feet with shielding is 0.8 milliroentgen per hour.

4. Numerically, shielding is a more effective way to reduce dose rate than distance because multiple layers of shielding can reduce the dose rate by repeated factors of ten, but distance reduces dose rate only by the square of the added distance from the source. However, it depends on the situation. In some cases, increasing distance is not an option, like in an enclosed space or when work must be done near the radiation source. On the other hand, since lead is very heavy, there is a practical limit to how much shielding can be used.

Developer
FASE Productions

Distributor
FASE Productions

Funders/ Contributors
ARCO

The Carnegie Corporation of New York

IBM

The John D. and Catherine T. MacArthur Foundation

NASA

National School to Work Office

National Science Foundation

U.S. Department of Education

U.S. Department of Energy

U.S. Department of Labor

FUTURES

With Jaime Escalante 1990, 1992

Videos supplement mathematics curricula, showing students how widely mathematics and science are used outside of school. The series features Jaime Escalante, the renowned East Los Angeles classroom teacher who inspired students of all backgrounds to master advanced mathematics. The broadcast-quality videos combine classroom scenes with visits to hundreds of workplaces across the country and behind-the-scenes interviews with professionals who use mathematics and science in their careers.

Videos: 2 12-episode sets (15-min. episodes) available @ $350/set ($500/both sets), $39.95/episode or $69.95/2 episodes; Curriculum guides: softcover, 47 and 71 pp., free with video set.

A 1998 School-to-Career edition is available.

Content Overview

Various Mathematics

Materials cover absolute value, algebra, area, arithmetic operations, averages, conversion, decimals, equations, exponents, formulas, fractions, geometry, graphing, inequalities, integers, networks, parabolas, percents, periodic motion, ratios/proportions, right triangles, scientific notation, statistics, symmetry, trigonometry, volume, and whole numbers. Although intended for use by mathematics teachers, the materials have been strongly supported by science educators. Also, the curriculum materials note that many vocational education teachers are using FUTURES in their classrooms.

Target Audience

All middle and high school students.

Duration

1 class session for each 15-min. video and accompanying activities.

Workplace Connections

Every aspect of the curriculum focuses on how mathematics and science are used outside the classroom. The mathematics problems that accompany each episode use authentic contexts related to the workplaces highlighted in the videos. For about three-quarters of the episodes, teachers are encouraged to bring in subject matter experts to talk and/or work with students on assigned projects. An overview of employment options is provided for the fields featured in each video.

Instructional Approach

These 2 video series motivate students to study mathematics and science, and are ideal for introducing or reviewing topics in mathematics, rather than for teaching new mathematical and scientific content. In a typical instructional sequence requiring 1 class period, teachers: (1) acquaint students with vocabulary words before showing a video; (2) show the video; (3) lead a class discussion to further stimulate students' thinking about the video's topics; and (4) assign related mathematics word problems, research assignments, and/or hands-on projects. These latter may entail individual, group, or class work and may require students to contact experts or visit workplace settings. For flexible implementation, the curriculum materials provide many different types of problems and follow-up activities; teachers should preview the videos and accompanying activities before showing them.

In the videos, Mr. Escalante introduces mathematics concepts and practitioners who use them in their careers, and encourages students to learn mathematics. The series features professionals from many cultural backgrounds as well as a balance of men and women.

Curriculum Components

Videos are color VHS with closed caption and stereo sound.

For each episode, the FUTURES guide contains six parts:

- *Warm-up*—preview, vocabulary review (5-22 words).

- *Workout*—4-7 discussion questions and/or student research assignments.

- *Extra Laps*—2-6 tougher mathematics word problems.

- *Chalk Talk & Scrimmage*—professionals who could come to the classroom to discuss their jobs and give demonstrations of mathematics principles involved in their fields; places that students could see people at work and the products they make (3-6 suggestions).

- *Players' Positions*—some careers and jobs in each field.

- *Pros*—resource directory; the companies listed participated in FUTURES and can provide information, pictures, kits, etc., upon written request.

For each episode, the FUTURES 2 guide contains five parts:

- *Summary*—descriptions of the people interviewed, ideas discussed, and mathematics highlighted in the episode.

- *Class Discussion*—3-8 ideas to further stimulate student thinking about the topics; suggested answers are provided for teachers.

- *Class Activities*—3-5 suggestions for places to visit, experts who can talk to the class, class projects, etc.

- *Resources*—companies or associations that have offered to provide technical assistance, printed materials, or local experts.

- *Career Opportunities*—overview of employment options in the field.

FUTURES 2 next provides sheets that can be photocopied and distributed to students; these contain:

- *Vocabulary*—lists and definitions of terms used in the video and curriculum materials (12-18 terms).

- *Math Problems*—these 7-12 problems span a wide range of ability levels; advanced problems are specially designated.

- *Research Assignments*—2-5 are suggested; some involve contacting experts; difficult assignments are specially designated.

- *Projects*—2-4 are suggested to give students hands-on experience in applying aspects of topics; these can be completed as individual, group, or class assignments.

In partnership with the National School-to-Work Office and PBS, Foundation for Advancements in Science and Education (FASE) Productions is augmenting and rereleasing FUTURES in a School-to-Work edition. The 24 episodes will be packaged in six sets of four shows each, in the following categories: design and engineering, applied arts, environmental sciences, life sciences, sports and fitness, communications, and government and civil engineering. The accompanying curriculum guide will feature interdisciplinary (including English, social studies, and graphic arts), theme-based projects; expanded career information; and biographical profiles of professionals featured in the videos.

Materials

None.

Assessments No explicit guidance is provided, although the mathematics word problems, activities, research, and projects could be used for assessment purposes.

Teacher Resources WNET's national teacher training institute in New York trains teachers to use the videos in classroom instruction and has lesson plans available to complement the FUTURES materials. Contact Sarah Feldman at 212-560-3519 or visit the WNET Web site, http://www.wnet.org/wnetschool/ntti/index.html.

A "Making Connections" kit provides instructions and materials for workshops on effective use of the videos in grades 6-12 mathematics classrooms. Developed with National Science Foundation funding, the kit can be used with small groups (such as within a math department) or larger groups (such as entire districts or regions). The workshop can range from 2-4 hours. Kits are available from FASE at 1-800-404-FASE.

Standards No information provided.

References FUTURES has earned more than 50 awards, including the George Foster Peabody Award (one of the most prestigious in broadcasting), the Action for Children's Television Award, and the Gold Apple (National Educational Film and Video Festival).

Sample Pages Pages 73-74, from the Architecture and Structural Engineering episode of Futures, include sections of the video synopsis, Warmup, Workout, Extra Laps, and Chalk Talk & Scrimmage. Pages 75-76, from the Personal Communication episode of Futures 2, include sections of the Class Discussion, Class Activities, Career Opportunities, and examples of student math problems, projects, and research. Page 77 is a project from the Environmental Science and Technology episode from Futures' new School-to-Work edition.

Ordering Information The School-to-Career edition is $150 for 4 tapes and accompanying teacher's guide.

FASE Productions, 4801 Wilshire Boulevard, Suite 215, Los Angeles, CA 90010; 1-800-404-FASE; http://www.fasenet.org/itv/pg_futures.html

PBS Video, 1320 Braddock Place, Alexandria, VA 22314-1698; 1-800-344-3337

For an instructional television license, contact the National Educational Telecommunications Association (NETA), 1-803-799-5517.

Table of Contents

(Number of pages in curriculum guide indicated in parentheses)

radio operators, or "hams" as they are called, in the world. These hams operate 2-way radio systems, usually out of their homes. 52.8% of all the hams in the world are in the United States. How many are in the U.S.?

Fractions, Decimals

6] A coaxial cable is a large cable about 3 inches in diameter containing copper tubes inside of which are copper wires. Each of these copper tubes is called a coaxial. For telephone calls, these coaxials work in pairs, where one carries the signals going in one direction and the other carries the return signals. Together, a pair of coaxials can transmit 132,000 calls simultaneously.

New York City has a population of 7.3 million. Suppose that 2/3 of the population have telephones and that up to 3/4 of these phone owners make calls simultaneously. How many coaxials would be needed to accommodate this volume of calls?

Circular Geometry

7] "Iridium" is a project to launch 77 communication satellites into an orbit of 765 kilometers above the Earth (called low-Earth orbit).

a. If the satellites are to be evenly spaced above the equator, how far apart must they be? (The Earth's radius is approximately 6300 km.)

b. If you were to make a call to a point 6165 km away, how many satellites would it relay through? How far must the signal of your call travel between satellites and from the ground to the satellites and back? (Assume the satellites are directly above the sending and receipt points of the call.)

c. How many seconds of delay is there in the 6000-km call in the above question? (The signal travels at 300,000 km per second.)

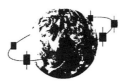

Trigonometry

8] Communications satellites receive signals from and transmit signals to Earth stations, which then send the signals to the receiving party. Suppose an Earth station were sending a signal, and the signal had to be directed within a 5-mile radius of the satellite. If the satellite is in orbit 22,000 miles above the surface of the Earth, by how much of an angle can the Earth station's signal diverge from a straight line to the satellite and still be picked up? (Use the trigonometric functions on a calculator to determine the angle.)

Projects

1] Design a means of personal communication through which you can reach anyone in the world (or in space). Will you speak through it, write through it, transmit computer data through it, or use some other method? Will it be portable? Will it use satellites to relay or transmit directly? Make a diagram showing your plan and explain to the class how it works.

2] This is a project for two or more people (preferably three). Look up "semaphore" in an encyclopedia which has a picture of all semaphore positions. Have each person make his own semaphore flags (out of cloth or construction paper). Now go outside (or into the hallway if it is long enough) and spread out as far as you can. Have the first person send a short message to the second person. Have the second person send the message on to the third person and so on. Then compare the messages. Did the first person's message get across clearly, or was it misunderstood? Send a few messages back and forth and see if you can

improve the accuracy of transmission. How far away do you think a semaphore signal could be seen? With relay points a reasonable distance apart, how far do you think a message could be sent without getting distorted?

Research

1] The telegraph was the first means of instant, long distance communication between people. Find out who invented it and when it was invented. When was the first cross-continental telegraph exchange established in the U.S.? When was the first transatlantic exchange established? What effect did the wide-spread use of the telegraph have on the world?

2] How has technology made it easier for the disabled to communicate? Find out about devices that will read printed material aloud (for the blind) or translate keyboard input into speech. How can such devices be used by the non-disabled to make communication easier or more effective?

3] Amateur radio users, or hams, have been able to broadcast signals hundreds and even thousands of miles. Some hams have communicated with people in Eastern European countries who received no other Western communication. Find out some of the methods hams use for sending their signals long distances.

4] In the near future, video communication may make the leap from flat, two-dimensional images to 3-D holograms. Find out what a hologram is and how it is produced.

5] How many geostationary communication satellites has the United States launched? About how many phone calls or other signals can these handle? What is the predicted life span of a geostationary satellite? What happens to them when they can no longer be used?

PROGRAM LENGTH: 15 MINUTES   **#103**

SYNOPSIS

Mr. Escalante and his students describe shapes like parabolas, triangles, and ellipses to introduce the professions of architecture and structural engineering. Pritzker Prize award winning architect Frank Gehry visits the classroom and describes how creating "cities" out of firewood as a child led him to his current work. Examples of his structural creations are shown, as he explains that turning ideas into real buildings requires an understanding of math. We then visit with structural engineer, Ysrael Seinuk, and take off on a visual trip through the building process. Structural engineering is the hidden art, he says, and he discusses how the artist designs the exterior while the engineer uses math and physics to build a support structure allowing the final form to take shape. Susan Bacas, Cantor/Seinuk Group's project manager, and Jaime Vasquez, project engineer, describe the variety of applications of structural engineering and the challenge of their work.

THE WARMUP

VOCABULARY REVIEW

Architecture: The art, science or profession of designing buildings.

Structure: (1) Something made of parts fitted or joined together (2) The main supporting part of something (3) The way the parts are fitted together. [from Latin *struere* - to build]

Engineering: The use of scientific principles for practical projects. [from Latin *ingenium* - talent]

Civil Engineer: An engineer trained in the design and construction of civil works (those related to a community or to citizens, e.g. roads, bridges).

THE WORKOUT

1.   **Discuss some of the man-made structures the students are familiar with.** [*e.g. Hospitals, museums, apartments, houses, skyscrapers, bridges, sewage plants.*]

a. **What are some of the shapes you see in these structures?**

b. **What are some of the stresses each of these structures must withstand?**

2.   **Different structures involve different stresses. What are some unique structural considerations for each of the following:**

a. **Oil platforms** [*e.g. Ocean currents, storms, safety features to avoid oil spills and fires.*]

b. **Tunnels** [*e.g. Replace ceiling support, maintain air flow, prevent collapse due to sound or other resonance.*]

EXTRA LAPS

1. As locations vary so do the construction needs. Look at your own neighborhood from a structural engineering point of view:

a. What types of buildings are being built?

b. Are there special considerations regarding soil, potential disasters, wind velocity, types of business?

c. What projects being undertaken in your area would you like to be a part of?

2. Resonance (continuing oscillation) is a feature that can tear apart a structure. For a bridge, two sources of resonance are wind and earthquake.

a. To demonstrate this effect, build a simple model bridge by stringing a rope between two blocks of wood. Can you move one or both of the wood blocks up and down in a regular pattern so that the rope begins to move regularly up and down? This is an example of resonance. Note how only certain patterns of block movement create resonance. Once the resonance is started, does it take much movement to continue it?

3. There are certain shapes which have unique characteristics. The triangle is particularly strong. You can find it as a support component of many bridges and within the framework of virtually every highrise building.

a. Build a rectangle with pieces of cardboard by taping the corners together. How easy is it to change this from a rectangle to a parallelogram (a four-sided figure with opposite sides parallel) by pushing down on one side?

b. Now turn the rectangle into two triangles by taping a cardboard strip diagonally across the rectangle. Is it now more difficult to distort?

c. Triangular elements are sometimes used to stabilize tall buildings. Do you see how this might work?

CHALK TALK & SCRIMMAGE

1. Have the students bring in pictures of skyscrapers from various locales, especially ones with innovative designs.

a. How do these buildings differ in architectural design?

b. Beyond support of the buildings themselves, are there any unique design features that the engineers needed to consider [e.g. *Unusual windows, exterior elevators, suspended walkways, rotating upper stories, attachment of stone facing.*]

2. Invite an architect, structural engineer or civil engineer to come to your class. Have him describe the types of projects he has pursued. What are some of the challenges he had to solve? Ask him to bring pictures of a favorite project and charts showing the internal structure if at all possible.

1 With current technology, we can speak on the telephone, write someone by FAX, send a message through a computer, or communicate in countless other ways. "Video phones," where both parties appear on a video transmission, are now becoming available, and science fiction authors have envisioned three-dimensional visual communication that makes it seem as though a distant person were in the same room with you.

a What are the benefits of visual communication? *You can show the other person what you are talking about; can see facial and body expressions.*

b Who do you think will be the first to buy such systems? *Corporation executives for whom more effective communication can mean more productivity and income; scientific and engineering establishments for whom the ability to show something is very important, etc.*

3 (Do this problem with students in class) A telecommunications network is made up of a number of nodes (points at which communication may be sent or received) connected together. For example, the network below consists of 3 nodes—A, B, and C:

This network has 3 connections. Find the total number of connections for a network with each of the following number of nodes. (It may be helpful to diagram these networks like the one above.)

4 nodes   5 nodes   6 nodes   7 nodes   24 nodes

Help students to make a chart and see the pattern that relates the number of nodes to the number of connections. Help them to notice that when you add the "nth" node, you add "n-1" connections. For example, when you add a 6th node, you add 5 (6-1) connections. When you add a 7th node, you add 6 (7-1) connections.

1 Visit a consumer electronics store. Ask for a demonstration of some of the newer pieces of equipment (such as car FAXES and mobile phones). What new products are expected in the next few years?

2 Visit a telephone switching station. Find out how the operators control the calls that come through. About how many calls does each operator handle in a day? How many calls are handled by the entire office?

3 Ask an engineer from a mobile phone company to speak to the class. Have her explain how the phones are set up to relay a signal. If possible, have her make a diagram on the chalkboard showing how a mobile phone communication is sent. Possibly she can bring some of the equipment she uses in her job to show the students. If many people in the same area try to make phone calls on mobile phones, will they run out of channels? If you are speaking on a car phone, does the signal have to switch to new mobile phone channels as you move out of range? What does the future hold for mobile phone technology?

Communications is a huge industry in the United States. The jobs available range from the very skilled technical positions requiring Master's or Bachelor's Degrees to on-the-job training positions available to high school graduates. Here is a sampling:

Telecommunication Engineers are known by the fields in which they specialize: *Electronics Engineers* and *Mechanical Engineers* design and run communications satellites. *Fiber Optics Circuit Designers (Optical Engineers)* specialize in fiber optics communication technology. *Laser Engineers* and *Electro-Optic Engineers* also specialize in fiber optics and the use of lasers in communication.

To: Local Environmental Consultants

From: Senior Recycling Planner, Seattle

Your city wishes to develop an effective recycling program similar to the one we have here in Seattle, and would like you to prepare a proposal for getting it done. I have been asked to explain to you what that proposal should include.

1) Landfill costs. Assume that the present cost for delivery of one truckload of garbage to your local landfill is $100.00, and that in two years this will rise to $250.00. (You are to estimate how many garbage cans full of trash are equivalent to one truckload, based on the approximate dimensions of garbage trucks you have seen and the dimensions of a typical household garbage can. This will give you an estimate of the cost to the city of delivery of one garbage can full of trash.)

2) Value of recyclable materials. Metal has an average value of $.75 per pound. Glass or plastic has an average value of $.10 per pound. Paper has an average value of $20.00 per ton.

3) Amount of garbage generated by typical home. I suggest you weigh the garbage produced in your own home for one week to determine this. Be sure to separately measure the weight of glass and plastic, paper, metal, and other garbage. (I suggest you keep it separate for a week before you weigh it, rather than trying to separate it out at the end of the week, which is a pretty messy job.)

4) If the recyclable material is not separated in the home, it will cost the city approximately $.03 a pound to have it separated.

   Based on this information, please calculate how much money would be saved by the city if glass, plastic, metal, and paper were recycled instead of sent to a landfill, and whether or not the city should require that such materials be separated in the home prior to being picked up.

You will need the support of your local population for this program to work, for they must at least be willing to separate out recyclable material from nonrecyclable material. I recommend that you survey some local people to determine their attitudes toward recycling, and determine what they would be willing to do and what incentives or fines the city could use to encourage compliance with its new recycling program.

You are asked to make a proposal to the city council which presents the information you have collected, your analysis of that information, and your recommendations for how to proceed in getting popular support for this program. Your presentation should be no more than ten minutes long. I suggest you develop visual aids for this to make it more understandable to council members. In my own experience, good pictures of garbage always have a lot of impact.

You must also summarize your proposal in a 1,000- to 1,500-word letter to the city council chairman.

Developer
Mathematical Sciences Education Board

Distributor
National Academy Press

Funders/Contributors
The Pew Charitable Trusts

High School Mathematics at Work

Essays and Examples for the Education of All Students *1998*

Collection of 15 essays and 14 illustrative tasks that suggest workplace and everyday contexts to strengthen the mathematical education of all students—those entering the workforce after high school as well as those going on to postsecondary education. Although the tasks do not comprise a curriculum, they highlight compelling contexts for central mathematical ideas.

Softcover, 192 pp., $27.95 ($22.36 if ordered from distributor's Web site)

Content Overview

Various Mathematics

Mathematics covered includes: data collection and analysis, estimation and approximation, optimization, proportions, iterative/recursive processes, mental arithmetic, exponential growth, weighted averages, geometric probability, translating verbal statements to symbolic equations, and geometric modeling. Task extensions often involve calculus.

Target Audience

". . . appropriate for a broad audience, including teachers, teacher educators, college faculty, parents, mathematicians, curriculum designers, superintendents, school board members, and policy makers—in short, anyone interested in mathematics education."

Duration

Each task requires 1 to several class periods.

Workplace Connections

A workplace context or everyday situation frames each task. Some tasks that use everyday situations discuss similar problems that arise in workplace contexts. Problems range from analysis of ambulance response times, to buying a used car, to determining how rounding off can be important in business.

Instructional Approach

All tasks are open-ended; many require students to make assumptions and draw from their everyday experiences to go beyond the information provided. Data collection is an integral component of 1 task (Buying a Used Car) and suggested for 3 others (Scheduling Elevators, Heating-Degree-Days, and Hospital Quality). In Back-of-the-Envelope Estimates, students are encouraged to create and solve problems similar to those presented. There is no discussion of pedagogy.

Curriculum Components

Each task follows the same general format: problem statement; commentary (elaboration of problem context and the nature and value of the mathematics embedded in the task); mathematical analysis; extensions; and references (when available).

Materials

Graphing calculators and spreadsheet software are recommended.

Assessments

Worked solutions are provided.

Standards

Two essays included on the role of Standards in problems connecting mathematics to workplaces. No information provided on specific relationship of 14 tasks to NCTM Standards.

Sample Pages

The majority of the text from one task (Rounding Off) is shown on pages 81-83, including problem statement, commentary, mathematical analysis, and extensions.

Ordering Information

Developer: Mathematical Sciences Education Board, National Research Council, 2101 Constitution Avenue, NW, Washington, DC 20418; 202-334-3294 (voice); 202-334-1453 (fax); mseb@nas.edu (e-mail)

Distributor: National Academy Press, 2101 Constitution Avenue, NW, Washington, DC 20055; 1-800-624-6242; http://www.nap.edu/bookstore/isbn/0309063531.html

Table of Contents

*(Number of pages indicated in parentheses; * denotes mathematics task)*

ROUNDING OFF

TASK. In a certain multi-million dollar company, Division Managers are required to submit monthly detail and summary expense reports on which the amounts are rounded, for ease of reading, to the closest $1,000. One month, a Division Manager's detail report shows $1,000 for printing and $1,000 for copying. In the summary report, the total for "printing and copying" is listed as $3,000. When questioned about it by the Vice President, he claims that the discrepancy is merely round-off error. In subsequent months, the Vice President notices that such round-off errors seem to happen often on this Division Manager's reports. Before the Vice President asks that the Division Manager re-create the reports without rounding, she wants to know how often this should happen.

COMMENTARY. We are often quoted rounded numbers that do not then turn out to be quite exact. Even a bank's approximate computational program for principal and interest can eventually drift far enough off the actual payment for the difference to be important. In any problem, we have to be concerned about which numbers are exact and about the accuracy of those that are not.

People don't often realize how huge the consequences of rounding numbers can be. Suppose, for example, that a company's board of directors has received a report indicating that each of the machines manufactured by their company will take up 2% of the freight capacity of their cargo planes, and the board wants to know how many machines can be shipped on each plane. In our standard notation, 2% represents a number somewhere between 1.5% and 2.5%. Solving the problem with each of these two exact percentages yields answers that are

quite different. Using 1.5%, the board will find that the plane can hold 100% ÷ (1.5%/machine) ≈ 66 machines; but by using 2.5%, the board will find that the plane can hold 100% ÷ (2.5%/machine) = 40 machines. So, in truth, all the board can say is that the answer is between 40 and 66 machines! Clearly, the report has not supplied accurate enough information, especially if the profitability of the shipment depends strongly on the number of machines that can be shipped.

If, on the other hand, the report had indicated that the board could assume another decimal place of accuracy, by stating that each machine accounted for 2.0% of the plane's capacity, then, with rounding, the board can be sure that the exact portion is somewhere between 1.95% and 2.05%. Using these exact percentages, the board can conclude that the plane can hold between 48 and 51 machines. One decimal place of additional accuracy in the reported data reduced the uncertainty in the answer from 26 machines to 3.

This problem is important for another reason as well, for its solution introduces a useful mathematical connection: the notion of geometric probability, where the range of options (technically, the "sample space") is represented by a geometric figure so that the probability of certain events correspond to the areas of certain portions of that figure. Geometric probability enables us to use our knowledge of the area (or length or volume) of geometric figures to compute probabilities.

MATHEMATICAL ANALYSIS. Fundamental to an understanding of geometric probability is the idea that on a portion of a line, probability is proportional to length, and on a region in a plane, probability is proportional to area. For example, suppose that in Figure 1, the areas of regions A, B, and C are 2, 1, and 3 respectively, for a total area of 6. Then a point picked at random from these regions would have probability of 2/6, 1/6, and 3/6 of being in regions A, B, and C respectively.

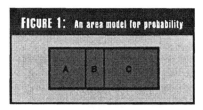

FICURE 1: An area model for probability

Note that the boundaries of the regions are not significant in the calculations because they have no area. Ideally (as opposed to in a physical model) these boundaries are lines with no thickness. Thus, the probability that a point from this rectangle will lie *exactly* on one of these boundaries, rather than close to a boundary, is zero.

In order to answer the question at hand, it must be stated more mathematically: Given a pair of numbers that both round to 1, and assuming that all such pairs are equally likely, find the probability that their sum rounds to 2. This assumption may or may not be reasonable in a particular business and would require some knowledge of typical expenses and some non-mathematical judgment.

A number that rounds to 1 is somewhere between .5 and 1.5. These numbers may be represented by a line segment, shown as the shaded portion of the number line in Figure 2.

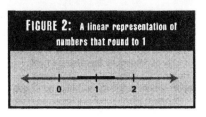

FIGURE 2: A linear representation of numbers that round to 1

To state this a bit more formally, a number x will be rounded to 1 if $.5 < x < 1.5$. (Again, we can ignore the boundaries, .5 and 1.5, because the probability that a number will be exactly on the boundary is zero.) Suppose y also rounds to 1, so that $.5 < y < 1.5$. If we consider a coordinate plane with points (x, y), these two inequalities determine a square of side 1. This square (Figure 3) represents all pairs of numbers where both could be rounded to 1. For example, point A represents (.8, .6), B represents (1.1, 1.1), and C represents (1.3, 1.4).

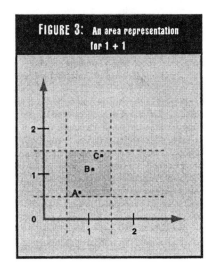

FIGURE 3: An area representation for 1 + 1

What can we say about $x + y$ for points inside the square? Most of the time, $x + y$ will round to 2, but sometimes it will round to 3, and sometimes it will round to 1. Note that the components of A add to 1.4, which rounds to 1; the components of B add to 2.3, which rounds to 2; and the components of C add to 2.7, which rounds to 3.

The probability that $1 + 1$ rounds to 1 is the fraction of the square containing pairs that, when added, round to 1. Now, $x + y$ rounds to 1 if $x + y < 1.5$, which will occur for points below the line $x + y = 1.5$. Similarly, $x + y$ rounds to 3 for points above the line $x + y = 2.5$. These conditions each cut off a triangular corner of the square (shown as the darker shaded regions in Figure 4).

The legs of these right triangles are each of length 1/2, so they each have area 1/8. Thus,

the probability that $1 + 1 = 3$ is 1/8, and the probability that $1 + 1 = 1$ is also 1/8. Finally the probability that $1 + 1 = 2$ is 3/4, the remaining fraction of the square.

EXTENSIONS. What's the probability that $1 \times 1 = 2$? This requires calculating the portion of the square that satisfies $xy > 1.5$ (Figure 5). Is this bigger or smaller than 1/8, calculated as the area of the upper triangle in Figure 4? A comparison of Figures 4 and 5 shows remarkable similarity. What is the precise relationship between the line $x + y = 2.5$ and the curve $xy = 1.5$? Solving the first equation for y and substituting into the second yields $x(x - 2.5) = 1.5$, a quadratic which simplifies to $-x^2 + 2.5x - 1.5 = 0$ or $2x^2 - 5x + 3 = 0$. This second equation factors easily as $(2x - 3)(x - 1) = 0$, yielding solutions $x = 1.5$ and $x = 1$. These solutions imply that the line $x + y = 2.5$ and the curve $xy = 1.5$ intersect the square at the same points. By the concavity

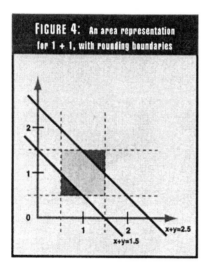

FIGURE 4: An area representation for 1 + 1, with rounding boundaries

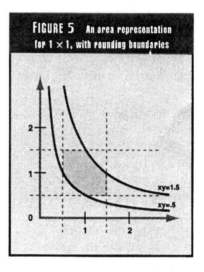

FIGURE 5 An area representation for 1 × 1, with rounding boundaries

Developer
FASE Productions

Distributor
FASE Productions
McDougal Littell

**Funders/
Contributors**
ARCO
*National Science
Foundation*
Toyota USA Foundation
U.S. Department of Energy

Interactions

Real Math—Real Careers 1994-1996

Motivates middle school students to study mathematics and science through videos showing the role math concepts play in solving real-life problems. Each video is based on a different theme and features several people who use mathematics in their jobs.

Videocassettes: 10-15 min., $435/12-program series or $39.95/cassette; Videodiscs: $1,080/6-module set (each module contains 2 of the videocassette programs) or $213.99/disc; Curriculum Guide: softcover, 104 pp., $10 (or free with purchase of cassette/disc set from developer's web site)

Content Overview

Various Mathematics, Science

Math covered includes decimals, exponents, fractions, functions, geometry, measurement, patterns, percents, powers of ten, proportions, ratios, and statistics.

Target Audience

For math and science classrooms in grades 6-9; "also ideal for many high school and college classrooms, vocational and career libraries, and for use by guidance counselors." Materials were intended to be used by mathematics teachers—all of the problems associated with each video episode are mathematical—but science educators have also made use of them.

Duration

Each video and its corresponding activities typically take 1 class period.

Workplace Connections

Every aspect of the curriculum focuses on how mathematics and science are used outside the classroom. The mathematics problems that accompany each episode use authentic contexts related to workplaces highlighted in the video.

Instructional Approach

"Interactions" motivates students to study mathematics and science and provides detailed contents for the study of specific topics. It is not designed to provide content instruction. In a typical instructional sequence, teachers (1) introduce the topic by reading or summarizing background information from the Teacher's Guide and asking students questions to get them thinking about the subject; (2) introduce vocabulary; (3) show video; (4) lead a class discussion of key elements from the episode, focusing on uses of mathematics; (5) have students work in cooperative groups on math problems (these may entail short calculations, making and interpreting tables and graphs, designing and conducting surveys, collecting and analyzing data, or writing short reports); and (6) assign a homework problem, which could involve short calculations, library research, and/or collecting and analyzing data over the course of a day or a week, for students to do with their families. Teachers should preview the videos and accompanying activities before use. The videos feature professionals from many cultural backgrounds as well as a balance of men and women.

Curriculum Components

(Number of questions/problems/items indicated in parentheses)

- *Videos*—color VHS with closed caption and stereo sound. For each video, the Teacher's Guide allocates 7-10 pp. to cover 5 features.

- *Overview*—general background information about video content.

- *Suggested Lesson Guide*—possible discussion points (2-3), vocabulary words and definitions (4-12), and key topics ("elements") in the video episode (5-9).

- *Interdisciplinary Activities*—activities that can be coordinated with teachers in other subject areas (4).

- *Additional Information*—content information beyond that covered in the video.

- *Memoranda*—reproducible outlines for student activity projects given in the form of memos from the professionals featured in the video episodes (2-3).

- *Answers and Sample Solutions*—solutions and solution methods for problems posed in the memoranda.

Materials

For videodiscs: Level 1 videodisc player; or, for Level 3 use, videodisc player with RS-232 computer connector, NTSC monitor, Macintosh LC or higher with 4 MB RAM.

Assessments

Although no explicit guidance is provided regarding assessment, the activities could be used for assessment purposes.

Teacher Resources   A "Making Connections" kit provides instructions and materials for workshops on effective use of videos in grades 6-12 mathematics classrooms. Developed with National Science Foundation funding, the kit can be used with small groups (such as within a math department) or larger groups (such as entire districts or regions). Workshop can range from 2-4 hours. Kits are available from FASE 1-800-404-FASE.

Standards   No information provided.

References   "Interactions" has received 17 awards, including a Distinguished Achievement Award (Educational Press Association), a Gold Medal (Worldfest/Houston International Film and Video Festival), a Parents' Choice approval, and a Silver World Medal (New York Festivals).

Sample Pages   Pages are from The Fashion Business episode. Pages 87-88 illustrate Memoranda-student activity projects given in the form of memos from professionals featured in the video. Page 89 is the Math at Home activity for this episode.

Ordering Information   **Videocassettes & instructional television license:** FASE Productions, 4801 Wilshire Boulevard, Suite 215, Los Angeles, CA 90010; 1-800-404-FASE; http://www.fasenet.org/itv/pg_interact.html

Great Plains National, P.O. Box 80669, Lincoln, Nebraska, 68501-0669; 1-800-228-4630. Broadcast licenses available.

Videodiscs: McDougal Littell (a Houghton Mifflin Company), P.O. Box 1667, Evanston, IL 60204

Table of Contents

(Number of pages in curriculum guide indicated in parentheses)

To	Costing assistants
From:	Michelle Branch/Merchandiser
Subject:	Costing jeans

The team designing jeans for next season have come up with an attractive design that they predict will be very popular. However, their design calls for a type of denim we haven't used before. We need to determine the cost for producing the new jeans.

As you look at the numbers in the table, remember that denim comes in rolls that are 6 feet in width. A "yard" of denim from such a roll is actually a piece that is 3 feet long and 6 feet wide.

Material	Amount used per 1000 jeans	Cost
Denim	1500 yards	$2.00 per yard
Cotton (for pockets)	300 yards	$0.50 per yard
Thread	25,000 yards	$0.005 per yard
Zippers	1000	$0.25 each
Rivets	6000	$0.015 each

1. Please determine the cost of materials for one pair of jeans (to the nearest tenth of a cent)

2. We could buy denim of a slightly higher quality for $2.20 per yard. By how much would the cost per pair of jeans increase if we used the higher-quality denim?

3. At our San Francisco plant we can make 5000 pair of the higher-quality jeans per day. We operate the factory 240 days of the year. The annual cost of this operation (not counting materials) is about 3 million dollars. What is the cost (to the nearest tenth of a cent) to make one pair of jeans, excluding materials? What is the total cost of manufacturing one pair of jeans?

56

MEMORANDUM

To: Market research assistants
From: Jill Lynch/Senior Marketing Specialist
Subject: Analyzing demographics

We have been studying the demographics of our north-central sales region where we would
like to sell more jeans. As a first step, we surveyed 1000 people and gathered the following information:

Age	Male	Female
0–11	54	43
12–15	59	62
16–24	96	105
25–45	168	172
over 45	114	127
Total	491	509

1. Please prepare a bar graph for the sales force showing the percent of people in
each age range. As you work on this project, apply these percents to the entire population,
not just the 1000 people that were surveyed.

2. We are considering marketing a style of jeans that we think will appeal to women
between the ages of 12 and 24. What percent of the population in the north-central sales
region would that range include?

3. One of our designs seems to sell best to men who are very active, which is about
80% of the men in the 12-15 age range, 60% of the men in the 16-24 age range, and 30%
of the men in the 25-45 age range. What percent of the total population in the north-
central sales region would those men represent?

4. We asked the people that we surveyed to tell us their favorite color of jeans, other
than the regular blue. Of the people in the 12-15 age range, 55% chose green, 20% chose
tan, and 10% chose light blue. I am interested to know if we would get similar results
from other populations. Please find another group of people in or near the 12-15 age
range. Survey them using this same question and report your results.

57

Dear Family,

We have been studying how mathematics is used by people in the fashion business. We have considered the cost of materials, determined profit based on regular and discount prices, figured out the effect of discounts on the rate of sales, and explored how math is used in making advertising decisions.

Here is a related activity about comparative costs that can be done at home. Please work with your daughter or son on this activity and discuss the results.

Sincerely,

_____

Making Clothing

With an adult, go to a clothing store and find an article of clothing you like. Note the type of material and the number of fasteners (buttons, snaps, zippers, hooks) used to make the clothing. Record the price.

Then go to a fabric store that sells patterns for making one's own clothing. Find a pattern for an item similar to the one that you priced in the clothing store. With the help of your companion and the fabric store salesperson, estimate the cost of making the item you have selected. First use the information on the pattern package to figure out how much material is required. Record the total cost for the item, including the cost of the material, thread, fasteners, and the pattern itself. (Some patterns may require other items such as trim or lining material.)

From your research, prepare to discuss with your group or class some advantages and disadvantages of purchasing ready-made clothing and of making your own clothes.

58

Developer
Adirondack Community College

Distributor
Adirondack Community College

Funders/ Contributors
National Science Foundation

Mathematical Applications for Business and Industry

1998

Applied mathematics course that can bridge the transition between high school and community college or high school and the workplace. All instruction is problem-based; problems focus on mathematics applications in real-world and business/industry settings. Written by community college and high school educators, and representatives from business and industry; sponsored by the National Science Foundation's Advanced Technological Education (ATE) program.

Loose-leaf notebook, 995 pp.; free

Content Overview

Various Mathematics

Although some chapters contain material not usually found in high school mathematics textbooks—e.g., dimensional analysis and statistical process control—most touch on a wide variety of typically found topics. For a course geared toward average students, the authors recommend covering chapters 1-5 and chapters 7-8. Precalculus students could cover the majority of the text (chapters 1-12).

Target Audience

High school seniors or community college freshmen who have successfully completed applied math 1, 2, and 3 or sequential math 1, 2, and 3 and are interested in applied mathematics for technical careers and/or work. Course was written for students in the middle 50% ability level.

Duration

1 year.

Workplace Connections

Many of the problem scenarios were written in cooperation with consultants from business and industry in the following areas:

allied health and medicine
environment
construction
transportation
telecommunications
marketing and retail

chemical and materials
military/law enforcement
sports
entertainment
finance

Some problems use specialized workplace terminology.

Instructional Approach

Concepts presented in multiple representations: graphical, numerical, algebraic, and verbal/written. Contains scenarios followed by several paper-and-pencil short-answer questions that may involve the use of graphing calculators. Students are sometimes expected to provide written justifications for their answers. Also included are hands-on laboratory investigations in which students follow explicit directions. The problems and labs are prescriptive and suitable for either individual or group work. No pedagogical recommendations are provided.

Curriculum Components

Chapters typically include:

* *Scenarios*—a context with accompanying paper-and-pencil questions.

* *Laboratories*—hands-on activities that involve materials.

* *Explorations*—graphing calculator-based explorations (not in every chapter).

* *Reflections*—nonmathematical paper-and-pencil questions to help students make sense of the content.

* *Exercises*—follow-up paper-and-pencil questions.

Capstone problems and projects—located at the end of the curriculum's 4 main modules, these complex and demanding activities require students to explore many aspects of problems over an extended period of time. Results are usually to be presented as a written report. Not all capstones are intended to be completed in the course; the teacher can select from the range of problems provided to best meet class interests.

The curriculum also contains a resource section (summary of formulas and algorithms) and an answer key (complete solution manual including solution processes).

Materials

Curriculum requires graphing calculators with statistical analysis capabilities; it recommends spreadsheets and data collection devices such as the Texas Instruments Calculator Based Laboratory (CBL) or Calculator Based Ranger (CBR). Internet access is desirable. Material lists are provided for laboratory activities. Most items are readily available and include mathematics resources (such as rulers and protractors); everyday items (such as gum, tomato juice, and cardboard boxes); and science resources (such as eye droppers, stop watches, weights, and spring balances).

Assessments

While problems in the chapters could be used for assessment purposes, no assessments are provided.

Standards

In developing this curriculum, attention was paid to the American Mathematical Association of Two-Year Colleges' *Crossroads in Mathematics: Standards for Introductory College Mathematics Before Calculus*, which references the 1993 SCANS report.

Sample Pages

Page 93 is a hands-on laboratory from the applied geometry chapter. Page 94 is a scenario and accompanying problems from the circular trigonometry chapter. Page 95 is a capstone project that follows the last module.

Ordering Information

Diane Doyle, Project Director, Adirondack Community College, 640 Bay Road, Queensbury, NY 12804; (518) 743-2228; doyled@acc.sunyacc.edu.

Authors currently distribute free copies; a publisher is being sought.

Table of Contents

(Number of pages indicated in parentheses)

Laboratory 2: Cardboard Packaging
Topics: measurement, scale drawing, ratio and proportion

Companies produce cardboard packaging to house the products they manufacture. Packaging production is a design process requiring planning based on product size and shape.

1. Using a cardboard package (cereal box, pizza box, equipment box, etc.) carefully open the package completely so the cardboard becomes a flat sheet. Assume that this shape has been cut from the smallest possible rectangular piece of cardboard. Companies are careful in production to minimize waste. Describe one method to calculate the amount of waste for your cardboard package.

2. The % waste is the ratio of waste to the original size piece of cardboard, multiplied by 100. Find the % waste for your cardboard package.

3. One way to introduce a new product to the public is to produce a trial size, a smaller version of the original. What factors need to be considered when making a trial size?

7 - 19

4. Develop a model trial size package of the package selected in Problem 1.

   a. Select the appropriate scale, using at least ½ reduction, to produce a scale model of this trial size.

   b. Make the scale model using plain white paper.

   c. Determine the amount of cardboard needed to produce the trial size.

   d. Is the % waste the same? Explain.

7 - 20

Scenario 5: Pipe Fitting

Topics: horizontal vs vertical plane displacement, 45-45-90, solutions t triangle, angle measure DMS conversions, scale drawing

Industrial facilities contain extensive piping systems to transport their feed and stock as well as their service utilities. Piping must be routed around tanks, equipment and other obstructions, thereby changing direction both horizontally and vertically. Pipe fitters must be able to compute actual pipe dimensions through these changes in planes.

1. The provided sketch shows a piece of pipe changing direction horizontally. (Top view of layout)

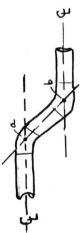

a. Redraw the pipe section showing only the pipe centerline. Label points a and b on the sketch.

b. Identify some methods that could be used to determine the distance between points a and b.

c. The perpendicular distance between the parallel pipes is known as the centerline distance. The centerline distance is 10'. Assuming 2 equal changes in direction in the horizontal plane, draw and label the diagram using the given information.

8 - 18

d. Calculate distance AB.

Angular directions in the horizontal plane are only described by north, east, south and west. Horizontal angles can range in value from 0° to 360°. Angular direction in the vertical plane are either positive or negative. Positive angles are above the horizontal plane; negative angles point below the horizontal plane. These angles range in value form 0° to 90° because the direction of the angle is first set in the horizontal plane. Changing more than +/ - 90° in the vertical plane causes the direction of the horizontal plane to change.

2. A horizontal pipe, 6" in diameter, must be reoriented at a 45° angle to avoid a pump. This reorientation gives a change in elevation of 6'- 4½". (The 6'- 4½" distance equals 76 ½" because the engineering graphics dash (-) symbol separates feet from inches.)

a. Draw and label the pipe layout before the change in orientation.

b. Draw and label the pipe layout with the new orientation using the provided data.

c. Calculate the length of pipe required for this change in elevation.

8 - 19

Capstone 23: Syringe Manufacturing

A medical equipment manufacturer makes two types of syringes -- type x and type y. These syringes require the addition of tips and grips before they are packaged.

1.   Each week the manufacturer has enough material available to produce 300 type x syringes and 300 type y syringes but the grips and tips must be special ordered. Each type x syringe comes with 5 grips and 7 tips while each type y syringe comes with 4 grips and 6 tips. Each week only 2600 grips and 3700 tips are available. The same number of type x and y syringes must be produced each week. Using the table feature on your graphing utility or a spreadsheet, generate a table showing the number of grips and tips required for each type of syringe.

2.   Use the table generated in question 1 to find the maximum number of syringes that can be manufactured each week.

3.   It takes an employee 3 minutes to assemble and package each type x syringe and 4 minutes to assemble and package each type y syringe. How long would it take one employee to package the maximum number of x and y syringes that could be produced each week?

C - 87

Developer
Gary Simundza,
Wentworth Institute of
Technology

Funders/
Contributors
National Science
Foundation

Mathematics for Technology

Laboratory Investigations 1996-1997

These 22 mathematics investigations introduce concepts in a real-world engineering and design context. The problems originally written for precalculus students taking community college courses in engineering, architecture, design, or management have been adapted for supplemental use in high school mathematics courses. They were created by a senior engineer at General Electric, Boston area high school teachers, and an interdisciplinary team at Wentworth Institute of Technology.

Spiral-bound, 164 pp.; contact developer for cost

Content Overview

Various
Mathematics

Problems cover geometry (shapes, area, volume, construction, translation, rotation, reflection); modeling (linear, geometric, use of variables, use of models to make predictions); algebra (equations, graphing and understanding lines, addition of functions, systems of equations, exponential functions, linear inequalities, ratios and proportions); measurement (significant digits, scientific notation, accuracy, precision); data analysis (average, mean, standard deviation, histograms, frequency distributions); logical reasoning (deductive reasoning, conjunctions, disjunctions); and miscellaneous topics (chart reading, introduction to vectors, scale drawing, variation, inverse square, golden ratio).

Target Audience

Adapted from materials developed for college freshmen for use in high school applied mathematics courses, including tech prep programs; a subset of the investigations also can be used to highlight workplace connections in algebra and geometry classes.

Duration

Investigations typically take 2 hours.

Workplace Connections

Introductory text for each laboratory investigation sets the activity's mathematics in the context of a specific real-world application. Careers highlighted include pilots, site excavators, engineers, architects, financial analysts, artists, and real estate developers.

Instructional Approach

The laboratory investigations are prescriptive and intended to be completed by students working in groups; they involve data analysis and often require data collection. A few investigations ask students to make predictions beyond the situation they are studying and/or require them to make oral presentations. The paper-and-pencil questions consist of both closed-form items involving calculations and open-ended items that have students justify their thinking or write a paragraph describing their sense of a situation. The instructional materials note where it might be helpful for the teacher to have the entire class work together through a set of calculations. No other pedagogical recommendations are provided.

Curriculum Components

Most of the 22 investigations begin with a list of mathematical topics, a list of prerequisite knowledge, a list of required equipment, and an introduction. The remaining sections vary with each lab.

Materials

All laboratory activities require equipment, most of which is either commonly found in mathematics classes (calculators, rulers, compasses, string); science laboratories (graduated cylinders, triple beam balances, ammeters, and vernier calipers); or households (bathroom scales, flour, nails, brooms). A minority of the equipment is specialized (visual flight rule charts and site plans).

Assessments

Materials do not illustrate how students should analyze data collected in their labs; no materials or advice provided for assessing student learning.

Special Preparations

Mathematics teachers may not be comfortable with students performing laboratory investigations, which is integral to implementing this curriculum. Also, some of the equipment used is unusual (visual flight rule charts, architectural plans); and some will be unfamiliar to most mathematics teachers (voltmeter, ammeter).

Teacher Resources

An edition for college freshmen is available: *Precalculus Investigations: A Laboratory Manual*, 1999, 336 pp., $25.00 est. (plus an Instructor's Manual), Prentice Hall, Saddle River, NJ 07458

Standards

The authors state that the curriculum is consistent with the current reform in mathematics education as promoted by the Mathematical Association of America, American Mathematical Association of Two-Year Colleges, and National Council of Teachers of Mathematics. No correlation between the curriculum and standards documents is provided.

Sample Pages

Pages 99-101 contain the first three of six pages from the Milling Traffic Signs investigation. Tasks 2-3 and homework are on the remaining three pages of the investigation (not shown).

Ordering Information

Gary Simundza, Project Director and Professor of Mathematics, Department of Applied Mathematics and Sciences, Wentworth Institute of Technology, 550 Huntington Avenue, Boston, MA 02115-5998; 617-989-4354; simundza @wit.edu (e-mail); http://www.wit.edu/events/mathtech/

Table of Contents

(Number of pages indicated in parentheses; followed by mathematics topics covered)

MATHEMATICS LABORATORY INVESTIGATION

MILLING TRAFFIC SIGNS

Topic: **Coordinate Geometry, Domain Restrictions**
Prerequisite knowledge: *Cartesian coordinates, Basic Algebra*
Equipment required: graphing calculator

I.   INTRODUCTION

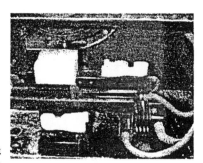

Milling is one of many processes used in manufacturing industries. When an object has to be cut precisely from a solid piece of stock material, it is milled. Common stock materials are wood, plastic and metal. Machine parts can be milled to very exact specifications. Molded plastic, glass or metal items are often cast in molds composed of a milled die. In another process, one pattern is created with a milling machine, several molds are made from that object and liquefied plastic, glass or metal is poured into the mold and left to harden.

II.   MODERN MILLING MACHINE OPERATIONS

Older milling machines can be dangerous to operate. Modern computer driven milling machines require less human contact and are safer. A modern milling machine is

pictured at right. An operator must instruct the computer how to direct the machine to cut out the desired object from the solid material. The operator's instructions must tell the machine where to begin and to end a cut, how deep to cut, and to cut in a straight line or circular arc. One method of instructing the computer driven machine is with codes. This, in effect, is writing a program to tell the machine how to cut from Point A to Point B and then from Point B to Point C and so on until the entire object has been cut from the stock material.

The geometry of creating machine instructions is similar to that used in many CAD (Computer Aided Design) programs. The process is the same for milling a pattern for your class ring or for creating an architectural drawing.

III. DESCRIBING THE MILLING PROCESS

The milling process can be described in many different ways. Different machines and different CAM (computer aided manufacturing) programs use different programming languages. This lab will be using a generic instruction language. Such machine independent languages are referred to as *pseudocode*. For the particular pseudocode of this lab, assume that the milling machine is capable of making only straight cuts. To see how the pseudocode works, consider the problem of milling a yield sign as shown below. Let us assume the corners are not rounded.

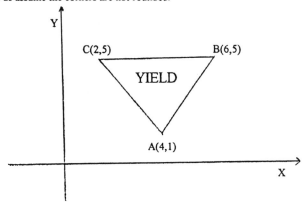

For this design, the pseudocode could read:

Go from (4,1) to (6,5) cutting a straight line
Go from (6,5) to (2,5) cutting a straight line
Go from (2,5) to (4,1) cutting a straight line

Notice that there are three points where the various cuts meets. These three *cut points* are called in this picture by A, B, and C, while the pseudocode refers to them by their coordinates.

Telling the machine where to start and stop is easy. It's a little more complicated to describe the milling process by using algebraic equations. The equations describe the line segments outlining the piece to be milled. In the case of the first cut on the yield sign, it is a straight line with a slope of 2 (rise/run) passing through the point (4,1), but only that portion from x = 4 to x = 6 is needed. This is called a *domain restriction*. Use of domain restrictions gives what are called *piecewise defined functions*. To get the equation of the function in this case, the *y-intercept* must first be found. The *y-intercept* is the number on the y-axis where the line crosses.

Using the slope intercept form of the equation $y = mx + b$, let m, the slope, be 2 and (x,y), the point be (4,1), the equation of the line can be found.

$1 = 2(4) + b$
$1 = 8 + b$, therefore b = -7

2

This gives us the equation of the line to be y = 2x - 7. The equation of the segment or the piecewise defined function would be as follows:

$$y = 2x - 7, (4 \leq x \leq 6)$$

TASK 1: Milling the Yield Sign

Using the space provided find the equations and the domain restrictions for the other two sides of the yield sign.

Complete the table below.

CUT	PSEUDOCODE	EQUATIONS	RESTRICTIONS
A to B	Go from (4,1) to (6,5) cutting a straight line	y = 2x - 7	$(4 \leq x \leq 6)$

The advantage of using algebra is that technology provides a way to check your equations so you can view your design before sending the pseudocode to the machine programmer. If your school has a modern milling machine, your code could be translated into its machine language and the shape would be milled from your design. Checking your design is important in the workplace. You don't want to gain a reputation for errors, which waste other employees' time and raw materials. Both of these are costly to the company, not just to one's self esteem.

Enter your equations into your graphing calculator to see if you get the yield sign. For TI calculators, use the syntax y = (function)/(restriction) with the restrictions written as $x \geq a$ and $x \leq b$. For example the cut from A to B would be entered as

$$y = (2x - 7)/(x \geq 4 \text{ and } x \leq 6)$$

You need to have a window with a square setting. To do this, press "zoom", and select Zsquare. Don't forget to set your domain and range values.

3

Developer
Agency for Instructional Technology (AIT)

Distributor
AIT

Funders/ Contributors
AIT

Mathemedia

1995

Video-based program to supplement, reinforce, and extend prealgebra curriculum. Each module focuses on a mathematics topic and includes a video showing applications of mathematics that are solidly and explicitly connected to workplace and everyday contexts. Modules have been correlated to the NCTM standards, SCANS competencies, and 30 commercial math textbooks from 14 different publishers.

Videos: 12 20-min. programs on 6 cassettes or 3 videodiscs, $495; Student ed.: spiral-bound, 320 pp., $15.95; Teacher's ed.: spiral-bound, 336 pp., $24.95; Software: Windows or Macintosh disk, $49.95; Individual videocassette and 1 Teacher's Guide: $75.00

Content Overview

Prealgebra

Covers graphs, decimals, exponents, logical reasoning, measurement, fractions, positive and negative numbers, formulas, ratios, percentages, area and volume, probability, and coordinates. Emphasizes problem solving and logical reasoning.

Target Audience

Can be used as the core of tech prep or applied mathematics courses.

Duration

Experienced mathematics teachers can use the video, text, and software materials as an entire year course. Also well-suited as supplementary resource: teachers could use portions to introduce topics in prealgebra classes or could cover key aspects of a video episode over 3-5 days.

Workplace Connections

While the content is organized by mathematical topic, workplace contexts are central to every module. Every video includes footage of mathematical activities or problems in actual business or industrial settings (including dairy farming, currency trading, construction, engineering, and landscaping). Videos also feature dramatizations in which teenagers solve workplace or consumer problems (e.g., buying tires, designing a cereal box).

Module 7 encourages students to visit a workplace (school kitchen or district food service office) or have staff from these sites visit the class.

Instructional Approach

The Teacher's Guide includes suggestions for facilitating group work and extensive pedagogical recommendations for each module. The recommended instructional approach for each of the 12 modules follows:

- *Overview of module*—students read the following sections in their text: "What You Will Learn in This Module, and Why You Need to Learn It," and "What You Will See on the Screen."

- *Video segment* (3 per module)—teacher should pause the tape at certain times to allow for student reflection, respond to student questions, and give demonstrations. Students read the text, view the video, answer paper-and-pencil questions, and engage in whole- and small-group discussions and debates. Requires students to mathematically analyze problems occurring in the video to predict likely outcomes; main possibilities are included in the remaining video, and the teacher can elect to play outcomes that match or conflict with student predictions. Some mathematics concepts are developed very quickly, so teachers should refer to the Teacher's Guide for suggested probing questions and explanations of formulas (these formulas often are presented in the videos without explanation).

- *Summary*—consists of 2 sections ("Hands On" and "Gearing Up for a Challenge"), each containing 2 problems and/or activities for individual or group work.

- *Assessment*—students watch a special section of the videodisc and answer 2-7 questions in their guide.

Curriculum Components

Video—Each module's video has 3 self-contained segments related to a particular mathematics topic. The first shows actual business or industrial settings where activities or problems demonstrate the use of the mathematics topic. The two other segments present dramatic situations–one involves workplace or consumer problems that may confront students (now or in the near future) and demonstrates how mathematics is used to solve common problems. Other segments show teens solving more abstract conceptual problems in non-workplace settings (e.g., calculating the probability of winning a game and counting rhythm in a school band). Interspersed throughout each segment are numerous questions or other prompts intended to generate discussion, debate, or problem solving.

The developers strongly recommend using the interactive videodisc format as opposed to the linear videotape. When the video presents students with several alternatives for solving a problem, barcodes permit teachers to play videodisc footage that shows the consequences of selected choices. By contrast, teachers who use the videotape format will need to stop the program for discussion and then play the consequences for each possible solution sequentially, stopping the videotape after each solution to make sure students understand it before moving on to the next. The bar codes on the videodisc also let teachers replay anything students may have missed or may need to review, or to skip ahead if the material has been learned. The videodisc for each module has a separate audio track that contains assessment items. The separate assessment track is not available on the videotape version, but the assessment items do appear in the printed Teacher and Student Guides.

Teacher's Guide—Each module includes teaching objectives, segment settings, key concepts, a list of required materials or preparation, and suggestions for implementing and directing the activities that appear in the Student Guide. Answers to all student exercises are provided.

Student Guide—Provides photos, drawings, tables, charts, and graphs for activities that support the lessons in each module. Space is provided for students to do calculations and to record the steps in their reasoning and conclusions from their work. Contains the following information and activities for each video module:

- *Connections*—previewing activities that link the topic or key ideas with students' prior experience and knowledge.

- Restatement of questions and prompts in the video segments to stimulate discussion and activities.

- *Putting It Together*—small group or team activities suitable for cooperative learning and portfolio assessment.

- *Hands On*—activity suggestions geared to students with alternative learning styles or special needs.

- *Gearing Up for a Challenge*—activities for academically inclined students, including those whose interests may lie in areas other than mathematics.

- *Assessment suggestions*—several paper-and-pencil questions that refer to the video.

Software—Consists of problem-solving activities using spreadsheets.

Materials

The Teacher's Guide lists materials required and recommended for each module. Most items are commonly found in mathematics classrooms (such as graph paper, rulers, scissors, and unit blocks) or are everyday objects (such as eggbeaters, liquid and dry measuring cups, cardboard, lumber, decks of cards, and maps). A few objects are commonly found in other teachers' classrooms (such as globes, balance scales, and Exacto knives).

Assessments

Each module's videodisc has a special assessment track containing several assessment questions that use selected video segments as prompts and cues. Students use this information to answer 2-7 paper-and-pencil problems in their books. These problems are either previously asked problems with 1 or 2 variables changed, or new ones requiring students to generalize what they have learned.

Special Preparations

Some modules have optional activities that require significant advance planning, purchasing of materials, and/or coordination of special facilities.

Teacher Resources

Three types of professional development workshops are offered to teachers: free presentations at regional/national meetings of the National Council of Teachers of Mathematics, free week-long training sessions at AIT (participants must cover their own travel expenses), and on-site workshops by AIT representatives for a fee. Contact the director of AIT professional development at 1-800-457-4509, ext. 212.

Standards

The Teacher's Guide correlates course content to NCTM Curriculum and Evaluation Standards (1989) and Professional Standards for Teaching Mathematics (1991).

Sample Pages

All pages are from module 7 (Formulas). Pages 107-108 are the first two pages of the module; they are atypical in the sense that the Useful Materials for this Module section is omitted because no materials are suggested for this module. Pages 156-157 illustrate part of the instructional sequence pertaining to the video. Page 158 is a section of the module summary, which includes a suggested visit to a worksite; this type of activity is atypical because worksite visits are uncommon in this curriculum.

Ordering Information

Agency for Instructional Technology, Box A, Bloomington, IN 47402-0120; 1-800-457-4509; http://www.ait.net/catalog/catpages/c372.shtml

Table of Contents: Teacher's Guide

(Number of pages indicated in parentheses)

7 Formulas

MODULE 7 MENU

Load Disc Side 4
(or appropriate videocassette)

PART A: FORMULAS BUY TIME

PART B: MILES PER BUCK

PART C: PLANE TALK

QUIT INSTRUCTIONS

Preview

Objectives: Students will demonstrate that they can

- construct formulas and equations
- solve equations in one variable
- use formulas in basic computer spreadsheets

Contextual Settings

- **Electronics store.** The manager explains the use of spreadsheets in predicting next year's sales and costs. Viewers are asked to help project next year's sales and expenses. ("Formulas Buy Time," beginning on page 7–3)

- **Health service association.** A nurse who needs to rent a car to drive a lengthy circuit is confused by the difficulty of comparing rates offered by different rental companies. Viewers are invited to advise her on selecting the best deal. ("Miles Per Buck," beginning on page 7–11)

- **Small airfield.** The pilot of a small private plane explains to two teenagers why he needs to plug the weight of gas, cargo, and even passengers into a weight formula before he can take off. ("Plane Talk," beginning on page 7–16)

7 Formulas

What you will learn in this module

As you have advanced in mathematics, you've probably come to realize that formulas are important for many calculations. In this module, you will look at formulas in general. You'll begin to understand what they are and how they operate, and you will see how they can make a lot of calculating easier and more efficient. You'll get some practice in using formulas when one quantity changes while others remain the same. You'll also see how computers use formulas to "crunch" hundreds of numbers in spreadsheets — and they do it faster than you can blink.

And why you need to learn it

If you have ever made money by babysitting, mowing lawns, or delivering newspapers, you probably used formulas to figure out how much you were earning — although your formulas may not have looked like the ones in the math books you have used. In babysitting, for example, you might calculate:

(N hours before midnight x $A) + (Y hours after midnight x $B) + $Z for an extra child = my pay

For mowing, your formula might involve:

hours x $rate + gas = payment

or

feet^2 x $rate = payment

Paper carriers might use a formula similar to this one:

(N daily subscribers x $profit per daily paper x A days) + (Y Sunday subscribers + $profit per Sunday paper x B Sundays) = earnings

Subtopics/Key Ideas

- Formulas are generalizations of procedures, patterns, and relationships.

- The use of formulas in spreadsheets allows for immediate adjustments and recalculations when any value is changed.

Useful Preparation for This Module

- You may wish to make arrangements for students to visit the school cafeteria or the district food-service office—or to have staff from these visit your class—to discuss the use of spreadsheets in tracking meals prepared and sold, as well as supplies and inventories.

What you will see on the screen

In Part A, "Formulas Buy Time," you will visit an electronics store and see some of the amazing calculations that a computer can make with data in a spreadsheet. By the time you finish this segment, you will understand how spreadsheets work, and you'll also get a good idea about how much cordless phones will cost next year.

Part B, "Miles per Buck," lets you share the problems of a nurse whose job is to drive hundreds of miles every day to visit clinics. When her car breaks down, she's at the mercy of car rental companies because she can't figure out the formula that will let her compare their rates.

Julia and Paige learn that to fly a small plane you must know how to use formulas for weight and fuel estimates. The safety instructions point in Paige's brother

Did you know that sometimes your own weight might make a difference in an airplane? In Part C, "Plane Talk," you will discover what happens when three young persons are ready to take a trip in a private plane. The pilot explains that using formulas to estimate weight and gas correctly can make the difference between reaching your destination and staying on the ground.

VIDEO TIME

■ Start the videodisc, and play Part A until it stops.

Talk This Over

■ Ask students to think about the question on what kinds of things a business can do with data stored in a computer, and have them list their ideas in their guides. Then encourage them to share their ideas. They might suggest "calculating prices" and "tracking inventory." Point out that a spreadsheet for a business that has many different kinds of expenses and many different types of sales can alert managers to costs that are too high, to merchandise that is selling well (or poorly), and to times when a certain type of sale is a success (or a failure). Spreadsheets also provide the information that managers need for figuring the taxes they owe and the sales taxes they have collected.

Ask students how much of this information would have been easily and quickly available in a handwritten ledger. Encourage discussion. After they have made several suggestions, swipe the barcode to continue.

VIDEO TIME

Talk This Over

Watch "Formulas Buy Time" to learn more about the way businesses use spreadsheets. The video will ask, "Once the raw data are stored in the computer, what kinds of things can a business do with the information?"

Think about this question in connection with a business you have observed or with which you've had experience. List some things a business owner can do with the data in the computer.

_____

_____

_____

_____

_____

Part A Formulas Buy Time

Continue

156 • *Mathemedia: Module 7*

Teacher's Guide

MATHEMEDIA ♦ 109

Figure It Out

■ The video presents a series of still frames that demonstrate how to construct a formula for predicting sales of cordless phones. Students are discouraged from making wild predictions and are told to focus on Zenith sales only. Discuss with them what will need to go into a formula for predicting next year's sales of Zenith phones. Also discuss what formula should be written for the first step, which is to find the percent of increase of this year's sales over last year's.

If students clearly understand that the formula for predicting sales must be based on percent of increase, and if they know how to calculate this, you may swipe the barcode to see the formula immediately. Otherwise give students a moment to create the formula for percent of increase, and then swipe "Break It Down" so they can compare their work with the video model to write the formula for percent of increase and/or to calculate the answer.

After students have had time to work, conduct a discussion of the formulas they have written. Then swipe the barcodes so they can compare their work with the video's explanations.

After showing the solution to the percent of increase in Zenith sales, the video offers a prompt related to next year's sales projections. Before pursuing either choice offered on the screen, challenge students to write the formula for predicting next year's Zenith sales.

Note: You may wish to stress the need to be careful when they use their results in the formula for predicting next year's sales. Specifically, they will need to use the decimal form (.052) of the percentage when they calculate.

When you have finished discussing the need to figure percent of increase in the previous year's sales and the role that these data play in the formula for predicting next year's sales, swipe for the solution.

FORMULA—NEXT YEAR'S ZENITH SALES

BREAK IT DOWN

SOLUTION—NEXT YEAR'S ZENITH SALES; BRANCHING OPTIONS

FORMULA—CALCULATING NEXT YEAR'S SALES PROJECTION

FORMULA—CALCULATING NEXT YEAR'S SALES PROJECTION (CONTINUED)

SOLUTION—CALCULATING NEXT YEAR'S SALES PROJECTION

Figure It Out

The video will pause again, presenting the data on the spreadsheet, asking a question, and giving you two alternatives for answering.

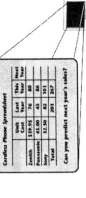

Cordless Phone Spreadsheet

	Unit Cost	Last Year	This Year	Next Year
Zenith	$19.95	76	80	
Panasonic	45.00	45	86	
Sony	12.50	82	101	
Total		203	267	

Can you predict next year's sales?

Can you develop a formula that might predict next year's sales? Sure you can. And here's a hint how to do it: Focus on the Zenith sales first.

What is the first thing you need to determine about Zenith phone sales, and how will you determine it? Discuss this question, and when you and your classmates have decided what you need to calculate, write the formula for this first step here:

Formula for first step:

Watch the video to see if you have correctly stated what the first step must be and if you have succeeded in writing the formula you need to carry out this step.

After you've compared your formula and your calculations with the ones on the video, a screen will ask:

> **Do you want to calculate next year's sales projection?**
> or
> **See a formula for doing this?**

Module 7
Wrap It Up

HANDS ON

Spreadsheets into Food

■ **Individual or team activity.** Arrange for the class to visit the kitchen supervisor at the school cafeteria or the district dietitian or food-service officer; as an alternative, invite a representative from one of these places to visit your class. School food services use spreadsheets to track numbers of meals prepared and sold, as well as to keep records of how many meals were eligible for federal subsidy. They also may use spreadsheets to track inventories and costs of staples, or to compare sales of different food items on menus. Have students prepare questions to ask the food-service employee about the use of spreadsheets in determining the meals that are served.

Secret Formulas

■ **Individual or team activity.** Have students do a research project that involves talking to sales representatives to learn about the formulas that determine a large number of everyday charges and purchases. The *Student Guide* contains a list of such items to help students get started, but they may be able to find other examples.

Student Guide, page 7–22

Module 7
Wrap It Up

HANDS ON

Spreadsheets into Food

Food services for schools use spreadsheets to keep track of daily meal purchases, numbers of subsidized meals, and sales of a la carte items (when available). They also use spreadsheets to find out which food items sell best or worst and to predict how many meals of a particular menu will be sold. Spreadsheets also track inventories of ingredients and supplies and show what needs to be ordered.

You may want to visit your school kitchen to see how spreadsheets are used there. Learn about the way spreadsheets determine what will be available in your cafeteria next week.

Secret Formulas

Many common products are governed by formulas. While the formulas are not exactly secret, few people really know what they mean. Do some detective work to discover the meaning of the formulas that are hiding all around you, whether you know it or not. Here are a few suggestions to get you started:

- octane rating of gasoline.
- rates for electric, gas, water, or telephone bills
- "proof" of alcoholic beverages
- "R" ratings for insulation
- insurance rates for young drivers
- motor oil classifications
- weights of different kinds of paper (a sheet of 20-lb. paper does not weigh 20 pounds!)
- USDA labeling standards for hot dogs, mayonnaise, and other prepared products

Talk to merchants and salespeople to learn about the formulas behind the various numbers, classifications, weights, or

Developer
Center on Education and Work, University of Wisconsin-Madison

Distributor
Center on Education and Work, University of Wisconsin-Madison

Funders
U.S. Department of Education, Office of Vocational and Adult Education

MathNet

1998

Focused on rigorous treatment of the mathematics used in several occupational contexts, this supplementary modular curriculum was developed by 8 interdisciplinary teams of mathematics and vocational/technical instructors at 7 high schools and a community college. Modules were designed for use in either a mathematics or a vocational/technical course.

8 modules: 6 softcover, and 2 three-ring binders; 17-194 pp. each; available on a cost-recovery basis

---

Content Overview

Varied Mathematics

Covers mathematics used in technical areas such as business and information management, construction, and automotive technology. Mathematics concepts covered include trigonometry, algebra, geometry, measurement, graphs, data collection and analysis, and statistics. Technology/vocational concepts include use of specialized tools; and concepts and skills related to surveying, solar energy, automobiles, welding, business, computers, electronics, multimedia, and physical science.

Target Audience

"Academic and vocational education teachers interested in developing integrated curriculum materials or in emphasizing workplace applications of mathematical computer modeling, graphing, statistics, and probability for all students to excel in mathematics."

Duration

2-6 weeks; some modules designed for block schedules

Workplace Connections

In each module, the mathematics topics are those needed in specific workplaces, but the amount of reference to the workplace varies by module. Examples of explicit workplace connections made in the modules follow.

- *Building for Bowser and Buck$*—teachers are encouraged to invite speakers to come to class to discuss market research.

- *Woofer Wise and Tweeter Smart*—students take a field trip to a local electronics store, or a salesperson from an electronics store visits the school and brings equipment and technical specifications.

- *Bridges—How Safe Are They?*—students identify careers and requirements needed to enter a variety of occupations.

Instructional Approach

The instructional approach varies considerably among the different modules, but each provides pedagogical recommendations. Although some have extensive sections in which students practice mathematical and technical skills on individual worksheets, in most modules, students spend the majority of their time working in teams in hands-on activities. Some activities are structured; others provide students with fewer directions as they progress through the module. Typical student activities include: brainstorming ideas, engaging in research, presenting results to the class, keeping journals of successes and difficulties encountered, peer teaching, and collecting and analyzing data.

Curriculum Components

Each module begins with an overview that includes a description of the local circumstances, interests, and resources of the team that developed the module; strategies for instruction and assessment; and practical considerations for implementation. In some modules, there is also a list of standards addressed. The overview is followed by the instructional materials; in some modules, this is divided into separate sections for teachers and students. The format of the instructional materials varies widely among modules.

There are 2 supplementary resources:

- *Integrating Mathematics in Occupational Contexts: A Sampler of Curricular Units* (88 pp.)—presents sample activities from each of the 8 modules.

- *Integrating Mathematics in Occupational Contexts: A Guide for Developing Standards-Based Units* (69 pp.)—provides a general 6-step framework for teams of instructors who want to develop integrated mathematics and school-to-work curricula that are "authentic" and standards-based.

Materials

All modules require some materials and/or equipment. Many materials are commonly found in mathematics classrooms, including computers with Internet access, spreadsheet software, calculators (scientific and graphing); graph paper (Cartesian, polar, and semi-logarithmic); and protractors.

Other materials generally can be found in school, technology, or science labs, including audio amplifiers, triple beam scales, weights, triangular drafting scales, levels, electronics equipment, sheet metal equipment, and carpenter squares. Some materials can be obtained from retail stores, local businesses, or homes. A few specialized materials must be obtained from vendors, such as specific computer software and kits for making toolboxes.

Assessments

Assessment techniques vary among the modules, but suggestions such as the following are provided in each: observing student handling of equipment, grading student responses to written questions, appraising the quality of student constructions, assessing students' written final reports and class presentations, grading the quality of student interactions, and grading students' journals and portfolios.

Special Preparations

Many modules recommend the use of team teaching and offer suggestions for its implementation. At a minimum, teachers are encouraged to maintain open dialogue with teachers in other disciplines when using the curriculum. If the curriculum is used by a mathematics teacher alone (not in conjunction with a technology teacher) he or she would need extensive time to become familiar with technical tools and equipment needed to implement the modules. Similarly, if the curriculum is used by a technology teacher alone, he or she would need to become familiar with the associated mathematics concepts.

Standards

Designed to be in alignment with the NCTM standards and with the National Consortium for Product Quality (NCPQ) criteria. Some modules reference competencies found in the SCANS standards. Some correlate specific concepts covered in the module to various standards documents.

Sample Pages

Pages 116-118 are taken from the unit Bridges - How Safe Are They? and illustrate the following components: hands-on investigations, a computer simulation activity, an example of incorporating industrial terms and concepts (steelworker rule), and a career note. Page 119 is a student activity from Discovering and Applying Mathematics and Automotive Technology.

Ordering Information

Developer: Victor M. Hernández-Gantes, Center on Education and Work, School of Education, University of Wisconsin-Madison, 964 Educational Sciences Building, 1025 West Johnson Street, Madison, WI 53706-1796; 608-265-4578; 608-262-3063 (fax); vhernandez@ soemadison.wisc.edu (e-mail); http://www.cew.wisc.edu/MathNet/

Distributor: Publications Unit, same as above, 1-800-446-0399 or 608-263-2929; 608-262-9197 (fax); cewmail@soemadison.wisc.edu

Table of Contents

(Because the contents of each module are very different, no sample table of contents is provided. Number of pages for each module is indicated in parentheses.)

MathNet Unit
School-To-Work

Univ of Wisconsin -Madison
River Dell Site (Oradell, NJ)

Page 9
Giglio/Ciccotelli/Piekielek

IMPROVING THE BRIDGE DESIGN

Train Truss Bridge over Mississippi River

Wide obstacles such as rivers are not easily spanned using a beam bridge. **The truss design** was developed to provide a means of spanning longer distances. **A truss** is a triangular arrangement of support. The power of the design is based in the fact that a triangle is the most rigid polygonal structure. Two of the forces that are exerted on a bridge are **compression** and **tension**. In a *truss*, these forces are in equilibrium at each of the verticies or *joints*. *Compression* is a force which pushes material together. Tension is a force which pulls material apart. The next activity will help you to explore the relationship between tension and compression .

Investigation Activity 3 Geometry of Forces: Which shape forms the stronger structure?

Purpose: To compare the rigidity of the triangle and the square.

Career Note: An **architectural technician** *builds scale models of structures. These models are used to test the properties of the structure. This is a very important step in the design process.*

Materials: Spaghetti 1 box (#9)
Marshmellows, small   1 bag
Rulers

Activity: 1. Build a triangle using 4 cm lengths of spaghetti as members and marshmellows as the joints.
2. Build a square with 4 cm lengths of spaghetti for the sides and marshmellows as the joints.
3. Hold the triangle in your hand and gently apply a horizontal force at the top joint with your finger. Notice what happens to the two member of that joint.
Record your observations. Which member is in tension? In compression?

4. Repeat step 3 on the square. Record your observations. Which member is in tension? In compression?

5. Which of the two structures is more rigid? Explain why .

6. Build a *cube* 4cm on each edge.

7. Build a *tetrahedron* 4cm on each edge. That is a 3 dimensional figure with 4 triangular faces.

8. Apply a horizontal force to a joint of the cube and a joint of the tetrahedron.

Portfolio Assignment 5

What do you observe about the rigidity of the two figures? Describe your observations in a few sentences. Which shape is more rigid?

Computer Simulation Activity 2: Geometry of Shapes

Purpose: To verify the results obtained in the previous investigation. Which shape is more rigid the triangle or square?

Materials: ModelSmart program

Activity:
1. Open a 70 cm by 50 cm grid with default material type
2. Construct an equilateral triangle 4 cm on a side with supports.
3. Apply a horizontal load to the top joint.
4. Execute an analysis of the structure.
5. Record the Total Applied Load
6. Select *Analysis* then View Results.
7. Compare the Actual Forces and the Actual Moments to the Ultimate Forces and the Ultimate Moments.
8. What was the cause of failure?
9. Repeat steps 2 to 8 for a square 4 cm on a side.
10. Do a comparison as in step 7.

Steelworker Rule

Steelworking is one of the trades that is used in the building of bridges. Steelworkers erect the bridge structure. Some of them do welding or riveting which joins two sections or members of steel. Others are responsible for preparing the materials that will be used in the structure.

The steelworker who cuts the *members* (lengths of steel) for the truss wants to have a rule to help determine the how many members (m) are to be cut based on knowing the number of joints (j) in the truss.

The number of *joints* depends on the on the overall length of the span and the length of a *member*.

MathNet Unit
School-To-Work

Univ of Wisconsin -Madison
River Dell Site (Oradell, NJ)

Page   11
Giglio/Ciccotelli/Piekielek

CONNECTED TRIANGLES

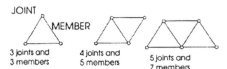

JOINT
MEMBER

3 joints and
3 members

4 joints and
5 members

5 joints and
7 members

> **Portfolio Assignment 6**
> **Look for a Pattern:**
> Copy the drawing of the 5 joint design.
> Draw another joint and the necessary
> members. Continue the drawing for 6, 7
> and 8 joints. Record the results in a table.
> *Look for a pattern*, **then develop a rule** for
> the steelworker to use relating the number
> of joints to the number of members.
> (Show your work on a separate page)
>
> **Extension:** *Look for a pattern based on
> the number of members in the bottom span.
> Examine the 1 triangle, 3 triangles, and 5
> triangles diagrams for the pattern.*

EFFICIENCY OF BRIDGE DESIGN

The bridge designer's goal is to build a strong bridge. However, **cost** is an important
consideration. Using more material than is needed will result in higher costs.
Consequently, the designer must aim to build the strongest bridge with the least material.
A way to evaluate the **efficiency** of a bridge design is to compute the *load to weight
ratio*. A bridge with a good efficiency rating would support a high live load compared to
the amount of material used to build the bridge Therefore, it is important to high
efficiency ratio in order to minimize costs.

Career note: The bridge design team must include an **accountant.** The accountant's
responsibilities include calculating the cost of the proposed bridge and managing the
budget while the bridge is being constructed.

CHECK IT OUT!!

Cost Accounting website
http://www.imbsen.com/edsrce.htm

Stone Arch Bridge 1983 Minneapolis across the Mississippi River. Truss section is a
replacement.

Scenario:

You are working as an automotive engineer. Ms. Julia Watson, the editor-in-chief of the trade journal, *Society of Automotive Technicians*, has contacted you about writing a response to a letter that the magazine has received. The letter states that the starting system of a 1988 Chevy S-10 has been working intermittently.

During an inspection of the starting system, a voltage drop of .4 volts across the ground connector was observed. The starter draws about 160 amps of current, and the battery is 12 volts.

Instructions:

Assist the technician in solving the starting system problem. Determine if there is excessive resistance in the ground connector? Make suggestions on what should be done to correct the problem. Provide reasons for what you suggest.

Evaluation:

To receive a proficient rating on this task, you must show all of the following:

1. Ability to analyze and solve the problem described in this scenario through your knowledge of:
   - effective use of Ohm's Law
   - acceptable voltage drop values in automotive circuitry
   - calculating resistance from the voltage drop
   - automotive starting system circuitry
   - effective use of graphs

2. Ability to communicate effectively with mathematics and in writing

Developer
Washington MESA

Distributor
Dale Seymour Publications

**Funders/
Contributors**
Discuren Foundation
*National Science
Foundation*

Real-World Mathematics Through Science

1994-1998

These activity-based supplementary modules teach mathematics within real-world science and engineering contexts. Students use mathematics, as do professionals in their careers, and learn about the science in these careers. A distinctive but minor feature is the curriculum's inclusion of family activities.

10 modules, softcover, 88-140 pp., $18.95 each

Content Overview

*Prealgebra,
Integrated Science*

Uses a variety of science and engineering contexts to teach prealgebra mathematics, including ratios, vectors, angles, factors, percents, and scientific notation. Covers earth, life, and physical science topics including paleontology, chemistry, aeronautics, meteorology, zoology, and seismology. Engineering/technology topics include manufacturing, criminology, and architecture. Modules typically contain a Writing Link and a History Link, which connect mathematics, science, and technology to language arts and history. The module titles are:

Classifying Fingerprints
Designing Environments
In the Air
In the Pharmacy
In the Wind
Investigating Apples

Measuring Dinosaurs
Measuring Earthquakes
Packaging and the
   Environment
Secret Codes

Target Audience

Not specified other than grade levels.

Duration

Some modules suggest 1-2 weeks; others suggest 3-4 weeks.

Workplace Connections

Each module includes 1 or more main activities in which students simulate aspects of a professional's job—e.g., filling prescriptions, cracking a code, creating a flight plan. Teachers are encouraged to invite real professionals into the classroom during a module. Each module includes 1-2 career profiles with descriptions of job responsibilities and working conditions; some modules profile an actual person (e.g., Susan Darcy, Boeing's first female test pilot).

Instructional Approach

In this entirely activity-based curriculum, students work in groups to solve problems and do investigations. Discussion questions are provided for teacher to prompt student reflection—e.g., to have students explain the reasoning behind their answers. Some activities require students to design their own experiments and present their opinions and findings as a group; others specify procedures and calculations for students. Every module includes a Writing Link that requires students to do research in the library or by contacting professionals in order to write a report. Some modules ask students to estimate and then explain their reasoning.

Curriculum Components

Only a single copy of a module is needed because each contains masters for duplication and class use. Each module has 5 or 6 classroom activities, a family activity, and completed sample student sheets. Each activity contains the following teacher information:

- *Overview*—outlines the amount of time the activity will take, purpose of the activity, required materials, and advance preparations.

- *Background Information*—discusses goals of the activity and use of student activity sheets.

- *Presenting the Activity*—provides detailed suggestions on how to teach the material, including classroom discussion and assessment questions.

In addition to student activity sheets, activities include Writing Links and 1-page readings about careers, topic-relevant history, and background information on science and technology concepts.

Materials

Each unit has a materials list which is generally composed of easily obtained materials.

Assessments

Completed student sheets illustrate possible student responses. Each activity contains 2-4 suggested problems for assessing what students have learned.

Special Preparations

While either mathematics or science teachers can use the curriculum independently, they would benefit from collaborating with each other.

Standards

Each module has a 1-page conceptual overview listing the specific NCTM standards (curriculum, teaching, and evaluation); mathematics content; and science topics covered.

Sample Pages

All pages come from the In the Wind unit. Pages 124-125 provide an overview of the unit. Each unit has a Career Link (p. 126) and page127 shows a student activity sheet.

Ordering Information

Developer: Washington Mathematics, Engineering, Science Achievement, Nancy Cook, Project Director, University of Washington, 353 Loew Hall, Box 352181, Seattle, WA 98195-2181; http://wa-mesa.engr.washington.edu:80/mesa/mesacu.htm#MIDDLE

Distributor: Dale Seymour Publications, 125 Greenbush Road South, Orangeburg, NY 10962; 1-800-872-1100; http://www2.awl.com/dsp/BookPages/22491_MESA.html

Table of Contents: Secret Codes

(Number of pages indicated in parentheses)

Each activity begins with the following teacher material:
Overview (1), Background Information (2), and Presenting the Activity (3)

ACTIVITY OVERVIEW

Overview

Many middle school students are familiar with the MESA module *In the Air*. As a result, they may know how to use a state map to chart an aeronautical course using navigation techniques. However, they are probably unfamiliar with how wind influences the path of an airplane, the methods pilots use to counteract this force, and the career of an aeronautical engineer.

Activities in *In the Wind* explore the mathematics and methods pilots use to navigate in windy conditions. They emphasize the mathematical connections for determining the correct headings to fly on a cross-country journey in a Cessna 172 when forecast winds are present.

If possible, invite a pilot or aeronautical engineer to visit the class. They will be able to answer questions and present specific instances of how wind affects flight and aircraft design.

Activity 1: Navigation and Aviation

Students review charting an aeronautical course. They use laminated state maps to chart course lines between airports. Using circular protractors, they determine directions then calculate distances and flight times. They discover mathematical relationships between parallel course lines and in the degree measures for initial and return flights. Working in pairs, students prepare a detailed flight plan for a 1,000-mile journey in a Cessna 172, incorporating a head wind and a tail wind. Finally, they examine an aeronautical sectional chart to locate familiar landmarks and to interpret symbols.

Activity 2: Drifting Apart

Students discover the path an airplane follows when continuously pushed off course by wind. They recognize how slight to moderate changes in a compass heading might effect their location. Using scale drawings on grid paper, students simulate aeronautical experiences as they extend course lines to examine the relationship between the distance traveled on an incorrect heading and the number of miles a pilot is off course. The concept of *drift angle* is introduced.

Activity 3: Blowing in the Wind

Students continue to investigate the path an airplane follows as it is continuously pushed off course by wind. Working in pairs, they use tractor-feed strips from used computer paper or Polystrips™ to build models of wind parallelograms, which are used to determine the actual flight path. Students investigate the effect wind has on the ground track and ground speed of an airplane. Through this, they are introduced to the concept of *vector*.

Activity 4: When the Wind Blows

Forecast information provides the direction from which the wind is blowing. Students use such data to determine the direction toward which the wind is blowing an airplane. After students are introduced to vectors, they use them to determine the effect wind has on a planned flight course, relating the situations to their previous work with wind parallelograms. Vectors are then applied to establish an airplane's ground track and ground speed.

Activity 5: Back on Track

Students revisit several previous flight situations to determine the true heading a pilot must follow to compensate for the prevailing winds. They explore a parallelogram method using tractor-feed strips or Polystrips™ before investigating a technique using vectors to identify the true heading and to calculate the adjusted ground speed. Students apply wind conditions to each leg of their original 1,000-mile journeys and complete detailed flight plans. The total times for their journeys are reassessed and compared to their original flight expectations from Activity 1, in which wind was not taken into account.

Family Activity: Wind Tunnel

Students are introduced to the forces involved in the theory of flight—lift, drag, weight, and thrust. With their families, they conduct several experiments that illustrate Bernoulli's principle, the scientific basis behind aircraft design. Families build simple wind tunnels in which to test the aerodynamics of various objects. Students begin to understand career aspects of aeronautical engineers.

x ACTIVITY OVERVIEW

Meteorologists

Pilots need current, accurate information about wind, storms, temperature, clouds, and other weather data. Keeping this flow of information coming is the job of meteorologists.

Meteorologists study weather conditions and forecast weather changes. They often use satellites and other specialized equipment to collect data about the atmosphere. They use observations, weather maps, and instrument readings to forecast the weather—a difficult task since weather is so unpredictable and depends upon so many factors.

Pilots are not the only people who need weather information. Ship captains, farmers, astronauts, and many others rely on weather forecasts. Meteorologists also tackle the task of identifying thunderstorms, hurricanes, and tornadoes—with the hope there will be enough time to warn communities before the fierce weather arrives.

Meteorologists may work for the federal government's National Weather Service, for television networks, for universities as teachers, or for private businesses.

To become a meteorologist, you need a bachelor's degree in meteorology. About 100 colleges now offer this major. You can also get graduate degrees and specialize in aspects of meteorology. The armed forces also offers training in meteorology. Salaries range from $20,000 to more than $50,000 a year depending on experience. Supervisors in private industry earn as much as $90,000 a year.

The National Weather Service and National Oceanographic and Atmospheric Administration have volunteer programs for students. This would be a way for you to explore the possibility of a career in meteorology.

Catch My Drift?

1. Why do you think the number of degrees a pilot is off course is referred to as the *drift angle?*

2. A plane intending to fly on a true course of 090° is actually flying on a ground track of 030°.

   a. Starting near the bottom, left-hand corner of your grid paper, use a circular protractor to chart and label a 090° course line that is 8 inches long.

   b. From the starting point on your grid paper, chart and label a ground track of 030° and extend it for 8 inches.

   c. According to your chart, the drift angle is _____ degrees.

3. As the plane continues on a 030° ground track, will it always be the same distance from the intended 090° course line? Explain your reasoning.

4. Let 1 inch equal 25 miles. Chart and measure the appropriate lengths on the true course and the ground track to determine the approximate distances off course this plane will be after flying 25, 50, 100, and 200 miles. Record your results in the table.

_____ Drift Angle

Miles Traveled	Miles Off Course
25	
50	
100	
200	

Developer
Contributors

Distributor
*Mathematical Association
of America*

She Does Math!

*Real-Life Problems From Women
on the Job* 1995

*This supplemental book of about 150 mathematics problems and
their solutions was written by 38 women in a variety of professions,
each of whom describes her career history and provides several
math problems typically encountered in her job.*

Softcover, 253 pp., $30.95

Content Overview

Algebra, Geometry

Problems are listed by the following subject areas: algebra, astronomy,
business, calculus, chemistry, computer science, geometry, health sciences, home economics, piloting a plane, physics, puzzles, statistics, and
trigonometry. Most of problems are in algebra, physics, computer science,
geometry, and trigonometry. The content covers a wide range of mathematical sophistication, from proportional reasoning through calculus.

Target Audience

This book was written to "encourage high school and college students—
especially women and minorities—to consider technical fields when
planning their careers."

Workplace Connections

Careers in mathematics are a prominent feature of this book, with 38
women from varied ethnic backgrounds describing how much high
school and college mathematics they took, how they chose their fields of
study, and how they ended up in their current job. Each woman describes
how math is used in her occupation and presents several problems typical
of those she solves on the job.

Instructional Approach

Each entry consists of 1-10 paper-and-pencil mathematics problems
(average number is 4). Many problems merely require the application of
formulas or conversion of units, while some others require creativity and
reasoning skills. No pedagogical recommendations are provided.

| **Materials** | Students may want to use calculators and computers with spreadsheet software to solve some of the problems. Other problems require easily accessible material such as scissors, tape, glue, and counters. |

Materials Students may want to use calculators and computers with spreadsheet software to solve some of the problems. Other problems require easily accessible material such as scissors, tape, glue, and counters.

Assessments Worked solutions are provided.

Standards No information provided.

Sample Pages Featured on pp. 130-132 is a complete entry for one woman (structural engineer), including her career history and sample problem from her work. Page 133 contains the solution to the problem posed.

Ordering Information Mathematical Association of America; P.O. Box 91112; Washington, DC 20090-1112; 1-800-331-1622; http://www.maa.org/pubs/books/sdm.html

---

Table of Contents

(Number of pages indicated in parentheses)

Linda K. Lanham
Structural Engineering

In high school I studied algebra, geometry, and trigonometry, but I was surprised to find myself needing these skills frequently when using drafting tools on computers. If you don't know geometry and trigonometry, you cannot really draw with the computer drafting tools. In fact, I often use a piece of scratch paper to figure out how to draw what I need on the computer, which was also not what I expected.

At my 9th grade science fair, I won a gift certificate from a drafting supply company. This started my interest in drafting, and resulted in several more scholarships. One was from a science fair, and another was the four-year General Electric National Scholarship from the Society of Women Engineers. I chose to attend an engineering college, the Colorado School of Mines.

After two years, I was getting a bit tired of school, so I accepted a cooperative education work assignment with the U.S. Forest Service. It was so much fun that I continued for three more years. I worked with older people, completed assignments, grew up, and gained experience towards a career, without knowing how it would work out. During my junior year, I also took one semester off to work fulltime with the U.S. Forest Service.

When I graduated with a BS in Mining Engineering, I went to work for the U.S. Forest Service, and have stayed with them ever since. I was an inspector of road and bridge projects and a road designer of low-volume roads in Colorado and Idaho. Now I am a bridge designer for the U.S. Forest Service Northern Region in Missoula, Montana.

Low-volume roads are unpaved timber and fire roads. The bridges I design are made of treated timber and concrete. I make a pre-design site visit, go back to my office to design the bridge, inspect the work in progress, and make a final inspection of the completed bridge.

One very easy math problem that many people find difficult is converting units—pounds per square inch, pounds over an area, volume, etc. In my work, I have to solve problems that involve conversions all the time. For example, a gabion is a rectangular wire cage filled with rock used in stream bank protection and headwalls. I measure its dimensions in feet and calculate its volume in cubic feet, but the material is ordered in cubic yards, not cubic feet. A simple error in conversion can translate into an expensive mistake.

73

Support for a Bridge

Timber is used to make bridges on unpaved fire roads through a forest. To build a bridge, calculate how large the wooden posts must be to hold the weight of the bridge and trucks that use the bridge.

Use the formula $F_c = P/A$ where:

$$F_c = \text{compressive stress or force; units lbs/in}^2$$

$$P = \text{force or load; units lbs}$$

$$A = \text{area; units in}^2$$

Problem 73. Determine the minimum dimensions of wooden post and steel-bearing plate when loaded with 100,000 lbs. (Ignore weight of wood post and bearing plate.)

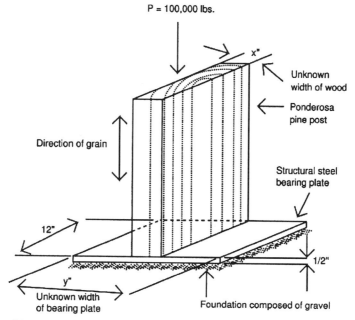

FIGURE 29
Wooden post and steel bearing

Step 1. Check compression parallel to grain—maximum crushing strength for the ponderosa pine post resting on the bearing plate. The mechanical properties of ponderosa pine for compression parallel to grain is 2450 lbs/in^2 (maximum). Given the force of compression, the total load, and the width of the board in one direction (12''), determine x, the unknown width of the wood.

Step 2. Check the compressive strength of gravel foundation material and the bearing plate. The ultimate bearing pressure for gravel is eight tons/ft^2. A good design for foundation bearing pressure is 2.0. Allowable bearing pressure, or compressive strength, for the gravel is four tons/ft^2.

First, convert the allowable bearing pressure for the gravel from tons/ft^2 to lbs/in^2. Next, given the bearing pressure for the gravel, the total load, and the width of the bearing plate in one direction, determine y, the width of the plate in the other direction. If the bearing plate was square, instead of 12 inches on one side and y inches on the other, what would its width need to be?

Step 3. Check the bearing plate's resistance to punching shearing stress due to the loaded wooden post. The ultimate shearing stress of structural steel is 25,000 lbs/in^2. From Step 1, the stress between the wooden post and bearing plate is Fc = 2450 lbs/in^2. Looking at one square inch of the steel material:

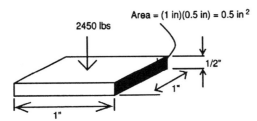

FIGURE 30
Steel material

The diagram shows that the area on the edge of the square inch is 0.5 inches, since the plate is 1/2 (0.5) inches thick. The formula for shearing stress, F_{shear}, is the same as F_c. Given the total force on the square inch, 2450 lbs, and the stress area, 0.5 inches, determine the shearing stress for the plate. Since the ultimate shearing stress of structural steel is 25,000 lbs/in, is the 1/2-inch plate adequate? Is a thicker plate necessary, or would a thinner plate do just as well?

Lanham—Structural Engineering

Problem 73. Step 1.

$$P = 100,000 \text{ lbs}$$

$$F_c = 2450 \text{ lbs/in}^2$$

$$F_c = \frac{P}{A}$$

$$2450 \text{ lbs/in}^2 = \frac{100,000 \text{ lbs}}{(12 \text{ in})(x \text{ in})}$$

$$x = \frac{100,000 \text{ lbs}}{(12 \text{ in})(2450 \text{ lbs/in}^2)} = 3.40 \text{ in}$$

Solutions

The unknown width of the post is 3.40 inches.

Step 2. To convert the allowable bearing pressure from tons/ft^2 to lbs/in^2:

$$\left(\frac{4 \text{ tons}}{\text{ft}^2}\right)\left(\frac{2000 \text{ lbs}}{\text{ton}}\right)\left(\frac{1 \text{ ft}^2}{144 \text{ in}^2}\right) = 55.6 \text{ lbs/in}^2$$

$$P = 100,000 \text{ lbs}$$

$$F_c = 55.6 \text{ lbs/in}^2$$

$$F_c = \frac{P}{A}$$

$$55.6 \text{ lbs/in}^2 = \frac{100,000 \text{ lbs}}{(12 \text{ in})(y \text{ in})}$$

$$y = \frac{100,000 \text{ lbs}}{(12 \text{ in})(55.6 \text{ lbs/in}^2)} = 150 \text{ in}$$

The bearing plate is 12 inches by 150 inches, so the required area for the bearing plate resting on gravel is 1800 in^2. A square bearing plate would be 42.5 in. wide since $\sqrt{1800 \text{ in}^2} = 42.5$ in.

Step 3.

$$P = 2450 \text{ lbs}$$

$$A = 0.5 \text{ in}^2$$

$$F_{\text{shear}} = \frac{P}{A} = \frac{2450 \text{ lbs}}{0.5 \text{ in}^2} = 4900.0 \text{ lbs/in}^2$$

Since the ultimate shearing stress of structural steel is 25,000 lbs/in^2, the 0.5-inch plate is adequate. A thinner plate or a bearing plate made of cheaper material could be used instead.

Developer
Department of Pure &
Applied Mathematics,
Washington State University

Distributor
Department of Pure &
Applied Mathematics,
Washington State University

Funders/
Contributors
National Science
Foundation

Tools of the Trade
Agriculture-Based Secondary
Mathematics 1999

Designed to supplement any secondary mathematics course, all 38 units cover important mathematical skills used widely in agricultural settings; many units start with an actual agricultural problem. In accompanying video, agriculture professionals advise students on the importance of learning mathematics; 5 short clips introduce several of the units.

Text: Binder, 404 pp., price TBA; Video: VHS, 45 min., price TBA

Content Overview

Varied Mathematics

The units cover a range of mathematics: routine arithmetic, geometry, hyperbolas, exponential functions, and calculus. A matrix provides suggestions for use in general math/prealgebra, algebra, geometry, algebra 2, precalculus, and calculus courses.

Target Audience

Any secondary student, rural or urban.

Duration

Several class periods per unit.

Workplace Connections

Units explicitly show applications of mathematics to agriculture-related problems. Video features information about mathematics-related careers in agriculture, and practicing professionals advise students about the importance of learning mathematics.

Instructional Approach

Various approaches are used including paper-and-pencil student worksheets, and mini-research projects in which simple mathematical models are constructed and tested. There is an abundance of computational problems, also some conceptual problems that require little or no computation. Most units can be used either for small group or individual student work.

All units contain expository text and student exercises. Some also feature issues for class discussion: Just Between You and Me (informal bits of extra information for students about the unit) and Just Between You and Your Parent (suggestions of issues for students to discuss with their parents, who may have valuable experiences to share).

Curriculum Components

Teacher and student pages are included for each unit. Teacher pages (Just Between Us Teachers) include the following pedagogical information for each unit: purpose, prerequisites, nature of the unit, references to video introductions (where appropriate), references to related units, teaching suggestions, complete solutions to exercises (answers and solution processes), suggested student assessments with answers (for approximately half the units), and—in units where experimental work is required—a full report on others' experiences.

The video contains 6 segments: A Career in Agriculture: What's Math Got to Do with It?; Wheat Production; Pesticides & Agriculture Aviation; Residue Cover; Volumes on the Farm; and Center Pivot Irrigation.

Materials

Calculators are required for many units; graphing calculators and computers are suggested for some units. Computer software (Mac) utilizing Geometric Sketchpad has been developed for 1 unit.

Assessments

Approximately half of the units have student assessment exercises, with accompanying solutions in the teacher pages.

Standards

No information provided.

Sample Pages

Pages 137-139 consist of three of four pages of the unit on Calibrating Tanks-Constructing a Dipstick. Pages 137 and 139 are teacher pages, and p. 138 is the student handout.

Ordering Information

Professors Dave Engelhard, Michael Kallaher, and Jack M. Robertson, Department of Pure & Applied Mathematics, Washington State University, Pullman, WA 99164-3113; 509-335-3142; robertso@delta.math.wsu.edu (e-mail)

Table of Contents

(Number of pages indicated in parentheses)

UNIT 28 – DRAFT

CALIBRATING TANKS - CONSTRUCTING A DIPSTICK

Just Between Us Teachers...

Just Between Us Teachers

Purpose of Unit: To give a problem solving cooperative learning project requiring students to calibrate a dipstick for a given tank; to give an application of volume formulas. (See Calibrating Tanks - An Overview preceding Unit 28.)

Prerequisite Skills: Volume formulas for cylinders and cones, ratio and proportion.

Type of Unit: Cooperative learning project for small groups followed by two related exercises.

Videotape Introduction: Volumes on the Farm.

Related Units: "Calibrating Tanks - Estimations", "Calibrating Tanks - Putting Them Together", "Calibrating Tanks - Using Calculus", and "Rain and Rain Gauges".

This unit can be introduced with the brief instructional videotape "Volumes on the Farm". It allows students to see some actual situations in the field on which the mathematics in this unit is based.

This first unit on calibrating tanks is very straight forward – what you see is what you get. Make sure students have or know the formulas for the volume of cylinders and cones. As the solutions show, ratio and proportion methods are used, so be ready for whatever problem that will cause your students. Calculators should be used.

1

UNIT 28 – DRAFT

CALIBRATING TANKS - CONSTRUCTING A DIPSTICK

Farmers have a variety of tanks for storing fertilizers, fuels and other chemicals. Normally the volume of the tank is known or easy to figure out. It is a partially filled tank, however, that presents the problem: How much is left in a partially filled tank?

Dipsticks are used to determine the amount of liquid in a partially filled tank. If the tanks have simple shape and orientation, such as an upright cylinder, the problem of calibrating the dipstick for the tank is very easy. The problem becomes more challenging when the tank is not so simple. The following project involves such a tank which could be found on any farm, in fact you have probably seen such tanks.

Project: Take a cash register tape whose length is 7 feet long and calibrate the tape for a dipstick for the tank shown in Figure 1. On one side of the tape enter the volume in gallons at 6″ intervals on the dipstick. On the other side of the tape place a mark for volumes of 50, 100, 150, ⋯ gallons, that is in 50 gallon increments. After you have finished check your answer against the tape other groups have constructed. Use the conversion 1 ft^3 ≐ 7.48 gallons.

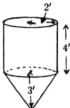

Figure 1

Follow up Exercises:

1. Calibrate a dipstick for the tank with cylindrical top and conical bottom shown in Figure 2. Use 6 inch increments only.

2. Calibrate a dipstick for the tank with a conical top and bottom as shown in Figure 3. Use 6 ″ intervals.

3. One group who did the project had marks for 50 gallon increments as shown in Figure 4. Without knowing any numbers or measurments how do you know there is an error?

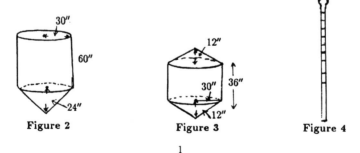

Figure 2   **Figure 3**   **Figure 4**

1

Solutions:

Project Solution: The conical part of the tank holds $V = \frac{1}{3}\pi r^2 h = \frac{1}{3}\pi(2^2) \cdot 3$ ft^3 $\doteq 94$ gallons using the conversion 1 ft^3 $\doteq 7.48$ gallons. The cylindrical part of the tank holds about 376 gallons for a total of 470 gallons.

To scale a dipstick for this tank we can begin with a 470 gallon mark 7 feet up and 94 gallons 3 feet up. Since the cylindrical top holds 376 gallons in 4 feet of tank, a convenient scale would be graduations of 47 gallons corresponding to lengths of 6 inches. (376 gallons divided by 8 equals 47 gallons; 4 feet divided by 8 equals $\frac{1}{2}$ foot.)

The taper at the bottom of the tank presents a more difficult situation. Assume the liquid in the cone stands at some height h. To find this volume we need both r and h. By similar triangles (see figure) we have $\dfrac{24}{r} = \dfrac{36}{h}$ so $36r = 24h$ or $r = \dfrac{2}{3}h$. Thus, $V = \dfrac{1}{3}\pi r^2 h = \dfrac{1}{3}\pi(\dfrac{2}{3}h)^2 h = \dfrac{1}{3}\pi\dfrac{4}{9}h^2 h = \dfrac{4}{27}\pi h^3$. We now substitute values for h in 6″ increments starting at the bottom with $h = 0$.

dipstick

amount gallons	height inches
470	84
423	78
376	72
329	66
282	60
235	54
188	48
141	42
94	36
54.5	30
27.8	24
11.8	18
3.5	12
.44	6
0	0

amount (gallons)	height (inches)
450	81.5
400	75.1
350	68.7
300	62.3
250	55.9
200	49.5
150	43.1
100	36.8
50	29.2

amount (gallons)	height (inches)
94	36
54.5	30
27.8	24
11.75	18
3.5	12
.44	6

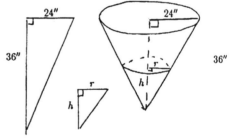

The 50 gallon increment locations are found similarly. For the conical portion using $V = \frac{4}{27}\pi h^3$ and setting $V = \frac{50}{7.48}$ ft^3 we get $h^3 \doteq 14.4$ and $h \doteq 2.4$ ft $\doteq 29.2$ in. For 100 gallons we must have 6 gallons in the cylindrical part of the tank since the conical portion holds 94 gallons. Setting $\frac{6}{7.48}$ ft$^3 = \pi 2^2 h$ we get $h \doteq .06$ ft $\doteq .8$ inch. So the 100 gallon tank is at 36.8 inches. Other marks are similarly computed.

2

Reviews of Science and Integrated Curricula **5**

This chapter presents reviews of the following 11 curriculum materials for science or technology, or science integrated with mathematics and/or technology. Each review is accompanied by 2-6 sample pages from the curriculum. Table 3.1 provides an overview the materials' dates of publication, funding sources, and intended grade levels. Appendix A provides brief descriptions of a few additional science or integrated curricula.

Developer
Center for Occupational Research and Development (CORD)

Distributor
International Thomson Publishing

Funders/ Contributors
Developer

Applications in Biology/Chemistry 2nd edition

A Contextual Approach to Laboratory Science 1999

Strongly connects science to workplace and other real-world contexts through videos, readings, and hands-on and laboratory activities. Describes science applications in a range of careers and includes activities that require students to contact professionals for information. CORD is funded in part by a consortium of over 40 state vocational education agencies.

Student ed.: 12 units, softcover, 150-250 pp., $6.75 each; Teacher ed.: 12 units, binder, 500-600 pp., $59.95 each; Video: 30-40 min., $35.00 per unit

---

Content Overview

Biology, Chemistry

The 12 modular units (listed below) cover a combination of biology and chemistry concepts; some units emphasize one field more than the other. Compared to a traditional biology textbook, the CORD ABC units place more emphasis on ecology, physiology, and genetics and less on taxonomy, evolution, and cell biology. Teachers can cluster units by content preferences.

Air and Other Gases	Nutrition
Animal Life Processes	Plant Growth and
Community of Life	Reproduction
Continuity of Life	Synthetic Materials
Disease and Wellness	Waste and Waste
Microorganisms	Management
Natural Resources	Water

Target Audience

"The course addresses the needs of contextual learners and is designed [for] students who learn abstract concepts through concrete experiences."

| **Duration** | 1 year; 4-6 units with 30-35 classes per unit. |

Workplace Connections

Workplace connections are integral to this curriculum. Contains job profiles and scenarios; these latter include interviews with workers about their daily job responsibilities (including lab processes) and their educational backgrounds. Videos depict on-the-job experiences and interviews with workers. Some unit activities are workplace-related (e.g., students contact the local agricultural extension service to find out what natural parasites are being used to control pests). Each lab is introduced by a workplace scenario, and many labs are similar to actual tests done in industry. At the end of each subunit, activities direct students to contact employers in the following occupational areas: agriscience, family and consumer, health occupations, and industrial technology.

Instructional Approach

Curriculum balances readings and activities/laboratory work in approximately equal proportions. Each unit contains 35-45 activities; these require students, working in small groups, to record results from short experiments, obtain information, or answer questions. Most of the activities and lab work ask students to address specific questions and follow established procedures; a few assignments are more open-ended in nature, such as when students perform text and electronic resources for research. Readings include explanations of science concepts, workplace scenarios, and job profiles; these are written at an 8th-grade level.

Curriculum Components

There are 3 required components to teach the curriculum: Teacher's Guide, Student Text, and video. Supplementary materials are also available, including worksheets ($19.95/unit), mini-modules, and a test generator databank.

Teacher's Guide—Includes black-line masters of graphs, charts, and other student handouts; detailed description of the videos; video discussion topics; organizations to contact for additional information; detailed laboratory implementation ideas; suggestions for classroom discussion; and tests.

Student Text—Each unit contains 4-6 subunits that begin with some framing questions. There are 4-9 goals and objectives for both the whole unit and for each subunit. Illustrations are used liberally through the unit to convey science concepts. Each unit generally contains these elements: science labs (8–10); job profiles (4-10); real-life scenarios (10-15); unit activities, some of which are occupation-related (35-45); and video segments (4-5). Activities and labs comprise at least half of the instructional time.

Video—For each unit, 4-5 video segments (5-10 min. each) are used to introduce a topic. They contain lab demonstrations; interviews with workers about challenges they face in their jobs; technical explanations (e.g., how a computer controls a greenhouse's environment); and problem-solving scenarios (e.g., how a worker would address a malfunction in the greenhouse).

Materials

Requires numerous consumable materials that most science teachers have on hand or that can be easily obtained. Microorganisms and Continuity of Life units require biotechnology workstations for their DNA labs.

Assessments

Each subunit contains study questions that ask students to explain their understanding of science concepts; these can be given as tests. Each unit also contains an End-of-Unit Test Bank, which includes descriptive questions related to the unit's labs, essay questions, and whole-class discussion questions. The Teacher's Guide contains responses to all questions. A test database is available.

Teacher Resources

Teachers are strongly encouraged to participate in a 1-week course offered by CORD ($750) before using the curriculum.

Standards

The Teacher's Guide correlates course content to the National Science Education Standards.

Sample Pages

The following curriculum components are illustrated using pages from the Animal Life Processes unit: a real-life scenario (p. 146), career profile (p. 147), student laboratory (pp. 148-149), research activities listed by occupational area (p. 150), and an activity (p.151),which is shorter than a lab. Research activities (p. 150) are provided only at the end of the 4-6 subunits of each unit. All other components occur frequently (see Curriculum Components).

Ordering Information

Developer: Center for Occupational Research and Development, P.O. Box 21689, Waco, TX 76702-5841; 1-800-231-3015; http://www.cord.org

Distributor: International Thomson Publishing, 5101 Madison Road, Cincinnati, OH 45227; 1-800-824-5179

Table of Contents:
A Detailed Description of the Animal Life Processes Unit
(Number of pages indicated in parentheses)

Teacher's Guide

Annotated Student Text

to determine that they are experiencing heat exhaustion, or **hyperthermia**.

Read on to find out how rescue personnel will respond.

A Cool Rescue

In the next few minutes, the immediate care rendered by rescue personnel could determine whether the firefighters will recover from their illnesses. Paramedics complete a primary survey to determine that all basic life functions are adequate. Then treatment begins.

The process of cooling the body is a reversal of the factors that created the overheating situation. The firefighters have been removed from the environment of the fire, but the outdoor temperature and the humidity are high. These two factors reduce the success of the cooling attempt by the body by reducing the rate of evaporation. The turnout gear and other clothing also prevent evaporation and convection, so they are immediately removed.

The paramedics place the patients in the back of the ambulance, thus providing a cooler environment. The patients are kept lying flat to prevent them from passing out again. Fainting occurs when the blood vessels enlarge to allow more blood to reach the skin where the heat can radiate to the atmosphere. The blood flow to the vital organs (including the brain) is thereby reduced, blood pressure drops, and a fainting response occurs. The body also attempts cooling through the respiratory system. This accounts for the rapid breathing pattern in these patients.

The paramedics will also aid cooling by bathing the patients with cool water. This carries heat away from the body by conduction and also cools by evaporation. Cold water will not be used, as it could chill the patients; shivering might produce additional heat.

Since the body has lost valuable salts and substances required for normal body functions through excessive sweating, the paramedics will start an intravenous solution (IV) for each patient. This solution will help replace lost fluids, salts, and other chemicals. The paramedics will also connect the patients to heart monitors. Electrolytes lost in sweat are important to normal heart function. Their loss could result in irregular heartbeat.

WHAT IS THE BEST COLOR OF CLOTHING TO WEAR IN HOT WEATHER?

Introduction

Our journalism class continued its tour of the school's athletic facilities with Mickey S., the athletic trainer. Mickey showed us the uniforms worn by some of the teams. "When judging proper clothing for athletes, I have to know what works to their advantage and what doesn't. For one thing, the type of cloth is very important, especially the wicking properties of the cloth."

"What's wicking?" Millie asked.

"Wicking is the ability of a cloth to move perspiration away from the skin's surface and allow the body to cool," Mickey responded.

"Is there a particular type of cloth that lets the athletes stay really cool?" Henry asked.

"Have you ever noticed," Mickey replied, "that early in the football season our players wear really loose-knit jerseys? In those jerseys, they get a good circulation of air. We used to have them wear wool jerseys, which were hot but would absorb a lot of moisture. Then we changed to nylon, but nylon was worse than the wool because it didn't absorb moisture at all. In fact, no air could get through it. Now, we use mostly cotton and some cotton-polyester blends.

"The color of uniforms is also important to staying cool. Just think about the baseball teams we play that have black shirts and black caps. They start having trouble with the heat about the sixth or seventh inning of daytime games because the black absorbs heat. On the other hand, in our gold uniforms, our players don't feel the heat as much. Our lighter colors reflect more of the heat, and they stay cooler."

Part B: Heat Absorption by Clothing

1. Obtain a piece of colored cloth from your teacher. Record the color of the cloth in your *ABC* notebook.

2. Place the sheet of aluminum foil, shiny side out, over the surface of the shoe box.

   - Fold the piece of cloth in half and wrap it around a thermometer as shown in Figure L8-1.

   - Secure the thermometer and cloth to the bottom of an empty shoe box with a rubber band as shown in Figure L7-1.

   - Leave the thermometer scale visible above 15°C.

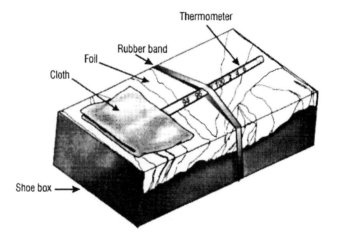

**Figure L7-1
Measuring
temperature of
the cloth**

3. Place the shoe box (with thermometer and cloth) outdoors in full sun, in a location where it will not be disturbed. As soon as you place the box, record the temperature of the cloth in your *ABC* notebook.

4. After at least five minutes of exposure to full sun, read the thermometer again.

   - Record the temperature of the cloth and time of day in your *ABC* notebook.

   - Continue to take temperature and time readings every minute until your teachers tells you to stop.

Applications in Biology / Chemistry

breathing to eliminate carbon dioxide and return the blood pH to a normal state.

CAREER PROFILE: RESPIRATORY THERAPIST

Lisa M. is a respiratory therapist who works in the pulmonary unit, the intensive care unit, and the neonatal care unit of a regional hospital.

"Many patients I treat have chronic lung diseases such as chronic bronchitis, asthma, or emphysema," explains Lisa. "Some are babies who were extremely premature or had low birth weights for their age and were born with hyaline membrane disease, the lung disease of prematurity.

Patients who are bedridden with respiratory disorders are often at risk of building up secretions in their lungs. These patients need to have their lungs suctioned periodically, which I do with a catheter attached to a suction machine. I also do chest percussion, clapping on the back, sides, and chest of the patient to loosen phlegm. I also use a nebulizer, a device that delivers medication as an aerosol to open the patient's airways and promote removal of secretions.

"Patients in the neonatal and intensive care units usually have their **blood oxygen saturation** monitored continuously by a pulse oximeter. The saturation represents a ratio of the amount of oxygen actually combined with **hemoglobin**, compared with the amount of oxygen at saturation. A 90% saturation means that 90% of the available hemoglobin is actually carrying oxygen and the remainder is in either a reduced or deoxygenated state. The normal blood oxygen saturation for any patient should be in the 95% to 100% range."

Lisa completed a two-year college program in respiratory therapy that included clinical training in a local hospital. She then went through the National Board for Respiratory Care examination and was credentialed as a Registered Respiratory Therapist (RRT).

If a patient has received an injury to the head, often the respiratory control center in the brain is involved. This patient has an inadequate air exchange that is characterized by slow, shallow breathing. In this instance, the problem originates in the respiratory system and the kidneys are

---

Applications in Biology/Chemistry

Activities by Occupational Area

General

Eating Habits and the Workplace

- Contact an occupational safety expert about the relationship between accident rate and dietary habits, such as is suggested in the scenario *Productivity and Nutrition*. If a relationship is found, what is it? How could a company address such a problem?

Agriscience

Transporting Livestock

- Contact a livestock farmer or extension agent and find out what kinds of feed changes, if any, are required when animals are about to be transported. Does the stress of being moved require additional calories?

Fattening Livestock

- In commercial feeding operations, the diets of young animals are designed to make them marketable. The marketable animal does not have a thick fat layer that must be trimmed as waste. The fat is dispersed throughout the muscle tissue (marbled) and causes the meat to be tender and juicy.

- Young animals are preferred for feeding because the feed conversion ratio (weight gained per pound of feed eaten) is higher than for mature animals and the meat from the young animals is more desirable. The higher feed conversion ratio gives the feeding operation a better return on the investment in the feed ration.

- Working in groups of four, research the cost of fifty 300-kg steers and feed expenses in fattening these steers from 300-kg body weight to a market weight of 400 kg.

  - Find the market value of fifty 300-kg (about 650 lb) steers.

  - Obtain the handout "Daily Nutrition Required for 1-Pound Daily Gain in Medium-Frame Steer."

Animal Life Processes 91

**Figure 3-6
Forms of
molecular
motion**

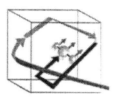

a. Translational

b. Rotational

c. Vibrational

When the temperature of an object increases, the molecules of that object translate, rotate, and vibrate faster. When the temperature of an object decreases, the molecules of that object translate, rotate, and vibrate more slowly. The amount the temperature increases when heat is added to a substance is determined by the heat capacity of the substance.

Activity 3-3

- Put 50 ml of water into a flask.

- Put 50 ml of denatured alcohol into another flask.

- Place both flasks on hot plates (not a gas burner) at low heat for 9 minutes. Do not to let the alcohol boil. Remove both from the heat.

- Record the temperature of each liquid as soon as the flask is removed.

- Record the temperature again at three-minute intervals until there is no temperature change in either solution— they have reached room temperature.

- Which substance has a greater heat capacity? Explain your answer.

As seen in Figure 3-7, a substance with a low heat capacity undergoes a large temperature increase when only a small amount of heat is added. By contrast, a substance with a high heat capacity undergoes a small temperature increase even when a large amount of heat is added.

Developer
American Chemical Society

Distributor
Kendall/Hunt Publishing Co.

Funders
ACS, NSF

ChemCom 3rd edition

Chemistry in the Community 1998

While the one-year ChemCom course covers most traditional chemistry topics and adds more organic, nuclear, and biochemistry, its organization around environmental/community issues and emphasis on collaborative work broadens the accessibility of chemistry to non-science specialist, college-bound students.

Student ed., 643 pp., hardcover, $47.90; Teacher's ed., 412 pp., softcover, $89.90

Content Overview

Chemistry

Unlike traditional chemistry textbooks that organize chemistry concepts according to the discipline, ChemCom teaches chemistry on a need-to-know basis. ChemCom includes the majority of traditional topics, but omits orbitals, equilibrium constants, and kinetics. ChemCom includes more nuclear, organic, industrial, and biochemistry topics. Eight units cover socio-technical issues such as water quality, food production, and nuclear chemistry. On average, only five units can be covered. The first four units are designed to be taught in sequence; the last four have been designed to be studied in any order.

Target Audience

Designed for college-bound students, especially those not planning on majoring in science.

Duration

One year; 8 units requiring 20-25 lessons/unit.

Workplace Connections

No visits to workplaces are required or suggested. Each unit contains two workplace profiles of individuals holding a job/career in a chemical field including their educational qualifications, working conditions, and how the job fits into the broader chemistry field. Unit 8, "The Chemical Industry: Promise and Challenge," has the strongest workplace focus, but all units provide detailed information about relevant industries and explanations of how devices operate (e.g., aluminum can recycling and metal reduction methods in the Resources unit; how a geiger counter works and radioactive waste disposal in the Nuclear unit). Professional organizations that have information about careers in science and technology are provided in the Teacher's Guide.

Instructional Approach

Each ChemCom unit begins with several framing questions. As the unit progresses, chemistry concepts are introduced that give students progressively more information that addresses these questions.

Most classroom instruction is structured around small-group work, including laboratory work. About half of the course is laboratory work. Students follow procedures that are provided, fill in lab data tables, and frequently are expected to answer questions on lab sheets. Algebra 1 is considered a prerequisite for ChemCom. There is a significant amount of reading in the curriculum. Many activities are class discussions; some are written assignments. Scientific concepts and ideas introduced in one unit are developed in later units, and are referred to in sidebars.

Curriculum Components

Each unit presents learning objectives and is divided into five to six parts; each part contains workplace profiles, laboratory activities, reflection questions, test questions, extension activities, and background information on relevant industries (via narratives and statistics).

Teacher's Guide—The Teacher's Guide does not reproduce pages from the student book. Rather, it provides suggested implementation strategies and answers to quiz questions. For each activity, the Teacher's Guide describes in detail the goal, the amount of time required, the class group structure, the teacher's role, some sample activities, and the number of each type of activity per unit. A teaching schedule is provided for each unit.

Student Book—Each ChemCom unit includes the following activities to promote decision making and problem solving:

- *Your Turn* asks questions that reinforce basic chemical concepts learned earlier in the unit.

- *Chemquandry* asks students to think about chemical applications and societal issues. These are open-ended problems that frequently do not have one correct answer.

- *You Decide* presents students with a societal/technological problem and asks them to collect and analyze data and develop, support, or refute hypotheses based on scientific evidence.

- *Putting It All Together* provides students with an opportunity to review and apply what they have learned. Students are expected to research issues and present scientifically sound findings that acknowledge the roles of economics, politics, and personal/social values.

- *Laboratory Activities* introduces and develops key chemical concepts and provides practice with laboratory skills.

Materials

Standard chemistry supplies; list of required supplies/equipment provided. Labs are microsized; macroscale versions included in the Teacher's Edition.

Assessments

Multiple-choice and free-response questions, multiple-choice answers, suggestions for scoring free response.

Teacher Resources

Professional development workshops; laserdisc of narrated video segments that support ChemCom topics; Teachers Resource Center on the web.

Miscellaneous

Japanese, Russian, and Spanish versions

Standards

Provides detailed cross-reference to National Science Education Standards.

Sample Pages

Page 156 illustrates that ChemCom sometimes presents the chemistry concepts of industrial processes. Each chapter begins with a You Decide feature (p. 158) that prompts students to consider what they need to learn. Page 157 is one of 20 career profiles, which sometimes include brief descriptions of the chemistry concepts used in occupations.

Ordering Information

Distributor: Kendall/Hunt Publishing Company, 4050 Westmark Drive, P.O. Box 1840, Dubuque, Iowa, 52004-1840; 1-800-KH-BOOKS (542-6657); http://www.kendallhunt.com/

Developer: Sylvia Ware, American Chemical Society, 1155 16th St. NW, Washington, DC, 20036; 1-202-872-4600; http://www.acs.org/education/currmats/chemcom.html

Table of Contents

(Number of pages indicated in parenthesis)

In earlier times, a relatively inexpensive way to increase the octane rating of gasoline was to add a substance such as tetra-ethyl lead, $(C_2H_5)_4Pb$, to the fuel. It slowed down the burning of straight-chain gasoline molecules, and added about three points to the "leaded" fuel's octane rating.

Unfortunately, lead from the treated gasoline was discharged into the atmosphere along with other exhaust products. Due to the harmful effects of lead in the environment, such lead-based gasoline additives are no longer in common use.

With this phase-out of lead-based additives in gasoline, alternative octane-boosting supplements have become increasingly important. A group of additives called *oxygenated fuels* are frequently blended with gasoline to enhance its octane rating. These substances are composed of molecules that include oxygen in addition to carbon and hydrogen. Although oxygenated fuels deliver less energy per gallon than do regular gasoline hydrocarbons, their economic appeal comes from their ability both to increase the performance rating (octane number) of gasoline and to reduce exhaust-gas pollutants. Two common oxygenated fuels are MTBE and methanol (methyl alcohol, CH_3OH).

United States production of methyl t-butyl ether (MTBE) started in 1979; in less than ten years annual production topped one billion gallons.

Flexible-fuel cars—designed to run on methanol, gasoline, or any mixture of the two—have been involved in demonstration programs in a number of major U.S. cities. A 10% alcohol-90% gasoline blend, sometimes called *gasohol,* can be used without engine adjustments or problems in nearly all automobiles currently in service. In addition to its octane-boosting properties, methanol's potential appeal also arises from the fact that it can be made from natural gas, corn, coal, or wood—a contribution toward conserving petroleum resources.

YOUR TURN

A Burning Issue

Methanol (CH_3OH) and ethanol (CH_3CH_2OH) are both used as gasoline additives or substitutes. Their heats of combustion are, respectively, 23 kJ/g and 30 kJ/g.

1. Consider their chemical formulas. Gram for gram, why are the heats of combustion of methanol and ethanol considerably less than those of any hydrocarbons we have considered? (See Table 4, page 189.) (*Hint:* What would happen if you tried to burn oxygen?)

2. Would you expect automobiles fueled by 10% ethanol and 90% gasoline to get higher or lower miles per gallon than comparable cars fueled by 100% gasoline? Why?

Other octane-boosting strategies involve altering the composition of petroleum molecules themselves. Since branched-chain hydrocarbons burn more satisfactorily than do straight-chain versions, a process called *isomerization* is commonly used. Hydrocarbon vapor is heated with a catalyst:

194 / *PETROLEUM C*

CHEMISTRY AT WORK

Keeping Food Supplies Safe for Consumers

State inspectors widen area for corn feed testing

Associated Press

RICHMOND — Inspectors from the Virginia Department of Agriculture expanded their search Thursday for a toxin in corn feed that has killed 18 horses.

Inspectors began taking samples of feed from manufacturers and dealers who mix their own feed in the area south of Interstate 64 and east of Interstate 95. The samples will be tested for Fumonisin B1, a mycotoxin that causes leukoencephalomalacia, also called molfy corn poisoning.

NEWS BRIEFS

SUFFOLK

19TH HORSE DIES: A horse from Suffolk has died and is suspected to be the 19th known victim of "moldy corn poisoning" in Virginia. The horse's owners, who were not identified, could not recall where they purchased the corn.

These actual newspaper headlines illustrate the deadly effects that certain microscopic toxins can have. Here, the consumers of the food were horses, but similar toxins can endanger human consumers as well.

Mary Trucksess is a chemist working to understand and prevent food toxins. She is Research Chemist and Chief of the Bioanalytical Chemistry Branch in the Division of Natural Food Products, Office of Plant and Dairy Food and Beverages. Mary and her fellow chemists at the FDA help ensure the quality of food and drugs (prescription and nonprescription) to protect people from harmful contaminants. Currently Mary is investigating fumonisins—a toxin found mainly in corn, caused by a common soil fungus—which can cause horses to develop a fatal disease of the brain. The FDA is investigating fumonisins to make certain that these toxins do not pose a threat to humans.

Mary's office analyzes other foods, such as peanuts and peanut butter, for aflatoxins. Aflatoxins are naturally occurring toxins that form when certain molds (*Aspergillus flavus* or *Aspergillus parasiticus*) begin to grow on peanuts. If not controlled, these and other toxins could threaten the health of consumers.

Mary also manages and directs other chemists as they conduct research. The chemists in her branch often discuss with her any problems they encounter in their research. She reviews progress reports from the chemists, and recommends different approaches as needed.

For several years, Mary—who holds undergraduate and doctoral degrees in chemistry—has supervised the work of high school honor students who have been selected to intern at the FDA. Mary develops specific projects for the students and trains them in laboratory procedures and data interpretation. Currently, for example, Mary is supervising a high school student who is working on a project to look for the presence of fumonisin in corn tortillas.

288

A.1 YOU DECIDE: THE FLUID WE LIVE IN

On a separate sheet of paper indicate whether you think each numbered statement below is true (T) or false (F), or whether it's too unfamiliar to you to judge (U). Then, for each statement you believe is true, write a sentence describing a practical consequence or application of the fact. Reword each false statement to make it true.

Do not worry about your score. You will not be graded on this exercise; it's intended to start you thinking about the wonderful fluid in which we live.

1. You could live nearly a month without food, and a few days without water, but you would survive for only a few minutes without air.
2. The volume of a given sample of air (or any gas) depends on its pressure and temperature.
3. Air and other gases are weightless.
4. The atmosphere exerts nearly 15 pounds of force on each square inch of your body.
5. The components of the atmosphere vary widely at different locations on Earth.
6. The atmosphere acts as a filter to prevent some harmful radiation from reaching the Earth's surface.
7. In the part of the atmosphere nearest the Earth, air temperature usually increases as altitude increases.
8. Minor air components such as water vapor and carbon dioxide play major roles in the atmosphere.
9. Two of the ten most-produced industrial chemicals are obtained from the atmosphere.
10. Ozone is regarded as a pollutant in the lower atmosphere, but as an essential component of the upper atmosphere.
11. Clean, unpolluted air is a pure substance.
12. Air pollution first occurred during the Industrial Revolution.
13. No human deaths have ever been directly attributed to air pollution.
14. Natural events, such as volcanic eruptions and forest fires, can produce significant air pollution.
15. Destruction of materials and crops by air pollution involves a significant economic loss for our nation.
16. The main source of air pollution is industrial activity.
17. The "greenhouse effect" is a natural warming effect that may become harmful because of excessive burning of fossil fuels.
18. In recent years, rain in industrialized nations has become less acidic.
19. Most air pollution caused by humans originates with burning fuels.
20. Pollution control has not improved overall air quality.

When you are finished, your teacher will give you answers to these items, but will not elaborate on them. However, each item will be discussed at some point in this unit.

The next section includes some demonstrations and at-home activities that illustrate the nature of the air you breathe.

Manufacturers have used large-scale techniques to reduce particulates coming from industrial plants. Several cost-effective methods, such as those described below, are used for controlling particulates and other emissions.

Electrostatic precipitation. This is currently the most important technique for controlling pollution by particulates. Combustion waste products are passed through a strong electrical field, where they become charged. The charged particles collect on plates of opposite charge. This technique removes up to 99% of particulates, leaving only particles smaller than one tenth of a micrometer (0.1 μm, where 1 μm = 10^{-6} m in diameter). Dust and pollen collectors installed in home ventilation systems are often based on this technique.

Mechanical filtering. This works much like a vacuum cleaner. Combustion waste products pass through a cleaning room (bag house) where huge filters trap up to 99% of the particles.

Cyclone collection. Combustion waste products pass rapidly through a tight circular spiral chamber. Particles thrown outward to the chamber's walls drop to the base of the chamber where they are removed. This technique removes 50–90% of the larger, visible particles, but relatively few of the more harmful particles (those smaller than 1 μm).

Scrubbing. This method controls particles and sulfur oxides accompanying them.

In *fluidized bed combustion,* air blows pulverized coal and powdered limestone (calcium carbonate, $CaCO_3$) into a combustion chamber where the heat from the burning coal decomposes the limestone (left side of Figure 18).

$$CaCO_3(s) + Heat \rightarrow CaO(s) + CO_2(g)$$

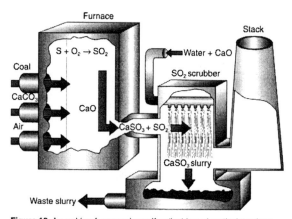

Figure 18 A scrubber for removing sulfur dioxide and particulates from products of industrial combustion processes. Dry scrubbing occurs in the furnace, and wet scrubbing in the SO_2 scrubber.

Developer
*Event-Based Science
Project, Montgomery
County Schools*

Distributor
*Scott Foresman - Addison
Wesley Publishing
Company*

**Funders/
Contributors**
*National Science
Foundation*

Event-Based Science

1996-1998

Through natural disasters keyed to historical events (such as the Loma Prieta earthquake of 1989), these supplemental modules engage students in science. Students watch "live" television news coverage, read newspaper reports, and solve problems related to the event. As they do, they take on the roles of various people whose expertise is needed. News media contributors include USA Today, CNN, *and* NBC News.

Student ed.: 18 modules, softcover, 50-75 pp., $7.95 each; Teacher ed.: 18 modules, softcover, 30-75 pp., and 5-min. video, $19.95 each

Content Overview

**Earth Science,
Life Science,
Physical Science**

Nine earth science modules cover topics in geology, meteorology, astronomy, oceanography, groundwater, and stream dynamics. Nine life/physical science modules cover topics in electricity, chemistry, ecology, and animal adaptation. Students learn science by taking the roles of experts who would be involved in solving problems. For example, in Earthquake!, students pretend that they are in the planning department of a land development company responsible for designing a city in an earthquake-prone part of the world.

Module titles follow; asterisked items are under development and will be available Spring 2000.

Earth Science	Life Science & Physical Science
Asteroid!	Tornado!
Earthquake!	Toxic Leak!
Flood!	Volcano!
Gold Rush!	Blackout!*
Hurricane!	Blight!
Oil Spill!	Fire!*

Fraud!	First Flight!
Gold Medal!	Survive?*
	Thrill Ride!
	Outbreak!

Target Audience

Materials are designed for middle school students.

Duration

5 weeks per unit.

Workplace Connections

In each module, students role-play a particular professional. They read about the job responsibilities of the position and the science they need in effectively fulfilling their role. Some roles are outside science—e.g., city planner, fire safety expert, architect. Each module includes up to six 1-page professional profiles; these include information on day-to-day job activities, education requirements, why the individual profiled chose his or her career, and career highlights.

Instructional Approach

Numerous readings provide background information; these are interspersed with hands-on science activities that let students make a number of decisions about how to proceed. Many of the activities model physical phenomena. Activities include design-and-build (e.g., create an earthquake-resistant building); models of real-world phenomena (e.g., demonstrate the movement of weather fronts); and design science tests (e.g., test the physical and chemical properties of fibers). In each activity, students write responses to general questions and explain what they have learned.

Teachers are encouraged to act as coaches, guides, and advisors as students work in groups to solve assigned problems. Each student in a group has an defined role. Students with similar roles are encouraged to work across groups and share information as well as work within their own group.

Curriculum Components

Teacher's Guide—reproduces pages from the Student Edition and adds implementation suggestions; these provide procedural information as well as the reasoning behind the suggestions. Each science activity includes information on the teaching objective, science outcomes, science concepts, a description of suggested teacher-student interactions, required materials, and a scoring rubric. Answers are not provided. Interdisciplinary and optional activities are provided.

Student Edition—Each module includes a story line, science activities, discovery files, workplace profiles, student interviews, interdisciplinary activities, and a performance assessment. Students are encouraged to use information from other sources such as textbooks, encyclopedias, newspaper and magazine articles, web sites, videos, and people within the community.

Materials

The majority of supplies are commonly found in science classrooms.

Assessments

Each science activity includes a scoring rubric that can be used as an assessment. There is also a performance assessment—and scoring guide—at the end of each module.

Teacher Resources

Training is available through the developer. Certified trainers are middle school teachers who have taught EBS modules and have been through EBS training. Minimum training is 1 day; this includes an overview of the EBS instructional approach and hands-on experience with at least 1 unit. Training can be customized for individual sites.

Standards

Teacher's Guide provides examples of sample indicators for each of the 6 Maryland Science Outcomes.

Sample Pages

All pages are from the Earthquake! unit. Pages 164-165 illustrate how each unit includes student questions and activities drawn from occupations that deal with the unit's topic. Each unit contains 3-4 hands-on science activities (p.166) and 3-4 job profiles (p. 167).

Ordering Information

Developer: Russell G. Wright, Event-Based Science Institute, Inc., 6609 Paxton Rd., Rockville, MD 20852; 1-800-327-7252; http://www.mcps.k12.md.us/departments/eventscience/ index.html

Distributor: Scott Foresman - Addison Wesley Publishing Company, One Jacob Way, Reading, MA 01867; 1-800-552-2259; http://www2.awl.com/corp/

Table of Contents: Earthquake!

(Number of pages indicated in parentheses)

Expert Tasks

Geologist: Conduct a geological study of the site of your community:

1. Draw a map of the actual site where the community will be built.

2. Locate a fault that runs through the site.

3. Identify where ground is likely to fail due to faults, liquefaction, or landslides.

4. Give a brief history of damaging earthquakes that have occurred in the region.

5. Estimate the probability of a damaging earthquake occurring in the region.

6. Identify areas that are suitable for housing (single-family houses, townhouses, apartments), industry, and commercial activities.

Chief of Transportation: Design a total transportation system for the community:

1. Draw a map or maps showing the location of each component of the transportation system. (The transportation system may include highways, bridges, railroad lines, airports, ports, marinas, and subways.)

2. Explain, in writing, special features that help adapt the transportation system to an earthquake zone.

3. Prepare plans explaining how the components of the system will work together to assist in providing emergency care and an orderly evacuation if necessary.

4. Consult with other experts so transportation facilities are located where they can best serve the community.

Director of Utilities: Plan the location of utility facilities (power plants, sewage treatment sites, water reservoirs, and pumping stations) and the distribution systems (pipelines, above-ground and underground wires, and so on):

1. Draw a map or maps showing the location of all community utility services (including water, electricity, sewer, gas, and so on).

2. Explain, in writing, special features that help adapt utility services to an earthquake zone.

3. Prepare an emergency-response plan that will help restore services and control losses due to interruptions following an earthquake.

4. Prioritize institutions that will need services restored immediately, and give reasons for the selected ranking.

---

5. Consult with other experts so utilities are located where they can best serve the community.

City Planner: Select the sites for all community facilities such as housing, shopping, industry, business, schools, hospitals, recreation facilities, fire and rescue stations, and police stations:

1. Consult with other experts on your team so community facilities are located where they can best serve the people.

2. Explain, in writing, features that help adapt the community to an earthquake zone.

3. Develop an emergency-response plan that will coordinate the efforts and resources of the agencies charged with public safety and assistance (police, fire department, hospitals, and so on).

4. Create a set of guidelines that can be used for damage assessment and emergency response.

Architect: Design buildings and assemble a three-dimensional model of the city plan:

1. Include one fault.

2. Include a body of water.

3. Include hills and valleys.

4. Include highways, bridges, railroad lines, airports, and so on as identified by the chief of transportation.

5. Include utility facilities as identified by the director of utilities.

6. Include buildings and other structures placed in the areas identified as safest by the team geologist.

Civil Engineer: Investigate design features necessary for the safest possible construction of roads, bridges, and buildings:

1. Consult with other experts so they are aware of your findings.

2. Design and build a model bridge that is earthquake resistant.

3. Assist the architect in constructing the city model.

4. Create a checklist of features that can be used to evaluate how earthquake resistant a house is. (Use the list to evaluate your own home and prepare a written report of suggested improvements.)

You and your team have the unique opportunity to benefit from the successes and failures of other city planners, architects, and engineers. By researching the construction methods and building materials—as well as the geology of the building site—used in other communities that have experienced an earthquake or other related disaster, your team can determine how to create a community that can withstand a large earthquake.

What Is Liquefaction?

Purpose

To investigate conditions that produce liquefaction during an earthquake.

Materials

- 2 large clear containers
- Tubing
- Water
- 2 rocks
- Sand
- Gravel

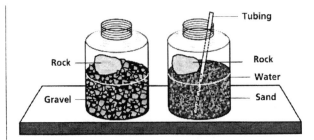

Activity

Background: You and your partners are experts on earthquakes. Your company just received a contract from the Alaskan state government to evaluate two possible building sites for a new state office building within Anchorage. Both sites are frequently shaken by earthquakes, but one site is located on sandy soil that is constantly saturated with water and the other site lies on bedrock. You and your partners decide to conduct an experiment before you write your recommendation.

1. Read Solid to Liquid in the Blink of an Eye, page 22.

2. Using the materials listed, construct a model of the two sites.

Note: When you add water to the sand, add it slowly and watch it fill the spaces between the grains. Keep adding water until it is just below the surface of the sand.

3. Wait a minute or two for everything to settle, then pound on the table with your fist to simulate an earthquake.

4. Pay particular attention to the rock. It represents a building or other heavy object on the surface.

Conclusions

Now prepare a brief memo for your supervisor in which you comment on the suitability of the two sites. Make your recommendation based on your understanding of liquefaction. State the reasons for your recommendation in words your supervisor will understand. (She is not a scientist.)

The Story—Part 2   23

Geologist

CAROL PRENTICE
UNITED STATES
GEOLOGICAL SURVEY
MENLO PARK, CALIFORNIA

After a big earthquake, there are thousands of aftershocks that continue for years. Often there is what we call "after-slip." During an earthquake, there is a certain amount of slippage, then over the next day, week, or even months, the fault continues to slip. It is very interesting to measure to see how fast that happens. In some cases, it may be that little pulses of "after-slip" happened with aftershocks.

When an earthquake occurs and you look at the seismogram, you do not know whether or not a particular event is a pre-shock or a main-shock. You do not really know until something bigger happens or does not.

There are two things I love about my job. The first is that I have a lot of freedom and get to spend time outside. Second, I feel that what I do is very relevant to people's lives, and that is important to me.

The main thing I do is dig trenches across faults. I go as deep as I can, but not so deep that I put my life in jeopardy. A typical trench is between 10 feet and 15 feet deep. I study the face of the trench inch by inch.

In the state of California there is a law that if you are building *near* what has been designated by the state as an active fault zone, you have to have a geo-technical report. If you are building within the zone, a geologist has to come and dig a trench to make sure there are no active faults where you plan to place the building. If I were part of your site development team, I would insist on the same process for your planned city.

Math and physical science (physics and chemistry) are important to a geologist. History is helpful to a paleo-seismologist. Camping skills are also helpful.

When you are talking about the size of an earthquake, there are really two different ways of thinking about it. There is the *intensity* of an earthquake, which has to do with the amount of shaking and damage. There is also the *magnitude* of an earthquake. Magnitude has to do with the amount of energy released. When we study California earthquakes that occurred in the nineteenth century, there is really no instrumentation to tell us much about the energy released. We try to estimate the intensity based on damage reports from newspaper articles and people's journals and letters. An intensity reading gives us a general idea of what the magnitude was. We measure intensity on the Mercalli scale.

Developer
CeMast, Illinois State University

Distributor
Glencoe/McGraw-Hill Publishing Company

Funders/ Contributors
Illinois State Board of Education

CeMaST, Illinois State University

National Science Foundation

Integrated Mathematics, Science, and Technology

1998

IMaST promotes hands-on learning for students and teaming among teachers from 3 or more disciplines. Curriculum is built on 1 major theme per module (such as food production and wellness); several key concepts related to this theme are presented within each discipline. Strong emphasis on problem solving, group work, and authentic assessment.

Per module—Student text: softcover, 127-176 pp., $14.99; Student journal: 3-hole punched, perforated-edge booklet, $5.99; Teacher's Resource Binder: 3-ring binder, 293-427 pp., $49.99

Content Overview

Integrated Science, Mathematics, Technology

Grade 7 modules address life and material sciences; discrete mathematics; and technologies of manufacturing, communication, and transportation. Module titles and objectives are:

Wellness—apply problem-solving skills to make informed decisions about nutrition, exercise, and communicable diseases to promote wellness. *Key concepts*: nutrition, exercise, communicable diseases.

Food Production—use a problem-solving process to make informed decisions about the appropriate use of materials and technology to produce food. *Key concepts*: select, prepare, nurture, propagate, harvest.

Waste Management—make informed decisions to promote active involvement in reducing, reusing, recycling, and rethinking ways of using solid waste. *Key concepts*: reduce, reuse, recycle, rethink.

Energy Transformations—cooperatively create and present a model of energy transformations linking wellness, food production, and waste management. *Key concepts*: harness, transform, store, distribute, use, control.

Manufacturing—design, produce, and evaluate a product that meets a need; demonstrates effective use of materials; generates little waste, and is affordable. *Key concepts*: quality, efficiency, design, production, materials.

Forecasting—develop, graph, and solve linear equations verbally, tabularly, graphically, and symbolically to make predictions. *Key concepts*: slope; describe and predict patterns symbolically, verbally, tabularly, and graphically.

Grade 8 modules address earth, environmental, physical, and biological sciences; algebra and geometry; and technologies in construction, transportation, and communication. Module titles and objectives are:

Animal Habitats—plan a balanced ecosystem that considers the impacts of and relationships among the physical environment and animal behavior. *Key concepts*: populations, behavior, ecosystem, measurement.

Human Settlements—design a sustainable human settlement that considers the impacts of and relationships among the built environment, human behavior, and the natural environment. *Key concepts*: design, community, infrastructure, sustainability.

Systems—make decisions about a system based on analysis of its function and the internal and external relationships among its characteristics (input, process, output, feedback) and boundaries. *Key concepts*: systems model, variables, relationships.

Communication Pathways—design an efficient communication system using objects; electrical current; and/or sound, light, electromagnetic waves. *Key concepts*: message, device, medium, efficiency.

Target Audience

Not indicated beyond grade-level designation.

Duration

3 class periods (approximately 120 min.) a day over 2 years.

Workplace Connections

Several relevant careers are listed at the beginning of each student activity. The corresponding pages in the Teacher's Resource Binder give additional information about these careers, including a description of practitioners, where practitioners are employed, and required education/training.

| **Instructional Approach** | Curriculum encourages students to be active learners who work in cooperative group situations while engaged in hands-on investigations. Students proceed through a module as follows: |

- The Challenge is an interdisciplinary activity designed to introduce students to concepts covered in the module.

- Investigations are mathematics, science, and technology activities (about 5 of each), which conclude with an assessment. After allowing students to construct their own knowledge, many investigations are followed by an article that provides a social/cultural context for the activity's theme.

- Putting It All Together is a wrap-up section tying what students have learned about the module's key concepts to real-world applications and considerations.

The IMaST program is intended to be delivered by 3 teachers (in mathematics, science, and technology) in approximately 120 min. of class time each day; preferably—but not necessarily—this will comprise 3 consecutive class periods.

Each of the modules incorporates a problem-solving approach abbreviated as DAPIC: Define (the problem or the challenge), Assess (the situation), Plan (how to solve the problem), Implement (the plan), and Communicate (the evaluated results to others). The curriculum also uses a 4-phase learning cycle: Exploring, Getting the Idea, Applying the Idea, and Expanding the Idea. Students frequently use DAPIC within these 4 phases and are thus engaged in 2 levels of problem solving throughout the program.

Curriculum Components

Each module features a student text, a student journal, and a Teacher's Resource Binder. This last includes the entire student text, teaching suggestions, handouts, information on correlation to national standards, suggestions for connecting materials to social studies and language arts curricula, and assessments.

Materials

Materials and equipment needed for each activity are listed in the Teacher's Resource Binder; all are commonly found in schools or can be purchased locally at minimal cost.

Assessments

The Teacher's Resource Binder provides 2 types of assessments and accompanying scoring rubrics: (1) assessments at the end of each mathematics, science, and technology activity (problem-based performance measures of both content and process skills that relate to that activity's objectives); and (2) an end-of-module assessment incorporating content and processes from all 3 disciplines. The latter comprises both a team process activity—a 2-period problem that requires student teams to apply DAPIC as well as concepts and skills they developed throughout the module's activities—and a portfolio—a 1-period essay assignment focusing on the module's key concepts, substantiated with materials from student work throughout the module.

Teacher Resources

Program involves decisions and group efforts by teachers from more than 1 discipline and is likely to require substantial teacher planning and instructional changes. The Teacher's Resource Binder contains suggestions on scheduling, team planning, and facilities/materials. Orientation workshops are offered to introduce the program to teams of mathematics, science, and technology teachers and their administrators; contact the Center for Mathematics, Science, and Technology (CeMaST).

Standards

The Teacher's Resource Binder provides matrices that correlate module activities to the National Council of Teachers of Mathematics standards (1989), the National Research Council science standards (1996), and the International Technology Education Association draft technology standards (1997).

References

An IMaST program assessment (results of subtests of the Third International Mathematics and Science Study administered at six pilot sites during spring 1997) is available at http://www.ilstu.edu/depts/cemast/ProgramAssessment.html.

Sample Pages

All pages are from the Food Production unit. Pages 173-174 show the range of student activities used. Page 175 illustrates making a strong connection to a workplace (agriculture business). Several career connections appear on pp.176-177.

Ordering Information

Developer: Dr. Franzie Loepp, Director, Dr. Robert Fisher, Co-Director, and Dr. Sherry Meier, Co-Director, Illinois State University, Campus Box 5960, Normal, IL 61790-5960; 309-438-3089; http://www.ilstu.edu/depts/cemast/imastwelcome.html

Distributor: Center for Mathematics, Science, and Technology, Glencoe/McGraw-Hill Publishing Company, P.O. Box 543, Blacklick, OH 43004-0543; 1-800-334-7344

Table of Contents

(Generic module)

Exploring

1 Carefully observe your plants for signs that they have reached maturity. (Your teacher will provide you with information about characteristics of a mature plant.) When the plants are mature, it will be time to harvest them.

2 Carefully remove the plants from the hydroponics system in the manner your teacher has demonstrated. Wash your harvested crop with fresh water and drain or pat dry to remove excess water.

3 Measure and weigh your crop **yield** from your two plants. Record this data in the appropriate space on the Data Collection Sheet you have been using to record data about your plants.

4 Store your harvested crop in a plastic container. Seal the container tightly and place it in a cool place to prevent spoilage.

5 Once the crop has been harvested and stored, the last step is to prepare the growing

yield: Amount or quantity produced; amount harvested from mature plants.

environment for the next planting season. For a farmer, this might mean plowing under the parts of the plant that remain after harvest. It might mean turning the soil and adding nitrogen or other fertilizers to replace some of the elements that have been removed during the growing process. In your case, the growing chamber must be cleaned, disassembled, and stored. Many of the parts will be used again next year; therefore, when the unit is taken apart, try to save as much of it as possible.

6 Use cleaning materials to thoroughly wash the main parts of the system, especially those parts that held the root system and delivered the nutrient solution.

7 After the reusable parts that you have cleaned are thoroughly dry, store them where your teacher indicates, and clean up the work area.

Getting the Idea

After a class discussion, record your responses to the questions in this section on Journal Sheet T7-1.

1 Compare your growing experience with that of other teams. Did all the plants mature at the same rate? Give some examples to support your answer.

Food Production **149**

2 Compare your growing experience with that of other teams. Were all the plants the same size? Explain.

3 What was the total weight of food produced by the class? Were the results what you and your team expected? Explain your answer.

4 How many people could be fed with all the food produced by the class?

5 Why is timing important when determining when to harvest a crop?

6 Did your plants seem to grow better or worse than the Wisconsin Fast Plants that were grown in your science class? Provide proof to support your answer.

Applying the Idea

1 If your hydroponics system were to be used on a larger scale of 20 to 30 acres, what design changes would be needed?

2 What type of hydroponics system would be required to feed a family of four for a year?

Expanding the Idea

1 Would it be **cost-effective** to produce tomatoes for stores in your area using the hydroponics method? Explain your reasoning.

2 Relate the harvesting process you used for your hydroponics crop to the harvesting of the *Brassica rapa* seed pods in science class.

cost-effective: Describes situation in which the earnings from the output exceed the costs of all the inputs. For example, in the case of a crop, the earnings from the sale of the harvested crop should be greater than the total combined costs of all the inputs, such as seed, fertilizer, equipment to plant and harvest, fuel to operate any machinery used, and the cost of transporting the crop to the market.

Understanding Technology Processes: Harvesting the Crop

Read the following article about the processes farmers use for harvesting their crops. Did you and your classmates take care that none of your crop was wasted when you harvested your hydroponics crop?

---

150 Food Production

Harvesting Technologies

The efficiency of harvesting techniques affects the crop yield. In the case of subsistence farmers, reduced yields could mean the difference between surviving and starving. In the case of commercial farmers, reduced yields could mean the difference between profit and loss.

Harvesting technologies vary around the world. The vast majority of farmers throughout the world rely upon harvesting by hand. They use very simple instruments like the hand sickle or the scythe. These farmers might also have access to an animal-driven harvester. In industrial nations, high-tech harvesters are used to bring in the crops. These expensive, motor-driven machines perform a number of tasks in a relatively short amount of time. Although harvesting technologies vary, the goal remains the same in each case: maximizing the amount of food taken from the field.

In Third World countries, harvesting is a slow, multi-step process. The farmer must pick the corn by hand. The corn kernels must be removed from the cob with hand-powered equipment, such as this corn sheller, which shells up to 10kg of corn in 20 minutes. Then the corn stalks must be cut down by hand. The stalks may be used for food or shelter for farm animals.

152 Food Production

CAREER CONNECTIONS

Below you will find selected information about a few careers that relate to the subject matter in this activity. You may wish to share this information with students by posting a copy on the bulletin board or by using it as the basis of a class discussion. For further information on these or other related careers, direct students to the *Occupational Outlook Handbook*, the *Dictionary of Occupational Titles*, and/or other available career resource materials.

Agronomist

Description: Agronomists study how field crops such as corn, wheat, and cotton grow. They work to improve the crops' quality and yield by developing new growth methods and determining the best means of controlling diseases, pests, and weeds. Some agronomists specialize in one type of crop or crop problem.

Where Employed: For the U.S. or State Department of Agriculture, state agricultural colleges or agricultural research centers, commercial research and development companies, agricultural service companies, and seed companies.

Education/Training: Usually at least a master's degree in agricultural science or a related life science.

Statistician

Description: Statistics deals with the collection, analysis, and presentation of numerical data. Statisticians design, carry out, and interpret the numerical results of surveys and experiments. In doing so, they apply their knowledge of statistical methods to a particular subject area, such as biology, economics, or engineering.

Where Employed: For manufacturers, financial analysts, insurance companies, business services offices, government agencies, hospitals, and colleges and universities.

Education/Training: For entry level jobs, at least a bachelor's degree with a major in statistics or mathematics or, for some jobs, a major in an applied field such as economics or a life science and a minor in statistics.

Electrician

Description: Electricians install and maintain electrical systems for a variety of purposes, including climate control, security, and communications. They also may install and maintain the electronic controls for machines in business and industry.

Where Employed: May be employed by a company that contracts to go to job sites to perform installation or maintenance/repairs or may be employed in large factories or in office buildings.

Education/Training: Usually, a four-year apprenticeship program that includes at least 150 hours of classroom training per year as well as a total of 8,000 hours of on-the-job training over the course of the four-year program. Classroom training includes blueprint reading, mathematics, electronics, electrical theory, electrical code requirements, and safety and first aid practices.

Developer
Northwestern University

Distributor
Northwestern University

Funders
*National Science
Foundation*

Materials World Modules

1997-1998

Topics relate to many industries in which modern materials are produced and used. Teaching method strongly and explicitly emphasizes the design and scientific inquiry processes used in many scientific and technical careers.

Student ed.: 9 modules, spiral-bound, about 40 pp., $8 each; Teacher ed.: 9 modules, spiral-bound, 140-150 pp., $30 each

---

Content Overview

Integrated Science, Mathematics, Technology

Materials science is an interdisciplinary field that employs science, technology, and mathematics in the discovery of new materials. This curriculum primarily supplements science (biology, chemistry, physics) and technology courses; the mathematics involved in each module is also briefly treated. The modules in this series are:

Biodegradable Materials	Food Packaging
Biosensors	Polymers
Ceramics	Smart Sensors
Composites	Sports Materials
Concrete: An Infrastructure Material	

Target Audience

Any high school students taking science, technology, or mathematics courses.

Duration

2-3 weeks per module.

Workplace Connections

Content is industry-relevant; additionally, each module has a sizable appendix with articles about the industrial production and uses of materials. For example, the appendix to the Composites module covers the following topics: chemistry of synthetic fibers, using Young's Modules to indicate elasticity of materials, and composites used in sports equipment and aircraft manufacturing.

Instructional Approach

Students are expertly guided through the processes of scientific inquiry and technological design. They make, test, evaluate, investigate, examine, and discover as they learn about the field of materials science. Activities are designed for pairs or small groups of students to design their own investigations within suggested parameters. During activities, students are encouraged to record their thoughts and predictions, and to modify these predictions based on additional learning and experiences. Students are also encouraged to come up with their own definitions (e.g., in the Composites module, they are asked to provide their own operational definitions of "strength" and "stiffness" prior to testing materials); design their own data tables for recording findings; and discuss the results of experiments. For classrooms where the learning is more directed, the curriculum provides data tables and suggested conversation points. Optional teacher demonstrations are provided for introducing or reinforcing concepts.

Curriculum Components

Teacher's Edition—contains extension activities and suggestions for implementing the curriculum in commentary that surrounds a reproduction of the Student Book.

- *Using Your Module*—includes information on the curriculum philosophy, topic background, and an overview of the activities and design projects. A 1-page Overview introduces the science topics addressed by each activity. The Module-At-A-Glance includes learning objectives, required materials, and an estimated time table. Suggestions are provided on ways to adapt the activities to students of differing abilities and to alternative teaching styles. A short bibliography contains citations for reference books, articles, and World Wide Web addresses.

- *Planning Guide*—for each activity, the Planning Guide provides information on the purpose, an activity summary, safety issues, any advance preparation information, and suggested alternatives when appropriate. Correlated to each event in an activity are common student responses, suggested questions or discussion topics, and ways to assign various readings.

- *Appendix*—includes substantial readings that provide background content information for both the teacher and the student, extension activities, and masters of data tables.

Student Book—contains the activities and design projects with some, or all, of the following main sections:

- *The Concepts Behind Composites*—presents the main idea of the activity in 1 or 2 sentences, and 1-2 pages of science explanations and real-world examples.

- *Procedures, Data & Observations*—includes student group discussion questions, instructions for the activity, and reflection questions.

- *Putting It All Together*—provides student questions, discusses the connections to the design challenges, and asks students to consider new questions they may have after doing the activity.

- *Expanding on the Concepts*—1-page section that discusses the science concepts students addressed in the activity.

Materials

Each module has a materials list, which is generally composed of easy-to-obtain materials.

Assessments

The Teacher's Guide provides suggestions for different modes of assessing student learning using the activities in the module: traditional assessment, self-assessment, science process skills, and portfolio assessment.

Teacher Resources

"Materials World Interactive" helps teachers make decisions about how to use Materials World Modules in the classroom. It is available on CD-ROM and via the World Wide Web at http://mwm.ms.nwu.edu/mwi/index.html.

Standards

No information provided.

Sample Pages

Pages 182-183, from the Biodegradable Materials unit, show a research activity and a hands-on science investigation, respectively. Pages 184-185, from the Composites unit, show some background information and a Design Challenge, respectively. Design Challenges are the overall organizer for instruction.

Ordering Information

Developer: Robert Chang, Northwestern University, 2115 North Campus Drive, Evanston, IL 60208-2610; 847-467-2489; http://mwm.ms. nwu.edu/

Table of Contents: Composites

(Number of pages indicated in parentheses;

each activity and design project is preceded by a 2-page planning guide)

Researching Biodegradable Materials

Dr. Linda Griffith-Cima is working on developing a biodegradable scaffolding on which liver cells could be grown and then implanted in patients with liver failure. The scaffolding consists of a synthetic polymer with channels running through it.

dental implants
fertilizers
medicine-delivery microcapsules
orthopedic implants
packing materials
sutures
tissue regeneration

Could biodegradable materials be used someday to make new body parts? Some researchers think so. They are presently developing biodegradable polymers that can be used to regenerate skin, bone, and other types of tissues. Human cells are grown on the polymers, which are then implanted in the body. The cells perform their specialized functions while the polymers degrade.

Biodegradable materials have many applications in medicine, engineering, agriculture, and other areas. Do research to learn about a biodegradable material that interests you. The list to the left may help you select a topic. You may also select from the list of biodegradable objects you identified in Activity 2. Your report will be due at the end of the module.

Use library references or online resources to find out how the biodegradable material you have chosen was developed, what it is made of, how it degrades, and how it is used. Look for at least three sources of information. These may be found in books, magazines, and on the Internet. Keep a complete bibliography of all your sources. You may also wish to contact and interview experts in the field, such as bioengineers and materials-science researchers.

After you complete your research, write a report describing the development, manufacture, and use of the biodegradable material. Your report should include an introduction, body, conclusion, and bibliography. In the introduction, tell whether the biodegradable material is synthetic or natural, what it is made of, and the use of the material that you will focus on. In the body of your report, tell how the material was discovered or developed; also describe details of its use; finally, evaluate the advantages and disadvantages of this material, incorporating an evaluation of economic and environmental aspects of its manufacture, degradation, and use. In your conclusion, propose new uses for the material. Explain how the properties of the material would allow it to be used in the ways you proposed.

Attach a complete bibliography to your report, using the following style:

For magazine articles:
Author. "Article Title." *Magazine Name*, volume (date), pages.

For newspaper articles:
Author. "Article Title." *Newspaper Name*, date.

For books:
Author. *Title*. Place of publication: Publisher, date, pages.

For online sources:
Author. *Title*. Internet address.

Let us dare
to read, think,
speak, **and write.**

John Adams,
Second president of the
United States

3 Processing Biodegradable Materials and Comparing Their Mechanical Properties
ACTIVITY

If you ever tried tearing apart a plastic bag, you probably found that it was difficult to do. One of the advantages of plastics, which most commonly are nonbiodegradable polymers, is that they are durable and relatively strong. Could a biodegradable polymer have the same properties?

PART A Processing Gelatin into a Gel and Films

In this part of the activity, you will process gelatin, a biodegradable polymer, into two different forms—a film and a gel.

Predictions Read the procedure for making the gel and films. What might happen when you add different amounts of gelatin to the solvent? Predict how the concentration of the gelatin will affect the solutions. Record your prediction.

▶ **Make a data table with the following categories:**
- your prediction about the concentrations of the gelatin solutions
- description of the gelatin capsules
- gelatin concentrations (weight percent) of the solutions
- mass of gelatin used to make each solution
- observations of each gelatin solution
- observations of the films and gel
- masses of the films and gel

▶ **Gather these materials for Part A:**
- 7 vials and caps with 10 mL HCl solution (pH 1) in each vial
- gelatin capsules
- mass balance
- scissors
- 6 plastic petri dishes
- wax pencil
- spatula

Think about these questions as you do the activity:
? How is gelatin processed into gels and films?
? How do the tested materials vary in strength and compressibility?
? How does the concentration of gelatin affect the strength of the films?

*D*esign Connection What do you think might be some practical uses for biodegradable gels and films?

Procedure, Observations, and Data
Safety Note: Wear goggles during this activity. Hydrochloric acid (HCl) is corrosive. Concentrated HCl can burn your skin and clothing. Do not taste or eat any of the materials.

1. Carefully observe a gelatin capsule. What does the gelatin look like? How does it feel? Record your observations.

2. Prepare three kinds of gelatin solutions that vary in weight percent of gelatin. A 1% weight/volume (w/v) gelatin solution is equivalent to 1 g of gelatin per 100 mL of HCl. Make three 5% w/v, three 10% w/v, and one 20% w/v gelatin solutions by adding the correct number of grams of gelatin to the 10 mL of acid solution in each vial. You will need to cut the gelatin capsules with scissors. Label the vials. Record the amount of gelatin you added to each vial.

3. Cap each vial and shake it under warm, running tap water until all the gelatin has dissolved. *Safety Note: Be careful not to spill any of the liquid, as it contains acid.* Observe the solutions you made and record your observations.

4. Label three petri dishes 5% w/v and another three petri dishes 10% w/v. To make films, pour all the gelatin solution from the appropriate vial into each petri dish. Leave the films overnight to dry.

5. To make a gel, let the vial with the 20% w/v solution sit overnight. Keep the vial capped.

6. The next day, examine the gel and the two types of films. Record your observations.

7. Peel off the films from the petri dishes and carefully scoop out the gel from the vial. Weigh the films and gel and record your data. Save the gel and films for Part B. Store the films in the appropriate petri dishes. Put the gel back in the vial.

4 INTRODUCTION

As you learned in Activity 3, some materials are very strong, but not very stiff, such as nylon rope. Other materials are rigid, but not very strong, such as chalk.

Composites in Sports Equipment

Filaments of graphite and other materials can be combined with polymers, forming a composite that can be used to make a strong, stiff, lightweight tennis racquet.

the Concept behind COMPOSITES

When a strong, flexible material is combined with a stiff, weak material, the result may be a composite that has desirable qualities of both components: strength and stiffness.

Any human-made composite material is specifically designed to take advantage of the best attributes of each of the materials that compose it. Sports equipment illustrates this point really well. Many are made of fiber-reinforced composites, which are strong, stiff, and light in weight.

In these composites, the bulk of the material is a plastic or plasticlike material called a polymer. Pure polymers used in sports equipment are light, but very weak. However, polymers can be combined with stronger materials, such as graphite fibers. The resulting fiber-reinforced polymer composite is many times stronger and stiffer than the pure polymer and much less dense than pure

materials, such as wood. In this composite, a weak but light polymer and strong, stiff graphite fibers are combined to form a material that is lightweight, strong, and stiff. And perfect for a tennis racquet.

The modern-day tennis racquet is a marvel of composite engineering. Compared with older tennis racquets, which have a wooden frame, tennis racquets made of composites are very light, stiff, and strong. A core of plastic foam forms the racquet frame and the handle. This material is similar to the foam beam in the activity you will do next. Layers of graphite-reinforced polymers are wrapped around the core. This strengthens the racquet frame and makes it stiff without adding much weight.

Racquets made of such composite materials help improve the game of all tennis players, amateurs and professionals alike. Being light in weight, the racquet is easier to handle and control. being strong, the racquet can withstand the force of the hardest hit balls; being stiff, the racquet doesn't distort when the ball hits it, so most of the racquet's energy contributes to the return shot.

The graphite-reinforced polymers are baked in a mold to harden. After 10 to 40 minutes in a 300° F oven, the racquet frame is unmolded.

Think about these questions as you work on your design:

? What are some important characteristics of a good fishing pole?

? How can you measure each of these characteristics?

? What are some benefits and drawbacks to using composite materials for your prototype fishing pole?

the Design CHALLENGE

Your task is to design a fishing pole, made out of a composite material that is based on a plastic straw. The winning fishing pole will be strong, light, and have maximum flexibility. To compete successfully in this contest, your group needs to complete the following steps:

Come up with a Proposal for a Set of Prototype Fishing Poles

Discuss different designs for fishing poles and decide on a set of prototype fishing poles, which vary in a single element of design. The prototypes must follow these constraints:

1. The design must incorporate the straws provided.

2. No fishing pole can have a diameter more than 0.5 cm greater than the diameter of the original straw.

3. No fishing pole can be longer or shorter than the original straw.

4. Each prototype set should include three to five fishing poles in which one feature is varied for the set; by testing a set of prototypes that differ in a single variable, your group will best be able to evaluate the effectiveness of your design.

Predict how the Prototypes will Perform

Make a prediction about which prototype fishing pole in your first design set will perform the best and give reasons for your prediction.

Develop and Follow a Repeatable Procedure for Constructing and Testing your Prototypes

List the steps in constructing the prototypes and describe how you will test the prototypes to evaluate their performance according to the criteria for the contest.

Record the Data from the Tests

Construct a data table for each test, record the data, and summarize the results of each test.

Interpret the Data from the Tests

Construct graphs of the data. Compare and contrast the graphs. Then, draw conclusions based on your interpretations of the data and give reasons for your conclusions.

Reflect on your original Predictions

Discuss how your results from the tests of the prototypes confirmed or differed from what you predicted would happen. Analyze sources of experimental error.

Present your Prototypes and the Results of your Tests

Describe your prototypes and how you made them. Explain the results of your tests on the prototypes. Invite classmates to evaluate your prototypes and your testing methods and write down their comments and suggestions.

Critique the Prototypes of your Classmates

Think about how the prototypes were constructed, how they were tested, and how the results were interpreted. Suggest ways of improving any of these steps.

Redesign your Fishing Pole

Come up with a new design for your fishing pole based on what you learned from working with your first set of prototypes and what you learned from critiquing the prototypes of other groups. Repeat the design cycle for building, testing, and critiquing your second set of prototypes.

Offshore Oil Drilling

A Coordinated Science Approach 1995

Developer
CSU Sacramento

Distributor
CSU Sacramento

**Funders/
Contributors**
*American Petroleum
Institute*

*California Department of
Education*

*National Science
Foundation*

Developed by teachers, engineers, and scientists, this module integrates topics in biology, physics, chemistry, and the geosciences as students analyze different aspects of oil exploration. The module strongly connects to the workplace by providing information about the oil industry and profiles of several types of engineers. Some lessons engage students directly in the activities performed by these professionals.

Spiral-bound softcover, 174 pp., $18

Content Overview

Integrated Science

Teaches the physics, chemistry, biology, and geoscience of oil exploration. Produced by California's Scope, Sequence, and Coordination (SS&C) Project to help implement the central idea of the National Science Teachers Association's SS&C Project: integrate middle and high school science so that every science field is taught every year. Module also covers political and economic aspects of oil exploration; instruction on the latter can incorporate the videotape *Math in the Oil Industry*, produced by Shell Oil Company.

Target Audience

Not specified other than grade levels.

Duration

23 class periods, 5 weeks.

Workplace Connections

The workplace is prominently featured, with frequent descriptions of industrial procedures and of the following jobs within the oil industry: economist, environmental/civil engineer, drilling engineer, and extraction mud engineer. Students role-play professionals in several activities.

Instructional Approach

Students learn through laboratory activities, brief background readings, role-playing, games, and discussion. Most student work takes place in groups with a specified division of labor; there are also some whole-class lessons and occasional individual or paired activities. Some lab activities have students design their own experiments; others require students to follow established procedures. In most lessons, students are to provide speculative or descriptive responses to questions posed in the curriculum. Modeling activities are used to teach abstract concepts such as energy transfer and the food web.

Curriculum Components

Each of the 4 units includes the following sections:

- *Teacher Background*—unit overview that includes length of task; Big Ideas; themes; objectives; and lesson descriptions that contain materials, set-up suggestions for how to teach, discussion points to be made, and questions to be asked.

- *Student Directions*—directions for short student activities.

- *Student Information Sheets*—background information for the activities.

- *Student Labs*—more extensive, in-depth laboratory activities, included for some units.

Materials

The majority of supplies are commonly found in science classrooms or at home.

Assessments

The last lesson, "Regulatory Hearing on Offshore Oil Development," is the curriculum's designated assessment activity. In this culminating activity, students make use of the module's scientific, economic, and political information by forming groups and assuming various roles within a committee to analyze a proposal for an offshore oil exploration and drilling permit.

Standards

Materials were produced to illustrate aspects of the California Framework for Science.

Sample Pages

Page 189 shows a career profile while page 191 is a description of job activities. Page 190 illustrates a hands-on science lab.

Ordering Information

California State University Sacramento, Helen Kota, SS&C, 6000 J Street, Sacramento, CA 95819-6120; 916-278-4766

Table of Contents

(Number of pages indicated in parentheses)

Student Information Sheet #8a

THE ENVIRONMENTAL/CIVIL ENGINEER

"I'm R. K. Rod Bogan, an environmental/civil engineer with Phillips Petroleum Company. From the time I was in high school I wanted to work for an oil company. In high school and college I worked in the oil fields getting first-hand experience. In college I majored in Civil Engineering with a specialty in Environmental Engineering. This has allowed me to work in several different careers within the oil industry. On graduating from college I went to work for Phillips. They had an excellent training program that allowed me a half-year of work in the oil field learning the (upstream) extraction end of the oil business and a half-year working as staff engineer learning about the design of surface equipment and operations. From 1978 to 1981, I worked in different production jobs within Phillips Petroleum Co. In 1984 I moved into the drilling part of the business and in 1984 worked with both drilling and production. I'm now a staff consulting engineer training oil industry personnel all over the world in the latest oil industry technology. I give many presentations and training classes to large and small groups on the environmental and safety concerns of the oil industry. I'm also asked to do trouble-shooting whenever a problem arises. I love my job. It has also given me an opportunity to travel extensively."

In this activity you are an environmental/civil engineer working with an offshore oil rig. There are many regulations that govern the drilling of offshore oil wells in the United States. All the oil companies must obey the rules and regulations of government agencies, including the U.S. Geological Survey, the Coast Guard, the Fish and Wildlife Service, the Environmental Protection Agency, the Army Corps of Engineers, and Minerals Management Service, among others. Everyone working on the oil rig gets extensive training in safety, fire-prevention, fire-fighting and environmental protection. Many of the environmental problems and issues associated with offshore oil drilling will be studied in the next unit.

For now, you are going to study an important problem that concerns all oil companies: how to prevent corrosion on an oil rig. Your expert group of environmental/civil engineers will be given two pieces of iron metal. Follow the Student Lab Directions to help your company decide which metal to use in building an oil rig.

Lesson 3c. Who Does What?   *Student Lab Directions (continued)*

Student Lab Directions (continued)

THE ENVIRONMENTAL/CIVIL ENGINEER

4. Keep the set-up to help with the assessment.
5. Place dry sand into petri dish #3 and position one nail so that it is about half-buried.

Figure 13. Lab set-up for petri dish #3.

6. Place damp sand in petri dishes #4 through #9 and do the following:

     a.   In dish #4, half-bury an iron nail.
     b.   In dish #5, mix one teaspoon of salt in with the sand and half-bury a nail .
     c.   In dish #6, bend a nail and cover it with damp sand.
     d.   In dish #7, dip a nail in oil and then half-bury in damp sand.
     e.   dish #8, half-bury a painted nail.
     f.   dish #9, half-bury a galvanized nail.

7. Leave overnight.
8. The next day, write down your observations for each petri dish, #1 through #9.

Extension

You have just finished an experiment where you have seen iron under certain conditions get a reddish color coating, which is called rust. Rusting is a form of corrosion. Another example of corrosion is when silver gets dull or darkish. Millions of dollars are wasted every year because iron and steel rust. Rusting can be prevented by keeping air away from the iron. Rusting is more rapid in air that is moist and in air that contains salt. Bridges are always being painted to keep the air from rusting them. A "tin" can is really an iron can coated with tin. The tin keeps the air away from the iron. Garbage pails are made of iron coated with zinc. Such iron is called "galvanized" iron. Some iron is coated with copper and some with chromium. Stainless steel is much less prone to rusting than ordinary steel. It is made by melting together iron, nickel, and chromium. Roller skates are protected from rusting with an oil covering.

Company problem

Your company is in charge of a huge oil rig. What types of preventive measures must your company use to solve the corrosion problem?

Student Information Sheet #8b

THE DRILLING ENGINEER

A Houston native, Juanita Alvarez found herself drawn to the oil industry, and particularly to what she now refers to as the "upstream" sector of the industry—those who are directly involved with the drilling and extraction of oil. To position herself properly to get a job with an operating company, Juanita interned with an oil company while studying mechanical engineering at Rice University. She joined the company as a drilling engineer after graduation, and is now a manager of international drilling at the company's headquarters.

Juanita has found that drilling engineers possess a unique attitude toward their role in the extraction process—they seem born to drill for oil or gas. Drilling engineers are responsible for the design of the well; drilling managers oversee the construction of the well. While the drilling engineers work closely with other members of the extraction team, it ultimately comes down to the drilling department to design the well and execute the drilling program in a safe, cost-effective, and environmentally sound manner. It is also up to the drilling engineer to acquire the optimum amount of geotechnical and petrotechnical information, and to leave the wellbore in a condition that guarantees that productive wells will yield the maximum commercial value to the company.

An considerable amount of work must be accomplished to prepare drilling sites. Obviously, one of the first tasks is to build the oil rig and assemble the various drilling systems, which include hoisting, rotating, circulating, power, and blowout prevention systems. Once the rig has been built, drilling can progress by one of two routes. In straight-hole drilling, an array of specialized down-hole tools located in the lower drill stem is used to regulate the weight on the bit and the rotation speed according to the parameters set during exploration. The other technique, known as directional drilling, usually occurs when space is limited at a particular site, or when a formation cannot be reached from directly above. Under these conditions, drilling engineers may opt to deviate the direction in which the hole is drilled in order to penetrate a specific target formation. To ensure that drilling proceeds smoothly, drilling engineers will continuously monitor the activity and recommend changes as appropriate. For example, they may replace or modify drill bits, bottom hole assemblies, mud properties, hydraulics, or casing strings to adjust to the conditions encountered during drilling.

Because oil sites may be located all over the world, drilling engineers must be willing to travel extensively in order to investigate new sites and monitor drilling operations. And even when at home, drilling engineers must be on 24-hour call in case a problem occurs during drilling. But for Juanita and other motivated, project-oriented people, the life of a drilling engineer is ideal.

PHYS-MA-TECH

1992

Developer
Northern Illinois University & five area high schools

Distributor
Curriculum Publications Clearinghouse

Funders/ Contributors
National Science Foundation
IL Board of Education
IL Depart. of Vocational Education
Northern IL University College of Engineering

Integrates physics, mathematics, and technology in various engineering applications, such as technological devices, systems, and processes. These 45 activities comprise an entire course, but can also be readily used as supplemental, stand-alone activities. Designed to encourage students who do not traditionally enroll in physics.

Ring binder, 706 pp.; $42.00

Content Overview

Integrated Physics, Mathematics, Technology

These materials stem from a realization that much of the technology in the workplace and home is hidden from users and beneficiaries. By opening up some of the tools and devices of technology to understand their structure and function in quantitative terms, it is hoped that students might find science, mathematics, and technology more appealing and less remote. Engineering applications covered range from the familiar—such as power tools—to thermally and optically activated electronic sensors; laser applications; and industrial automation such as robots, machine tools, and CAD/CAM.

Target Audience

Aimed at encouraging students who do not traditionally enroll in physics to do so, without diminishing the content or rigor of the physics.

Duration

Activities require 1-6 class periods; most take 1-2.

Workplace Connections

Workplace knowledge is incorporated in all problem contexts. Visits to industrial sites are encouraged as follow-up to approximately half the activities. Guest speakers are encouraged as follow-up to a few activities.

Instructional Approach

Designed to be team taught by three subject-matter teachers—in physics, mathematics, and technology—and each activity includes a suggested teaching strategy with roles outlined for the three teachers. Five models for staffing an integrated course are given. Materials may, however, be more easily implemented by a single teacher trying to make the curriculum more interdisciplinary.

Most activities follow this sequence: (1) review of prerequisite material; (2) presentation of new concepts; (3) teacher demonstration and/or student engagement in small groups in a laboratory activity (with step-by-step instructions for students to follow); (4) write-up of lab (including filling in data tables) and paper-and-pencil post-lab worksheets and mathematics worksheets (these ask students to define terms, explain phenomena, perform mathematical calculations, and solve physics problems based on learning in that activity); and (5) possibilities for extensions to the activity.

Curriculum Components

Activities typically include the following: technological framework; purpose; Illinois Learner Outcomes; concepts; prerequisites; materials, equipment, apparatus; time frame; teaching strategies; teaching methodology; further fields of investigation; reference information; procedure; anticipated problems; methods of evaluation; follow-up activities; references, resources, vendors; and post-activity questions/worksheets.

Materials

Each activity lists required materials, equipment, and apparatus. Most of these can be found in shop or engineering/physics classrooms; essential equipment for a few activities will require special arrangements (e.g., trucks with hydraulic jacks). A list of vendors and contact information is provided for each activity; estimated costs are not included.

Assessments

Assessment suggestions are briefly presented for each activity (e.g., teacher-generated quizzes and tests, teacher observation of students while engaged in lab activities, evaluation of worksheets provided for each activity). No grading criteria are provided.

Teacher Resources

Most activities require specialized shop, engineering, physics, and/or construction equipment. A 1-hour in-service videotape for professional development, available for $15.75, discusses the curricular materials and their implementation, particularly integration of physics, mathematics, and technology. Teachers opting for the team-teaching approach intended by this curriculum would need to invest time in joint planning.

Standards

Each activity lists the associated Illinois State Learner Outcomes. No reference is made to national math, science, or technology standards.

References   J.D. Scarborough and C. White, "PHYS-MA-TECH: An Integrated
                        Partnership," *Journal of Technology Education*, Vol. 5, No. 2 (1994).

Sample Pages   Pages 195-198 show most of the Programmable Home Thermostat labora-
                        tory. The bottom of page198 is a related Mathematics Worksheet. Page 199,
                        taken from the Variable Resistor laboratory, is an example of Post-Lab
                        Questions, which are provided for some labs.

Ordering Information

Developer: Dr. Jule Dee Scarborough, Principal Investigator, Department
of Technology, Northern Illinois University, DeKalb, IL 60115

Distributor: Curriculum Publications Clearinghouse, Western Illinois
University, Horrabin Hall 46, 1 University Circle, Macomb, IL 61455-1390;
1-800-322-3905; http://www.wiu.edu/users/micpc/

Table of Contents
(Number of pages indicated in parentheses)

MATERIALS, EQUIPMENT, APPARATUS:	A programmable thermostat (Hunter Model 42204 or similar product), 24-V/110-V transformer, bell wire, 24-V bulb and base (or 24-V pilot light), junction box, 110-V single pole switch, ceramic disk heater (or similar heating device), 1/4" peg board 8-cubic foot enclosure, fiberglass insulated 8-cubic foot enclosure, computer interfaced temperature probe.
TIME FRAME:	1 class period to teach concepts, 1 class period to install and program thermostat, a class period to collect and interpret data.
TEACHING STRATEGIES:	Mathematics teacher--temperature scale conversion (as a linear relationship), graphing and proportions (change in temperature), assist in laboratory activity.

Physics teacher--thermometers, temperature scales (including Kelvin), discuss kinetic theory, assist in laboratory activity.

Technology teacher--construction of enclosures, instruction on installation of thermostats, assist in laboratory activity.

Assembly and installation takes place in the Technology lab. Testing and interpretation take place in the Technology lab or classroom (enclosures are mobile).

<u>Activity One</u>: Students will work in pairs installing the programming thermostats.

<u>Activity Two</u>:

    Option 1. Students collect data from Super Champ temperature in teams (pairs).

    Option 2. Data are collected as a class. Students will graph data individually.

Brennan/Miner/Skeen
Aurora West High School
Activity 6
Programmable Home Thermostat

page 568

PHYS·MA·TECH

AN INTEGRATED PARTNERSHIP

TEACHING METHODOLOGY:	<u>Activity One</u>: Students work in pairs for installation and programming of thermostat on mock-up walls.

> Period 1: Cover temperature conversion concepts, kinetic theory.
>
> Period 2: Students will be provided with a "wall" with three wires coming from it (as if they had just removed a home thermostat). Using the instruction manual and student worksheet, students will install and program the thermostat as per directions on worksheet. This will allow for collecting data during the class on the next consecutive day.
>
> Period 3: Students will verify programming of thermostat.

<u>Activity Two</u>: An 8-cubic-foot peg board enclosure (2 x 2 x 2) with a ceramic heater will be the "room" where the temperature data are collected for 5 minutes. The heater will be turned off and data collected for a 10-minute cooling period. Then the enclosure will be insulated with 3 1/2" fiberglass batts and temperature data will be collected again.

Students will use Super Champ (or other computer-based) temperature probe to collect data from the heating and cooling of the two enclosures. Students will sketch two heating graphs of temperature as a function of time on one set of axes and two cooling graphs of temperature as a function of time.

<u>Activity Three</u>: Students will work in small groups and complete graphs to convert temperature scales.

FURTHER FIELDS OF INVESTIGATION:	Home, business, and industrial environment control.

Brennan/Miner/Skeen
Aurora West High School
Activity 6
Programmable Home Thermostat

page 569

PHYSICS

PROCEDURE:

Activity One

Step 1: Read installation instructions from thermostat manual and install thermostat as directed.

Step 2: Read programming directions from thermostat manual and program as indicated on Programmable Thermostat Worksheet.

Step 3: Complete the Programmable Thermostat Worksheet.

Step 4: (Next day) Observe the "pilot" light and determine if your programming is correct.

Activity Two

Step 1: Collect data on non-insulated enclosure from Super Champ (or other computer-based) temperature probes for heating periods: 5 minutes on, 10 minutes off.

Step 2: Place insulated enclosure over the peg board enclosure and collect data for the same time periods.

Step 3: On one graph, sketch heating temperature as a function of time for non-insulated and insulated enclosures.

Step 4: On a second graph, sketch cooling temperature as a function of time for both enclosures.

Activity Three

Temperature Scale Conversions Worksheet (attached)

ANTICIPATED
PROBLEMS:

Thermostat should be programmed in such a way that it will run the next class day. You do not want to start this activity on Friday, unless you restructure your initial time on the thermostat.

Brennan/Miner/Skeen
Aurora West High School
Activity 6
Programmable Home Thermostat

page 570

PHYS·MA·TECH

AN INTEGRATED PARTNERSHIP

METHODS OF EVALUATION:	Successful programming of thermostat is observed by students and teachers. Worksheet is completed and reviewed.
FOLLOW-UP ACTIVITIES:	In industrial visits, ask about environment control systems.
	Environment survey of student homes.
	Presentation by home energy conservationist (insulation, caulking, thermal windows, etc.).
	Suggestions for change: environmental control, heat transfer, effects of insulation. Plot temperature as a function of time and do temperature scales. Determine R-factor of insulation.
REFERENCES, RESOURCES, VENDORS:	Hardware store
	Energy research companies (e.g., Potential Energy, Inc., Chicago, IL)
	Local gas company (e.g., N.I. Gas)

TEMPERATURE SCALE CONVERSIONS: MATHEMATICS WORKSHEET 2

1. Graph Fahrenheit versus Celsius using freezing point and boiling point to determine the linear relationship.

2. What is the vertical intercept? _____

3. What is the slope? _____

4. Write the linear equation (y = mx + b) _____

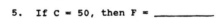

5. If C = 50, then F = _____

6. When the Celsius scale reads 10°, the Fahrenheit reads _____

7. 15°C = _____F   8. –5°C = _____F   9. 25°C = _____F

10. To the nearest degree, 34°C = _____F

11. Rewrite the equation in (4.), solving for C = _____

12. If F = 86, then X = _____

PHYS·MA·TECH

AN INTEGRATED PARTNERSHIP

VARIABLE RESISTOR POST-LAB QUESTIONS

1. Compare the current calculated flow for each fluid.

    (a) Which fluid had the highest current flow?

    (b) Which fluid had the lowest current flow?

2. Why do sensors need to be used to detect gas leaks?

3. Why is the cold resistance much higher than the hot resistance?

4. The resistance in a sensor is 252 KΩ. The sensor is switched on and a voltage of 12 volts is measured across the sensor. What is the current flow in the sensor?

            I = _____mA;   I = _____A

5. Name two local industries which would have gas sensors installed for safety reasons.

Allen/Crowns/Peterson
Grayslake High School
Activity 4
Variable Resistor (Gas Sensor)

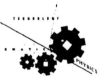

page 51

Developer
COIN Educational Products

Curriculum and Instructional Materials Center

Distributor
COIN Educational Products

Funders/ Contributors
Oklahoma Department of Vocational and Technical Education

Practical Exercises in Applying Knowledge

PEAK Science Packet 1995

PEAK contains 60 4-page student activities that can supplement other curricula. Each activity provides a detailed job profile of a professional in a workplace context that uses specific science or math. A problem likely to be encountered in that occupation is discussed, and students then solve similar problems. A broad range of occupations is highlighted. An analogous PEAK mathematics product is available but not reviewed in this book.

Class masters, 3-ring binder, 310 pp., $195 (includes site license for duplication)

Content Overview

General Science, Biology, Chemistry, Physics

See Table of Contents (below) for list of all student activity worksheets. The chemistry activities are written at a 9th-grade level rather than 11th, which is when students typically take chemistry.

Target Audience

Reading level is about 2 grade levels below the grade when the relevant course is usually taken.

Duration

Each activity takes approximately 1 class period.

Workplace Connections

Each science topic is embedded within a workplace context. A detailed job profile for a professional relevant to the workplace context is given, including information about working conditions, environment, job responsibilities, and the science addressed on the job. When a technology (e.g., lasers) is featured, multiple applications are also described. One noticeable omission is a list of the careers featured in the activities cross-referenced to the academic content covered.

Instructional Approach

After a specific science topic has been taught, the materials may be used to introduce students to the topic's workplace relevance. Alternatively, a PEAK student activity worksheet can be used before teaching a new science concept as a way to motivate students. Student activity worksheets typically include 1-2 pages of reading followed by paper-and-pencil activities such as performing mathematical calculations, writing an essay, answering short questions, and drawing and interpreting graphs or maps. Worksheets are designed for individual student work, but some small-group implementation strategies are provided in the introduction.

Curriculum Components

Each 4-page student activity worksheet has the same format and includes these components:

- *Key Topic*—identifies the academic subject matter (e.g., center of gravity, levers).

- *Key Topics on the Job*—gives a brief statement about 2 occupations that use the same academic subject matter in different ways.

- *Your Job*—describes a profession in some depth. Students then assume the role of an individual in that profession (e.g., profession—statistician, role—census taker) as they answer questions on the worksheet.

- *Information You Must Know*—presents academic subject matter students will need to know to answer the questions, including mathematical formulas.

- *Your Solution*—contains up to 10 questions with space provided for students to do the work. Each worksheet emphasizes 1 of the following problem types: mathematical calculations, essays or short written answers, multiple-choice questions, graphing, and interpreting results or reading diagrams.

- *Your Next Options*—includes a list of suggested ways students can obtain more career-related information and a list of 54-102 careers that use the curriculum content (algebra, biology, etc.) featured in the activity. This page is identical for all activities within the same content area.

The curriculum also includes Your Solution Check, which contains the solutions to the problems in the student activity worksheets and evaluation suggestions for open-ended items.

Materials	No materials are needed; all worksheets are limited to paper-and-pencil activities.
Assessments	Not explicitly addressed.
Standards	The curriculum predates National Science Education standards.
Sample Pages	Pages 204-207 present the entire Earthquake activity (Science #9). The last page (p.207) is the same or very similar for all of the PEAK activities.

Ordering Information

Developer: Coordinated Occupational Information Network Educational Products, 3361 Executive Parkway, Suite 302, Toledo, OH 43606; 1-800-274-8515; http://www.coinep.com

Oklahoma residents: Oklahoma Department of Vocational and Technical Education, Curriculum and Instructional Materials Center, 1500 West Seventh Avenue, Stillwater, OK 74074-4364; 1-800-522-5810, ext. 195; http://www.okvotech.org

Table of Contents

(Number of pages indicated in parentheses)

PRACTICAL EXERCISES IN APPLYING KNOWLEDGE

SGS-9
KEY TOPICS:
Earthquake Waves,
Epicenter, Seismograms

The Key Topics On the Job:

• Geodetic surveyors study the land forms of the earth. By studying earthquake waves and seismograms, they can find the epicenter of an earthquake. Once they know where an earthquake took place, they can make a map showing this information.

• Structural engineers, especially those who work in places where earthquakes are common, use information about earthquakes. They want to make sure that the buildings they build will not collapse during an earthquake.

Your Job: Geologist

You are a geologist. Geologists study many things about the earth. They may study how mountains were formed. Geologists may work with rocks, minerals, and fossils. They are sometimes experts on earthquakes or volcanoes.

You work at an earthquake recording center operated by the U.S. Geological Survey. The station you work at is in Denver, Colorado. You run the *seismograph* at the center. A seismograph is an instrument that records earthquake waves. The seismograph draws wavy lines on a piece of paper. This is called a *seismogram*. The wavy lines on the seismogram are caused by earthquake waves. By studying the earthquake waves, you can find out how far away from your center an earthquake occurred.

During a recent earthquake you recorded the earthquake waves on this seismogram:

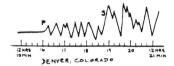

DENVER, COLORADO

Earthquake stations at Seattle, Washington and Los Angeles, California both recorded the same earthquake waves. These stations sent you copies of their seismograms.

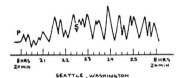

SEATTLE, WASHINGTON

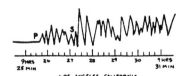

LOS ANGELES, CALIFORNIA

Now that you have three seismograms, you are to find the *epicenter* of the earthquake. The epicenter is the point on the earth's surface directly above the earthquake location.

SGS 9 — 1

Information You Must Know:

An *earthquake* is the shaking of the earth caused by the sudden, quick release of energy. The energy moves in all directions from the *focus*. The focus is the point inside the earth where the rocks moved and caused the release of energy.

The energy released by the moving rocks travels in the form of waves. Three types of waves are made when the rocks move:

- *Primary waves or P-waves*
  arrive first at the recording station

- *Secondary waves or S-waves*
  are the second to reach the recording station

- *Surface waves or L-waves*
  are the last waves to arrive at the recording station.

With seismograms from three earthquake stations, the epicenter of the earthquake can be found. Remember that *the epicenter is the point on the earth's surface directly above the focus*. The focus is where the earthquake really took place inside the earth.

Use this graph and map for your solution:

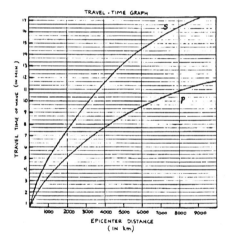

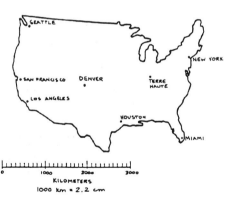

SGS 9 — 2

Your Solution:

1. As you work, fill in the earthquake data table with your answers.

EARTHQUAKE DATA TABLE

Earthquake Station	Arrival Time of Waves		Difference in time $(S_1 - P_1)$ (min, sec)	Distance to Epicenter (km)
	P-wave (P_1) (hr, min, sec)	S-wave (S_1) (hr, min, sec)		
Seattle, WA				
Denver, CO				
Los Angeles, CA				

2. By reading the given seismograms, find out:

    •   the time the P-waves arrived (hours, minutes, and seconds).
    •   the time the S-waves arrived (hours, minutes, and seconds).

    Estimate the seconds.

3. Subtract the arrival time of the P-wave from the arrival time of the S-wave to find the difference in arrival time.

4. Use the travel-time graph for the earthquake waves, to find the distance to the epicenter from each recording station. To find out how far the earthquake waves had to travel from the epicenter to reach a station, do the following:

    •   Lay the edge of a piece of paper next to the travel-time of wave scale (on the left side of the graph).
    •   If the difference in arrival time was 4 minutes 20 seconds, put a mark on the edge of your paper at the point (0,4 min. 20 sec.) and at the point (0,0).
    •   Move the edge of your paper along the P and S curve until the mark at 4 min. 20 sec. is on the S curve and at the same time the mark at 0 is on the P curve.
    •   When the marks on your paper are exactly on the P and S curves, you can find the distance by following the edge of your paper down to the epicenter distance on the graph (4,000 located at the bottom of your time travel graph).

5. When you have found the distance to the epicenter for each station, find the epicenter for the earthquake:

    •   Use the map given. Use the map scale to set your compass at the distances to the epicenter from one of your stations.
    •   Place the point of the compass at the station. Draw a circle around it.
    •   Do this for each station. The epicenter is where all three circles meet. In some cases the circles may not meet. Then make a triangle of arcs. The epicenter will be in the center of the triangle.

Your Next Options:

- Visit your Career Resource Center in your school's media center for more information on this career.

- Research career information on a computerized career information system such as COIN Career Search.

- Ask for help or assistance from your teachers, counselors, librarians, and your advisor.

- If your school does not have a Career Search Program available to you, ask your teacher or counselor where to find more information on careers.

Careers Using Science Skills:

The more you know about careers relating to subjects you are taking in school, the better prepared you will be to make career choices. Learn more about any of the following careers by using the Career Search Program:

Aerospace Engineer
Agricultural Scientist
Air Traffic Controller
Airplane Pilot
Animal Caretaker
Architect
Archivist and Curator
Biological Scientist
Blue-Collar Worker Supervisor
Broadcast Technician
Ceramic Engineer
Chemical Engineer
Chemical Equipment Operator
Chemist
Chiropractor
Civil Engineer
Clinical Laboratory Technologist
College Faculty Member
Commercial Artist
Dental Assistant
Dental Laboratory Technician
Dentist
Dietitian & Nutritionist
Diesel Mechanic
Electrical/Electronics Engineer
Electrician
Electronic Equipment Repairer
Elementary School Teacher
Energy Conservation and Use
  Technician

Engineering Technician
Firefighter
Fish and Game Warden
Food & Beverage Service
  Worker
Forester & Conservation
  Scientist
Forestry Worker
Geographer
Geologist and Geophysicist
Industrial Engineer
Industrial Hygienist
Inspector, Tester, and Grader
Laser Technician
Librarian
Library Technician
Licensed Practical Nurse
Mathematician
Mechanical Engineer
Metallurgical/Materials Engineer
Meteorologist
Nuclear Engineer
Nuclear Medicine Technologist
Numerical Control Tool
  Programmer
Nursery Worker
Occupational Therapist
Ophthalmic Lab Technician
Optician

Optometric Assistant
Optometrist
Pharmacist
Photographer
Physical Therapist
Physician
Physicist and Astronomer
Plumber and Pipe Fitter
Power Plant Operator
Radiologic Technologist
Range Manager
Registered Nurse
Respiratory Therapist
Robotics Technician
Sales Engineer
Science Technician
Solar Energy System Installer
Speech Pathologist and
  Audiologist
Sports Professional
Surveyor
TV and Radio Repairer
Teacher Aide
Telephone Installer and
  Repairer
Travel Agent
Ultrasound Technologist
Vending Machine Mechanic
Veterinarian

SGS 9 — 4

Developer
Center for Occupational Research and Development (CORD)

Distributor
Agency for Instructional Technology
South-Western Educational Publishing

Funders/ Contributors
Consortium of 40 state vocational educational agencies

Principles of Technology

2nd ed. 1990-1994

Applied science course introducing students to technology and its underlying principles by focusing on the physics concepts involved. Physics is taught in a context of 4 energy systems: mechanical, fluid, electrical, and thermal. Text materials are integrated with many hands-on lab activities, cooperative learning opportunities, teacher demonstrations, and videos. Course includes extensive treatment of the mathematics inherent to the physics topics.

14 units—Student ed.: softcover, 75-150 pp., $4.50 each; Teacher ed.: binder, 200-360 pp., $49.95 each; Videos: 35-60 min., $75 each

Content Overview

Physics, Technology, Mathematics

Course teaches a subset of traditional physics concepts in the context of technologies that make use of 4 energy systems: mechanical, fluid, electrical, and thermal. The course explains physics principles of technological devices and processes in the workplace rather than the derivation and manipulation of physics formulas. Curriculum emphasizes mathematics, so strong prealgebra skills are a prerequisite. However, the units do extensively cover the mathematics needed to understand and apply the physics principles. (Also see Pedrotti, 1996.) The 14 units are:

1. Force
2. Work
3. Rate
4. Resistance
5. Energy
6. Power
7. Force Transformers

8. Momentum
9. Waves and Vibration
10. Energy Converters
11. Transducers
12. Radiation
13. Light and Optical Systems
14. Time Constants

Units 1-7 are currently available; units 8-14 are due in early 1999.

Target Audience   Aimed at middle 50 percent of high school students; ideal for implementation in tech prep programs and other school-to-work initiatives.

Duration   Each unit generally takes 26 1-hour sessions; can be used over 1 or 2 years, with complete course requiring 2 years.

Workplace Connections   Workplace contexts are integral to the text, video, and laboratory exercises. For example, each unit's introductory text features a technician who outlines how he or she uses the concepts in his or her occupation, the videos showcase workplaces and technicians who use the specific concepts, and many subunits identify workplace applications where technicians use the concepts introduced. The workplace connections are, however, less extensive than those in CORD's "Mathematics in Context" (see p. 50) and "Applications in Biology/Chemistry" (see p. 142).

Instructional Approach   "Principles of Technology" is a lab-intensive class; roughly 40% of a student's time in any subunit is spent in a hands-on lab. By the end of the course, a student will have completed about 90 labs and will have been exposed to nearly 200 different equipment items. In general, the videos include scenes inside workplaces where technology is used, animation that shows how technology operates (inside views), and interviews with people who use technology in their jobs. The course's 14 units, which are intended to be taught over 2 years, each build upon the previous units. They follow a similar instructional sequence:

1. Overview of unit
   a. Whole-class discussion to tap prior knowledge of unit's main ideas
   b. Video and whole-class discussion

2. For each subunit (2-4 subunits per unit)
   a. Whole-class discussion to tap prior knowledge
   b. Video and whole-class discussion
   c. Text: presentation of new physics information, teacher demonstration (1 per subunit), example problems are worked out
   d. Student exercises: fill-in-the-blank, short answer
   e. Mathematics Skill Laboratory: students use calculators to solve paper-and-pencil short-answer questions; some examples are worked out
   f. Lab activities: hands-on technology labs (2 per subunit)
   g. Review: video is viewed again, followed by a whole-class discussion; review of objectives and main ideas of subunit

3. Summary
   a. Whole-class discussion: reinforcement of major ideas
   b. Video and whole-class discussion
   c. Student exercises: paper-and-pencil questions (short answer, matching, multiple choice)
   d. Teacher-performed demonstrations

Curriculum Components

Three components are needed to implement the curriculum: videos, student text, and annotated Teacher's Guide. The latter includes the full student text as well as discussion questions; content/background information; demonstrations; solutions to student exercises; pedagogical recommendations (regarding pacing and difficulty of material); and points to raise with students (clarification of text, explanations of formulas, equipment issues, and references to other sections of text).

Supplemental materials that are available but not crucial to implementation include: Student Resource Book (key formulas, tables for unit conversions and constants, comprehensive glossary, and 18 remedial mathematics laboratories for students who need to review prealgebra); Test Databank (print) and Test Database (electronic version, in PC and Macintosh formats); and A Closer Look at Principles of Technology (includes unit and subunit objectives, math activity objectives, laboratory objectives, lab and demonstration equipment lists, lab management).

Materials

The Math Skills Laboratories require students to use scientific calculators. A Closer Look at Principles of Technology contains detailed lists of laboratory equipment needed to complete the lab activities and teacher demonstrations; this includes facilities requirements and list of vendors that support the course.

Assessments

The student text and Teacher's Guide do not contain any assessments, although the student assignments can be used for assessment purposes. No scoring guidelines are provided. The supplementary Test Databank and Test Database contain tests, quizzes, and worksheets with free-response, multiple-choice, and fill-in-the-blank items; these can be customized.

Teacher Resources

Three types of professional development workshops are taught by CORD-endorsed master teachers: 3- to 5-day comprehensive workshops for $150-$750 at the Roney Teaching Center in Waco, TX; customized topic workshops and teacher training developed according to teacher needs in local regions; and technical assistance and short courses available through CORD's Virtual Teaching Center (accessed through local teleconferencing). Call CORD at 1-800-231-3015 or send e-mail to training@cord.org.

Other Languages

Spanish

Standards

National Technology Education Standards were not available when materials were developed.

Sample Pages

All pages are from the Unit #4, Resistance. On page 213, a technician describes how unit concepts are used on the job. On page 214, concepts are strongly connected to industrial settings.

Pages 215-216 illustrate student exercises and a part of a laboratory.

Ordering Information

Text materials: South-Western Educational Publishing, 5101 Madison Road, Cincinnati, OH 45227; 1-800-824-5179; http://www.swep.com/science/index.html

Videos: Agency for Instructional Technology (AIT), Box A, 1800 North Stonelake Drive, Bloomington, IN 47402-0120; 1-800-457-4509; http://www.ait.net/catalog/catpages/c249.shtml. For broadcast pricing of videos, contact AIT's Broadcast Service Department, 1-800-457-4509, ext. 236.

Note that Year 1 (units 1-7) and Year 2 (units 8-14) curriculum sets may be purchased, package prices are available for sets of units; and all prices cited are for purchases in CORD's 40 partner states.

Table of Contents: Unit 4. Resistance

(All units are similarly formatted: this is included as a partial example)

Student Text

Overview of Unit 4, Resistance
Subunit 1, Resistance in Mechanical Systems
- Topic explanation and examples
- Student Exercises
- Math Skills Lab: Rearranging symbols in equations to isolate unknowns; Solving mechanical resistance problems insulation
- Lab Activity: Investigating friction
- Lab Activity: Streamlining shapes to reduce air drag
- Review

Subunit 2, Resistance in Fluid Systems
similar to Subunit 1, including:
- Lab Activity: Measuring fluid resistance in tubes
- Lab Activity: Measuring resistance in air filters

Subunit 3, Resistance in Electrical Systems
similar to Subunit 1, including:
- Lab Activity: Ohm's Law and series circuits
- Lab Activity: Ohm's Law and parallel circuits

Subunit 4, Resistance in Thermal Systems
similar to Subunit 1, including:
- Lab Activity: Measuring resistance of thermal
- Lab Activity: Effect of thermal insulation

Summary
Glossary
End-of-unit Student Exercises

Teacher's Guide

Notes on Teacher's Guide
Breakdown of Unit (teaching paths)
Subunit 1, Resistance in Mechanical Systems
- About the video (for this subunit)
- Notes, answers, etc. for each page of student text
- Answers to student exercises
- Notes, answers, etc. for math labs
- Notes, sample data, answers, etc. for lab activities
- Hints and notes for review

Subunit 2, Resistance in Fluid Systems
(similar to Subunit 1)

Subunit 3, Resistance in Electrical Systems
(similar to Subunit 1)
Subunit 4, Resistance in Thermal Systems
(similar to Subunit 1)
Hints and notes for Summary

Answers to End-of-unit Student Exercises
- Demonstration: Mechanical friction and lubrication
- Demonstration: Resistance to airflow
- Demonstration: Electrical resistance and Ohm's Law
- Demonstration: Thermal resistance

A TECHNICIAN TALKS ABOUT RESISTANCE...

I'm an electromechanical technician.

I maintain the equipment for a plant that makes fiberglass insulation. Since we operate on a high-volume production schedule, much of our work is done by computer. Our equipment has to work within certain performance limits. If we don't meet these performance limits, our product won't meet government standards. And if it doesn't, we can't sell it.

That's why my job is important.

When we make fiberglass insulation, we move things around a lot. For example, huge, elevated storage tanks hold dry ingredients. Ground-level tanks hold liquid ingredients. We run them through pipes to a mixing station. Our product is shaped, packaged and transported by machines that use conveyors, knives, packaging machines and storage transporters. Therefore, resistance occurs throughout the manufacturing process.

Resistance can work for us—or against us. The process begins when we mix the liquid and dry ingredients. An electric current moves through the mixture. This heats it. Then the molten glass is spun into fiberglass.

There are three variables that I worry about during the melting process. First, there's the distance between the electric conductors (called "electrodes"). Then there's the voltage difference across the electrodes. And third, I know that the composition of the mixture determines the heat produced by the resistance path through the material.

I adjust the machines to make the best use of electrical energy. In this case, resistance works for us. However, in other cases, resistance works against us.

For instance, air and hydraulic fluid move through lines that are designed to keep resistance low. We want to avoid turbulence because turbulence creates friction. When we put in these lines, we choose their size, interior surface, valves and fittings carefully. We know that friction can cause small particles—impurities—to be rubbed off into the fiberglass. We have to make the right adjustments when we move ingredients from the elevated storage tanks through pipes into the mixers—or we won't have a product we can sell.

We also try to reduce friction in conveyor systems and packaging machinery. Reducing friction improves machine efficiency and cuts down on waste heat. We use rollers and roller bearings to minimize energy losses due to friction because rolling friction is less than sliding friction. Machine wear also is minimized by a good lubrication program.

When I do my job right, our production line works smoothly and efficiently. At almost every step, what I know about resistance—how resistance helps and hurts the production process—is important. And what I know about resistance also helps me troubleshoot and repair the equipment that makes fiberglass insulation possible.

WHAT'S RESISTANCE?

Pretend you're in a speedboat (Figure 4-1). Push the throttle wide open. At first, the boat's speed increases rapidly. The force of the engine causes the boat to go faster and faster. But soon, the boat reaches some top speed. It goes no faster. The engine pushes as hard as before, but the speed doesn't increase. That's because something holds the boat back with a force equal to the forward push of the engine.

That "something" is **resistance.** As the boat moves through water, a mechanical resistance called "drag" occurs. Force pushes water out of the boat's path. Force also moves the sides and bottom of the boat through the water. These forces add up to produce **drag.** As the boat's speed increases, drag increases. At top speed, backward drag equals the forward push of the engine.

Usually when one force *causes* motion, another force *opposes* motion. This opposing force is called "resistance." Think of **resistance** as **opposition to motion.**

Fig. 4-1 Resistance limits a boat's speed.

WHAT ABOUT RESISTANCE OF PIPES IN SERIES?

Suppose several pipes are connected in series. Total resistance of the string of pipes is the sum of the individual resistances. You just add them.

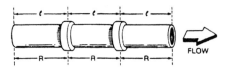

Fig. 4-27 Pipes in series.

Figure 4-27 shows three identical pieces of pipe in series. Their total length is three times the length of one piece. So it makes sense that their total resistance is three times the resistance of one piece. Adding more pieces of pipe in series increases resistance.

WHAT ABOUT RESISTANCE OF PIPES IN PARALLEL?

Figure 4-28 shows two pipes connected in parallel. In this case, the main flow divides and follows two paths. Increasing the number of pipes in parallel increases the cross-sectional area. This has the same effect as using a larger

pipe. Fluid resistance is reduced. and the flow rate is increased for a given pressure difference.

Fig. 4-28 Pipes in parallel.

WHY IS FLUID RESISTANCE IMPORTANT IN TECHNOLOGY?

Fluid resistance is an important factor that affects flow rate through a pipe, tube or duct. Figure 4-29 shows four examples where fluid resistance must be considered. There are many other examples. Fluid resistance is present in any system that uses a liquid or gas. Therefore, knowing about resistance is important if you need to control flow through a fluid system.

Practical problems involving fluid resistance usually involve an adjustment of flow rate at a fixed pressure. Flow-control valves (sometimes called "gates") control flow rate by controlling resistance. Closing the valve produces a constriction (narrowing) that increases fluid resistance. It's important to remember that fluid resistance for any given fluid can be reduced by using larger cross-sectional-area pipes. shorter lengths—and fewer bends along the flow path.

a. Oil pipeline

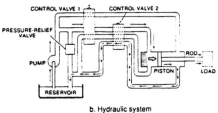

b. Hydraulic system

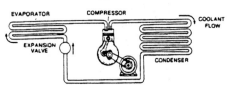

c. Refrigeration system

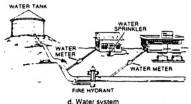

d. Water system

Fig. 4-29 Applications where fluid resistance is important.

44   *Principles of Technology*

Example 4-C: _Calculation of Fluid Resistance_ ─────────────────

Given: Fluid flows through a certain length of pipe at a flow rate (Q_V) of 0.05 m³/sec. It undergoes a pressure drop (Δp) of 1000 N/m².

Find: Fluid resistance of the pipe.

Solution:

$$R_F = \frac{\Delta p}{Q_V} \qquad \text{where: } Q_V = 0.05 \text{ m}^3/\text{sec}$$
$$\Delta p = 1000 \text{ N/m}^2$$

$$R_F = \frac{1000 \text{ N/m}^2}{0.05 \text{ m}^3/\text{sec}} = \left(\frac{1000}{0.05}\right)\left(\frac{\text{N/m}^2}{\text{m}^3/\text{sec}}\right)$$

$$R_F = 20,000 \frac{\text{N/m}^2}{\text{m}^3/\text{sec}}$$

Notice that resistance units are units of pressure (N/m²) divided by units of volume-flow rate (m³/sec). They're cumbersome, but they "explain" themselves.

───

Example 4-D: _Fluid Resistance Affects Flow Rate and Pressure Drop_ ─────────

Given: A certain length of hose has a flow rate of 5 gal/min when the pressure drop from one end of the hose to the other is 20 lb/in².

Find: a. The fluid resistance of the hose.

b. The flow rate along the **same** hose when the pressure drop along it is 40 lb/in².

c. The pressure drop along the same hose when the flow rate is reduced to 3 gal/min.

Solution: a. Solve for resistance (R_F) where: Δp = 20 lb/in² and Q_V = 5 gal/min.

$$R_F = \frac{\Delta p}{Q_V} = \frac{20 \text{ lb/in}^2}{5 \text{ gal/min}} = \left(\frac{20}{5}\right)\left(\frac{\text{lb/in}^2}{\text{gal/min}}\right) = 4 \frac{\text{lb/in}^2}{\text{gal/min}}$$

Once again, units of resistance are units of pressure divided by units of flow rate.

b. Solve for flow rate (Q_V). To do this, the equation, $R_F = \Delta p / Q_V$, must be rearranged to isolate the symbol Q_V. When done correctly, this gives:

$$Q_V = \frac{\Delta p}{R_F}$$

Substitute given values for Δp and R_F: Δp = 40 lb/in² and $R_F = 4 \dfrac{\text{lb/in}^2}{\text{gal/min}}$.

$$Q_V = \frac{40 \text{ lb/in}^2}{4 \dfrac{\text{lb/in}^2}{\text{gal/min}}} = \left(\frac{40}{4}\right)\left(\frac{\text{lb/in}^2}{\dfrac{\text{lb/in}^2}{\text{gal/min}}}\right)$$

Note: The units in the denominator are in a "fraction" form. Simplify the units. Invert the fraction in the denominator. Multiply it times the numerator. as follows:

$$\frac{\text{lb/in}^2}{\dfrac{\text{lb/in}^2}{\text{gal/min}}} = \text{lb/in}^2 \times \frac{\text{gal/min}}{\text{lb/in}^2} \qquad \text{(Cancel lb/in}^2\text{.)}$$

The simplified answer for units is gal/min—which is the unit that flow rate (Q_V) should be in. Finally, then, the answer is:

$$Q_V = \frac{40}{4} \text{ gal/min, or 10 gal/min}$$

c. Solve for pressure drop. To do this, the equation, $R_F = \Delta p / Q_V$, must be rearranged to isolate Δp. This gives:

$$\Delta p = R_F \times Q_V, \text{ where: } R_F = 4 \frac{\text{lb/in}^2}{\text{gal/min}} \text{ and } Q_V = 3 \text{ gal/min}$$

Then,

$$\Delta p = 4 \frac{\text{lb/in}^2}{\text{gal/min}} \times 3 \text{ gal/min} \qquad \text{(Cancel gal/min.)}$$

$$\Delta p = (4 \times 3) \text{ lb/in}^2 = 12 \text{ lb/in}^2$$

The pressure drop is 12 lb/in².

───

Subunit 2: Resistance in Fluid Systems 41

LABORATORY

EQUIPMENT

Airflow assembly with 12-V DC fan
Three assorted drag objects, all with same
   diameter equal to approximately 60% of
   airflow-assembly tube ID
DC power supply, 20 V, 10 A
Spring scale. 8-oz (2.5 N) or 16-oz (5-N)
   capacity
Support stand, rods, and clamps
Monofilament line

PROCEDURES

1. Set up the airflow apparatus and power
   supply as shown in Figure 2. Be sure
   power supply is OFF before plugging it in.

2. Calibrate the spring scale so that it reads
   zero when suspended above the airflow
   column with no object attached.

3. With the power supply OFF (fan is NOT
   RUNNING) attach the flat disk object to the
   free end of the line tied to the spring scale.
   Make sure object is centered in the airflow
   column.

4. Turn the power supply ON, with voltage
   selector on zero volts. Gradually turn the
   voltage up to 8 volts. If the fan is working
   properly, as the voltage is increased, the
   fan will speed up and cause increased
   airflow past the test object. The drag force
   on the test object will cause the spring
   scale to extend and indicate a force
   reading.

5. Read the force indicated on the spring
   scale and record value in the appropriate
   area in the Data Table.

6. Gradually increase the voltage in one-volt
   steps to 12 volts. At each voltage setting

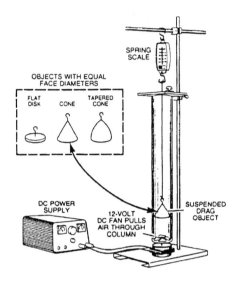

Fig. 2 Lab setup.

(9, 10, 11, and 12 volts) read the force on
the spring scale and record the value in
the Data Table.

7. Turn the power supply OFF. Replace the
   flat disk test object with the cone-shaped
   object. Repeat Steps 4 through 6.

▲*CAUTION: Do not exchange test objects while fan is running. If you drop the test object you will ruin fan blades.*

DATA TABLE: DRAG FORCE DUE TO AIRFLOW PAST TEST OBJECT

Test Object	Voltage Applied to Fan				
	8 V	9 V	10 V	11 V	12 V
Disk Shape					
Cone Shape					
Optional Shape (See your teacher.)					

Subunit 1: Resistance in Mechanical Systems   33

Developer
American Chemical Society

Distributor
W. H. Freeman

**Funders/
Contributors**
*National Science
Foundation*

Science Technology: Knowledge and Skills

1998 (Draft)

SciTeKS is a multimedia, modular science program in chemistry, biology, and the earth sciences designed to introduce 11th and 12th grade students to science technology in industrial contexts through laboratory investigations. Curriculum was developed in partnership with industries and is being field-tested during 1997-99. Provides students with experiences that extensively and realistically simulate the work of science technicians. There will be 14 modules in all.

For each module: Student ed.: stapled, 30-65 pp.; Teacher's ed.: stapled, 55-80 pp.; Video: 15-20 min.; CD-ROM: PC or Macintosh format; all costs TBA

Content Overview

Chemistry, Biology, Earth Sciences

This multidisciplinary science curriculum presents a wide variety of topics in the chemical, biological, and geoscience industries. High school biology is a prerequisite. The following 10 of the eventual 14 modules are in various stages of development.

The Carbonated Beverage Industry

Wastewater Treatment

Plant Tissue Culture Industry

Plant Research and Development

Food Safety Technology

Petroleum Refining

Polymer Research and Development

The Paper Industry

The Semiconductor Industry

Technology of Criminal Forensics

Target Audience

Designed to introduce science technology in an industrial context to 11th- and 12th-grade students, particularly those in tech prep programs.

Duration

Each module takes 5-6 weeks to complete; each lab takes approximately 45 min.

Workplace Connections

Provides students with detailed knowledge of technicians' responsibilities in their workplaces. Students assume the roles of technicians: they conduct tests and follow laboratory procedures, keeping in mind safety precautions and the cost-effectiveness of materials and/or tests; keep accurate laboratory notebooks, signed and dated by their peers; work in teams; and communicate results to their peers. Each module lists workplace skills students should master. Students and teachers are encouraged to contact local companies to arrange visits and/or invite guests to speak to the class. A goal of the curriculum is to increase student awareness of career opportunities in the science technology arena.

Instructional Approach

After learning background information from the video and CD-ROM, students conduct about 10 laboratory-based investigations in which they follow prescribed directions. They conclude by engaging in an open-ended investigation in which they apply their knowledge to a new situation and devise the steps of the investigation. All work is to be done cooperatively in teams, with students dividing tasks and sharing responsibilities. Throughout each module, students are encouraged to share their findings and thoughts with the entire class—either informally or through formal presentations. The Teacher's Edition provides extensive pedagogical, procedural, and technical information.

Curriculum Components

All curriculum components for each module are closely linked; for instance, references to the video and CD-ROM are embedded in the text, and images from the video are used throughout the CD-ROM.

Teacher's Edition—includes, in addition to an annotated student's edition, the following components:

- *SciTeKS Program Goals*—overview of the curriculum.
- *The Virtual Workplace*—how workplace elements are incorporated.
- *Materials*—list of supplies.
- *Sources of Supplies*—places to purchase supplies.
- *Background Information*—module-specific content information and instructional strategies for using the multimedia components.
- *Performance-Based Assessment*—suggestions for using the CD-ROM, scoring scales, lab notebooks, and ongoing assessments.
- *Teacher Support Materials*—detailed specifications for laboratory experiments, data analysis suggestions, and answers to CD-ROM practice and assessment items.

Student Edition—consists of the following:

- *Introduction*—includes philosophy of the SciTeKS curriculum; module overview and brief background information; statement of the problem; and important concepts, processes, and skills for the module.
- *Orientation*—background information.
- *Laboratories*—main section, containing a sequence of about 10 laboratory exercises.
- *Application and Reflection*—presentation of results and reflection on module's learning.

Video—15- to 20-min. introductory video for each module, presenting an overview of a particular industry. The role of quality control is a theme for many of the videos. The videos highlight the role technicians play in the production process, the teamwork involved, the tests performed, and the importance and role of computers in industry. Interviews with lab technicians cover what a typical day involves, as well as a discussion of their skills, training, prospects, and job satisfaction.

CD-ROM—provide students with information and testing opportunities that are difficult to achieve in normal high school classroom settings. The main component of each module's CD is an interactive plant or lab tour describing the functions of each aspect of the particular industry. The tours use stills, graphics, videos, text, and simulations to provide students with an overview of what happens in industry, either in the production process or in the research and development labs. One component of the CDs is a reference section consisting of a glossary and encyclopedia of module-specific terms.

Materials

Numerous materials are required, including some standard materials found in high school chemistry, biology, and earth science laboratories. Other materials must be ordered from specialized vendors. Materials lists and vendors are provided. Internet access is required to take advantage of referenced web sites.

Assessments

Assessment is integral to the SciTeKS curriculum. Teachers are urged to work with their students to design the actual criteria by which individual students and groups of students will be assessed. Student notebooks, products, laboratory findings, and performance are the primary ways in which data are collected on student achievement and proficiency as students test their skills and abilities in performing their workplace roles. Also, the CDs contain practice and assessment sections that allow students to operate various parts of industrial plants, run lab tests, and check their knowledge of equipment and procedures.

Special Preparations

Time and money are needed to purchase and become familiar with specialized equipment. Time is also needed to establish connections with local companies.

Standards

Relevant standards documents were reviewed to develop an overall list of concepts, skills, and processes appropriate for technicians in training. The documents reviewed included *National Science Education Standards*, *Benchmarks for Science Literacy*, *Voluntary Industry Standards for Chemical Process Industries Technical Workers*, *Gateway to the Future: Skill Standards for the Bioscience Industry*, and *What Work Requires of Schools*.

Sample Pages

All pages are from the Wastewater Treatment unit. Pages 223 and 225 help students understand a technician's job. Page 224 illustrates that students learn science concepts, processes, laboratory skills and employability skills. Page 226 is a sample laboratory investigation.

Ordering Information

Developer: American Chemical Society, 1155 16th Street, NW, Washington, DC 20036; 202-872-4600; http://www.acs.org/education/currmats/sciteks.html

Distributor: W. H. Freeman, Von Holtzbrinck Publishing Services, 6365 James Madison Highway (U.S. Route 15), Gordonsville, VA 22942; 888-330-8477; 800-672-2054 (fax); http://www.whfreeman.com

Table of Contents: Upgrading the Wastewater Treatment Plant

(Number of pages indicated in parentheses)

Your Role in Solving the Problem

Your job, as a technician at the plant, is to learn about the new processes, equipment, and EPA guidelines involved in the plant upgrade. You will do this by visiting a neighboring plant - either as a field trip or as a computer simulation - that has implemented activated sludge in its secondary treatment.

As a part of your own training, you will be modeling the various steps of wastewater treatment, and learning the lab tests that monitor these steps. Once you have mastered these, you will design, and carry out, a training program for other technicians who are anticipating plant upgrades.

Keep in mind, as you learn about the wastewater clean-up process, what details might be important to pass onto fellow technicians in the plant, particularly in terms of what it takes to monitor an activated sludge system.

You will need to build into your training program various problem-solving strategies so that technicians can handle any sudden emergencies that are linked to an activated sludge upgrade. You may wish to use the multimedia to help with this, or a selection of the hands-on laboratory activities that you will be doing yourself.

You will be learning about possible emergencies that occur at wastewater treatment plants throughout the course of this module. Some of these might include:

- how to deal with a sudden influx of wastewater (due to a big storm, for example)

- what to do when various indicators are too high or too low in the plant (such as the dissolved oxygen level or the pH level in the activated sludge tank)

- where to take samples that will provide the information needed to assess a problem situation

- how to carry out the appropriate tests for different "wastewater variables" connected to the upgrade.

The laboratory notebook, a class journal, and multimedia notebook will help you to keep track of what you have discovered about wastewater treatment. You can then use these resources to design your training methods.

INTRODUCTION

Multimedia Links

The multimedia provides you with detailed information on just what is done in a wastewater treatment plant.

You will be able to track the process that wastewater goes through as impurities are removed from it using a variety of different techniques. By clicking on the different parts of the plant diagram, you can access detailed information on each of the plant's components.

Important Concepts, Processes and Skills For This Module

Science Concepts

When you finish this module, you should be able to *define and give examples of:*

- Suspension components (wastewater)
- Characteristics of organisms (sludge-dwelling organisms)
- Water and its special properties
- Concentrations and dilutions
- pH in terms of monitoring sludge
- Requirements for a living system (biotic and abiotic)
- Stream velocity and carrying capacity

Science Processes

When you finish this module, you should be able to:

- *Define* problems to be investigated
- *Generate* questions and hypotheses
- *Test* explanations
- *Use* models
- *Construct* a valid experimental test
- *Gather* and *record* data
- *Organize* data into charts and graphs
- *Analyze* data using graphs
- *Arrive* at conclusions based on data
- *Communicate* results

Laboratory Skills

When you finish this module, you should be able to:

- *Take* samples at appropriate places and times
- *Follow and devise* directions for an experimental test
- *Measure* biochemical oxygen demand, dissolved oxygen, turbidity, chlorine, and density
- *Set up and monitor* a model of activated sludge treatment
- *Follow* appropriate safety procedures
- *Measure* pH using a pH meter
- *Calibrate* instrumentation as needed
- *Identify and count* microorganisms using a microscope

Employability Skills

When you finish this module, you should be able to:

- *Establish* a timeline
- *Read and understand* a standard operating procedure and standard laboratory analysis method
- *Develop* a standard operating procedure
- *Design* instruction for a familiar topic
- *Access* computers as necessary (including using the internet)
- *Interpret* a process diagram
- *Troubleshoot* a system
- *Work cooperatively* with team members

 Multimedia Links

The multimedia *encyclopedia* can provide you with extensive background information on the science concepts listed on this page.

In addition to textual explanations, you will be able to see animations illustrating some of the concepts, as well as still photographs and graphics. You will also be able to print out the entries in the encyclopedia so that you can refer to them later, as needed.

-8-

The First Session: Getting Ready for the Plant Representative's Visit

The purpose of this first session is to inform you, the wastewater treatment plant operators, about the physical processes used in cleaning up wastewater. This is to ensure that you are all operating from the same knowledge base with regard to the upgrade. Another important part of this first session is the research component. You will be accessing both the internet and the computer-based multimedia to conduct research on what is entailed in upgrading a wastewater treatment facility from trickling filters to activated sludge.

Here is the nature of the work for this first session. You and your teammates will:

- **work** through a series of mini-labs which illustrate what is meant by a physical process or change (as the first phase of wastewater treatment involves physical changes)
- **become introduced** to the wastewater treatment process through the multimedia
- **research** wastewater treatment topics using the internet and other resources
- **set up and operate** a model of primary treatment
- **follow and write** standard operating procedures (SOPs)
- **follow** standard laboratory analysis methods (SLAMs)
- **compare** the tests you use with your model of primary treatment to those in the multimedia
- **keep an accurate record** of how these first parts of the wastewater treatment process contribute to the overall cleanup effort.
- **establish a timeline** for future work on the problem.
- **interview** a local treatment plant representative.

Part 1: Understanding the Problem
What Are Physical Processes?
Building the Primary Treatment Models
Investigating With the Primary Treatment Models
Writing a Standard Operating Procedure
Using a Standard Laboratory Analysis Method
Conducting Research on Wastewater Treatment

Part 2: Setting the Task
Presentation By Plant Representative
Interviewing Plant Representative
Developing a Timeline

D E F I N I N G   T H E   P R O B L E M

Reminder: Prior to this first session, you will have set up a **model of an activated sludge tank** using directions provided by your teacher. This will need to be set aside in a safe place to become operational over the course of a week.

 Multimedia Links

Access the Plant Tour in the multimedia to find out about what the actual equipment involved in primary treatment looks like and does at the plant.

Remember to click on key words in the tour to access glossary and encyclopedia terms. Use the multimedia notebook to make a record of any information you might find useful later on.

Laboratory 4: Analysis of Monitoring Data

Laboratory Objective
In this activity, your team members will compare your test results from using the SLAMs to test results from the multimedia simulations.

Background Information
You may have used the Plant Operations section of the multimedia quite a bit as you learned about how to monitor your activated sludge model.

In this activity, you will be applying your knowledge of the testing procedures to new activated sludge conditions simulated on the multimedia. You will need to use your own data set, your SLAMs, and your standards tables to determine if the test data that you generate from the multimedia is within the industry standards.

If the data show that the simulated system is operating outside the standards, you will have the opportunity to make adjustments to the simulated system, then to re-test for the effects of your adjustments.

You will need to record all of your test results, as well as your adjustments and re-test results in the multimedia notebook (you can print this out to append to your laboratory notebook). Operating the simulated test procedures will help you and your teacher to assess how well you have learned and can apply your activated sludge monitoring knowledge and skills.

Materials
- multimedia Plant Operations
- your laboratory notebook
- SLAMs for the qualitative tests
- standards for the tests (both qualitative and quantitative)

Safety
- no special safety procedures are required for this activity

Procedure
1. Your teacher, in conjunction with your team, will provide a schedule for using the multimedia Plant Operations. Prior to accessing the multimedia, you will need to meet with your

 Multi-media Links

This time, when you use the multimedia, it will be to assess your proficiency with the tests used to monitor activated sludge. You will be running the tests on a simulated situation, comparing the data that you generate to the type of data you generated with your model. You will then make adjustments to the operation of the system based upon your data interpretation. It is important that you keep complete records throughout the assessment process.

- 39 -

Developer
TERC

Distributor
TERC

**Funders/
Contributors**
The Pew Charitable Trusts

Working to Learn
*Integrating Workplace and
Classroom Learning 1996*

*Three 6-week curriculum units—Cardiovascular Diagnosis and
Physiology; Heating, Ventilating, Air Conditioning, and Heat Flow;
and Water Testing and Aquatic Ecology—with 3 half-day or full-
day workplace experiences integral to each. Units are introduced by
and organized around questions that professionals would ask and
need to answer. Scientific investigation is the curriculum's central
activity.*

*3 units, shrink-wrapped, 3-hole punched, 150-196 pp., $24.95
each*

Content Overview

*Biology, Chemistry,
Ecology, Physics*

Cardiovascular Diagnosis and Physiology—biology, chemistry,
physics. Provides students with a basic understanding of the anatomy and
physiology of the circulatory system. Students are introduced to common
diagnostic techniques for determining if something is wrong with a
patient's heart, circulation, or blood.

**Heating, Ventilating, Air Conditioning, and Heat Flow
(HVAC)**—chemistry, physics. Teaches students about heat flow and
phase change by examining how both heating and cooling systems operate. Students are introduced to these concepts via classroom laboratory
experiments and investigation of HVAC units in the school or in other settings. The HVAC unit requires an understanding of algebra.

Water Testing and Aquatic Ecology—biology, ecology. Focuses on
how communities monitor and maintain water quality. Curriculum gives
students a basic understanding of the ecological concepts of niche, food
webs, and chains of causation. Students are introduced to common water-
quality testing techniques (pH, turbidity, suspended solids, fecal coliform)
and perform tests at a local study site.

Target Audience

"Especially designed for schools where work-based learning is used to set the context for classroom learning."

Duration

Each unit takes 23-25 classroom sessions, requiring 5-6 weeks. The developer suggests that the curriculum would be ideal for block scheduling.

Workplace Connections

Each unit includes 3 Common Workplace Experiences (CWEs), which are either full- or half-day events. Each CWE builds upon science content learned in the classroom. Students prepare for the visit in their classroom and are expected to answer questions during their visit. Information sheets are provided for the workplace supervisor. Student worksheets ask them to share factual data gathered during the visit, discuss the kind of work done and why, discuss the physical work environment, and answer questions that reinforce classroom learning. The curriculum also recommends unit-specific internships. The Water Testing and Aquatic Ecology unit contains 2 additional visits to a water study site for student fieldwork.

Instructional Approach

Using an approach called "mapping backwards," each unit begins with an essential question that workers in the field would ask and need to answer. The curriculum then maps backwards to the science concepts that students need to understand in order to answer this essential question.

Small-group and whole-class discussions occur frequently throughout each unit. Curricular activities are hands-on and include clinical activities a worker would perform (such as a dissolved oxygen test or taking blood pressure). In the science labs, students work in pairs or small groups. All units have data collection/analysis and graphing activities. When students are asked to record data, they are also asked to explain what the results mean and why they have obtained certain results. In the Water Testing and Aquatic Ecology unit, students and teacher choose a study site, define the research question, and design and implement a river study.

Curriculum Components

Each unit consists of a Teacher's Guide with student activity sheets and readings placed at the end of each lesson for duplication; there is no separate student book.

Teacher's Guide—includes descriptions of each activity plus background on the science concepts addressed, lesson-by-lesson suggestions on how to teach the activity, and black-line masters. Suggestions are given on how to establish and maintain relationships with employers who can provide workplace expenses for the students.

Student activity sheets—contain instructions for hands-on activities and questions for students to answer, including open-ended questions. Cardiovascular Diagnosis and Physiology unit activities include modeling the workings of the heart and circulatory system, dissection of a heart, and watching teacher demonstrations and videos. The HVAC unit activities include building a model of an air conditioner, measuring indoor air quality, designing experiments to test heat transfer, and developing a guide for choosing an appropriate thermostat location. Water Testing and Aquatic Ecology unit activities include observing, identifying, and classifying macro invertebrates, conducting interviews, designing a research study, and water-quality testing.

Workplace materials—describe for the workplace supervisor what students have been learning in the classroom, how to structure the workplace visit, and what topics need to be covered. For students enrolled in an internship program, the curriculum provides suggested activities for the supervisor that will complement current classroom learning.

Materials

For the Cardiovascular Diagnosis and Physiology unit, the teacher must obtain (among other items) blood samples, animal hearts, hemocytometer kits, and sample EKG records. The HVAC unit requires (among other items) radiators, thermostats, an air conditioner, tubing and scrap materials, air filters, and veterinary syringes. The Water Testing and Aquatic Ecology unit requires (among other items) water testing kits, kick nets, and community topographical maps.

Assessments

Each curriculum unit culminates in a presentation in which students demonstrate their mastery of the content. Students choose a topic to explore in depth. They present and defend a detailed explanation of the science behind the topic for an audience consisting of teachers, students, workplace supervisors, parents, and other members of the community. The Water Testing and Aquatic Ecology unit also contains a river case study that assesses student learning. Students are asked to describe what is occurring, explain why it is happening, and make recommendations to correct a situation. The HVAC unit challenges students to design a working heat transfer system.

Special Preparations

Identifying local sites that are willing and able to participate requires advance planning. Teachers must arrange for both CWEs and student internships before the curriculum begins. All units need some specialized materials, and particular textbooks are recommended. Suppliers for some items are included. Occasionally, experiments require significant advance preparation of materials; this is detailed in the curriculum.

Standards

Each curriculum addresses several content and skills frameworks from the AAAS Benchmarks for Science Literacy. The curriculum's introduction provides detailed information.

Sample Pages

All pages are from the Cardiovascular Diagnosis and Physiology unit. Page 233 illustrates classroom activities that prepare students for their workplace experiences. Pages 234-236 show the detailed instructional information provided to workplace supervisors. Page 237 is part of a worksheet that students complete during a workplace experience.

Ordering Information

TERC, Margaret Vickers, Project Director, or Working to Learn, Administrative Assistant, 2067 Massachusetts Avenue, Cambridge, MA 02140; 617-547-0430; http://wtl.terc.edu/aboutwtl.html

Table of Contents

(Number of pages indicated in parentheses)

DIAGNOSING BLOOD DISORDERS

Follow the directions below to determine whether you or your classmates might have a blood disorder and to make diagnoses on other "patients."

ESSENTIAL QUESTION 1: HOW DO YOU KNOW IF SOMETHING IS WRONG WITH THE BLOOD?

Here are some simple techniques that indicate possible anemia. These tests do not allow you to distinguish anemia from the aftermath of a hemorrhage. Form pairs to conduct the first test, and conduct the second and third tests on yourself.

First, gently pull down your lower eyelid, while the other student looks at the color.

- Is it white or pink?
- **IF** it is white, **THEN** this is a sign of possible anemia.

Second, press on your fingernail then let it go.

- How much time elapses before the nail is pink again?
- **IF** it takes 2 seconds or more, **THEN** this is a sign of possible anemia.

Third, pinch the skin on the back of your hand.

- How much time elapses before the skin flattens? Does it "tent"?
- **IF** it "tents," **THEN** this is a sign of dehydration.

If a person has suffered from a hemorrhage, then he or she is likely to show all three signs. A hemorrhage reduces the total volume of blood in the body. A patient who has had a recent hemorrhage will show signs of dehydration as well as signs of anemia.

ESSENTIAL QUESTION 2: WHAT IS WRONG WITH THE BLOOD?

In this activity, you will be given data about four teenage patients, each of whom has suffered either *blood loss* (through a hemorrhage, an accident, or an ulcer) or has *leukemia*, or some type of *anemia*. You have to decide among these three conditions: blood loss, leukemia, or anemia.

If you decide upon anemia, then your next task is to determine what type of anemia it is.

In their last lesson, the students "followed a drop of blood." They walked around a large floor diagram of the body; the students who were acting as "blood drops" actually picked up and delivered colored blocks (or paper squares) to and from different organs. Although they have learned about the substances the blood transports, most of the students will know very little about the immune system and the functions of white blood cells.

VIEWING BLOOD SMEARS

Use a set of teaching microscopes if you have them or, if not, use transparencies and a projector to show blood samples. This will be the first time that the students have seen magnifications of blood samples. Explain how the slides are made and what level of magnification is used.

Show a slide of a normal blood sample that includes red blood cells and at least one or two white blood cells. Ask the students to draw what they see, using colored pencils. Discuss the drawings, and help the students label the different kinds of cells correctly. Draw a cross section of a red blood cell, and explain why red blood cells look like pink rings that are pale in the center.

If possible, demonstrate how a blood smear is applied to a microscope slide. Show an unstained slide, and compare it with a stained slide. Ask the students to describe the differences between the two slides. Why are stains useful? When might one want to use them?

Now show a slide in which some of the red blood cells are affected by sickle cell anemia. Encourage the students to look closely at the affected cells and compare them with the unaffected cells. Our bodies replace red blood cells all the time because, on average, they last only 120 days. But misshapen red blood cells are fragile and do not last as long as normal red blood cells. Therefore, a person whose blood contains a large proportion of misshapen red blood cells will be anemic.

DIAGNOSTICS: THE HEMATOCRIT

Ask the students:

> What do your red blood cells do for you?
>
> What happens if you don't have enough of them?

Show the students the two tubes of blood (one anemic, one normal).

> Do they look the same? (They do.)
>
> But maybe they are *not* the same.

One can't see whether there are enough red blood cells in these tubes, because both tubes just look red. But one can use a centrifuge to spin the cells down and separate the cells from the plasma, in order to see whether the right amount of red blood cells are in the tubes.

Put the two samples (Tube A and Tube B) in the centrifuge, and while they are spinning, hand out several clean hematocrit tubes (one for each pair of students).

Point out the calibration lines on the hematocrit tubes, and ask the students what function these lines might serve. Write on the blackboard the normal hematocrit ranges for male and female blood, then discuss the techniques involved in making an accurate hematocrit reading. Now show the students the two tubes (Tube A and Tube B) from the centrifuge. Ask several different students to "read" the results from Tube A and from Tube B. Some students should write down two or three readings for Tube A, and the others should write down the readings for Tube B.

Now discuss the results: The patient whose blood was in Tube B has a problem. What could be wrong? Ask the students to come up with suggestions, and list these on the blackboard.

Is there a consistent reading for Tube A? What is it? And for Tube B? The students should record these results on their workplace sheets.

The patient could have had a recent hemorrhage or may have leukemia or anemia. How could one tell? All three of these conditions could cause a low hematocrit reading. Describe some of the most common physical symptoms of a person with anemia.

Ask the students what they know about anemia and other blood disorders, and encourage discussion. For example, they may think leukemia causes hair loss. Explain that this is not caused by the blood disease, but is a side effect of radiation treatment.

There are several different kinds of anemia. Describe two or three of these, and explain how they differ. Unless doctors know which type of anemia a patient has, he or she will not be able to treat the condition properly. To diagnose blood disorders, doctors request a complete blood count. This is done in a special laboratory.

This might be a good time for a break. Tell the students that they will learn about the complete blood count during the laboratory tour after lunch. Alternatively, you may want to introduce the complete blood count now, and revise it during the laboratory tour.

TOUR OF THE HEMATOLOGY LABORATORY

Plan to provide a tour that begins at the outpatient clinic (where blood is drawn), moves to specimen drop-off then to the laboratory (where some samples are actually tested). Complete the cycle by showing how test results from external laboratories as well as those from the hospital's own laboratories are recorded and conveyed to the medical records department and to the practitioners who need the results. Demonstrate the role of computers in information storage and transfer.

THE OUTPATIENT CLINIC

This setting allows students to consider how specimens are actually collected and why, and to discuss the patient's own experiences with blood drawing. Most people show fear and apprehension at having their blood drawn. The supervisor from this lab should talk with the students about how they deal with this fear. He or she might also discuss how drawing the blood or collecting a specimen is a more complicated process than just performing the task. One must have an ability to work well with people and to help allay their fears.

Walk the students through the process of collecting a blood sample. Explain that all specimens are labeled with the patient's name, hospital number, date, time, and initials of the phlebotomist. Outline the safety precautions that protect both patient and phlebotomist. Explain how phlebotomists and hematologists protect themselves from possible infection and avoid contamination of samples.

Show the students the equipment used for preparing samples; that is, clean specimen containers, complete blood count labels, #20 gauge needles, #22 gauge needles, and lavender-topped vacuum tubes. Explain how each item is used. For instance, the lavender-topped vacuum tube contains EDTA to prevents the coagulation of the blood.

SPECIMEN DROP-OFF

The students should be shown the procedures followed, including how the blood is labeled, how it is shipped to and from the hospital, and how preliminary information identifying the samples is entered into the computer. (Final results of the tests are entered later, adding to each of the records created here.)

THE LABORATORY

During the tour, the students should take notes on their workplace sheets. Ask them to sketch a flow chart that shows where blood samples are collected in the first place, where the specimen drop-off occurs, where the lab is, where the results are coded and entered into hospital computer, and finally, who uses the results and where the users are.

Ideally, the students will observe the actual testing of blood samples. If this is not possible, they should see how a specimen is put into the machine that conducts the analyses. Provide each student with a sample printout. Cover or delete the patient's name, and use printouts that provide results for different forms of anemia. Show the students how to find and read the data for a complete blood count, focusing on the hematocrit, red blood cell count, white blood cell count, and hemoglobin level. Discuss what each of these measures represents and how each is measured. Back in the classroom, the students will focus on diagnosing certain anemias, and only use these four items (hemocrit, red blood cells, white blood cells, and hemoglobin) in their "diagnoses." Mention that the printout gives other measures, including cholesterol levels. The students may be interested in the range of things they can learn from the printout, therefore allow some time to answer their questions.

5. What is the difference between normal red blood cells and sickle cells?

Your supervisor will show you a slide that contains "sickle-shaped" red blood cells. Draw a few of these cells and label them.

Why do people who have red blood cells with this shape develop the symptoms of anemia?

6. What is the hematocrit test?

The hematocrit (often referred to as the 'crit) is a simple, quick, and inexpensive test that can reveal whether a patient is anemic, normal, or polycythemic. It involves spinning down a sample of blood so that one can see what percentage of the blood is made up of red blood cells. A patient is anemic if he or she has too few red blood cells; a patient is polycythemic, if he or she has too many. In either case, a full set of diagnostic tests needs to be ordered.

Your supervisor will demonstrate the hematocrit test, using a blood sample from Patient A and one from Patient B. During this activity, you should fill in the following table.

What is the sex of your two patients?   Patient A _____   Patient B _____

Compare the hematocrit readings for Patient A and Patient B with the range of normal values for a person of that sex. What can you conclude about each patient (normal hematocrit, above normal, or below normal)?

Patient A_____

Patient B_____

Did either patient have a hematocrit reading that suggests something might be wrong? If so, what disorders do you suspect might be involved? What further tests should be ordered?

_____

_____

_____

References

Alba, A. (1999). Prime time math. *Mathematics Teaching in the Middle School, 4*(7), 480.

American Association for the Advancement of Science (AAAS). (1993). *Benchmarks for scientific literacy*. New York: Oxford University Press.

American Federation of Teachers (AFT). (1996). *Reaching the next step: How school-to-career can help students reach high academic standards and prepare for good jobs*. Washington, DC: Author.

Bailey, T. (1997). *Integrating academic and industry skill standards*. Macomb, IL: National Center for Research in Vocational Education.

Bailey, T. (1998). Integrating academic and industry skill standards. *Institute of Education and the Economy IEE Brief*, No. 18. IIE, Columbia University, New York.

Bailey, T., & Merritt, D. (1997a). School-to-work for the college bound. *Institute of Education and the Economy IEE Brief*, No. 15. IIE, Columbia University, New York.

Bailey, T., & Merritt, D. (1997b). *School-to-work for the college bound*. Macomb, IL: National Center for Research in Vocational Education.

Black, P., & Atkin, M. J. (Eds.). (1996). *Changing the subject: Innovations in science, mathematics, and technology education*. New York: Routledge.

Bottoms, G., & Sharpe, D. (1996). *Teaching for understanding through integration of academic and technical education*. Atlanta, GA: Southern Regional Board.

Britton, E., & Raizen, S. A. (Eds.). (1996). *Examining the examinations: An international comparison of science and mathematics examinations for college-bound students*. Boston: Kluwer Academic.

Cannon, M. (1999). Life by the numbers. *Mathematics Teaching in the Middle School, 4*(7), 488.

Center on Education and Work. (1996a). *Integrating vocational & academic education, Vol. 1: A handbook featuring four demonstration sites including students from special populations*. Madison, WI: Author.

Center on Education and Work. (1996b). *Integrating vocational & academic education, Vol. 2: A handbook featuring three secondary demonstration sites including students from special populations*. Madison, WI: Author.

Gaskell, P., & Hepburn, G. (1997). Integration of academic and occupational curricula in science and technology education. *Science Education, 81*(4), 469-481.

Grubb, W. N. (Ed.). (1995a). *Education through occupations in American high schools, Vol. 1: Approaches to integrating academic and vocational education*. New York: Teachers College Press.

Grubb, W. N. (Ed.). (1995b). *Education through occupations in American high schools, Vol. 2: The challenges of implementing curriculum integration*. New York: Teachers College Press.

Harwell, S., & Blank, W. (1997). Connecting high school with the real world. In W. Blank & S. Hardwell (Eds.), *Promising practices for connecting schools with the world*. Tampa, FL: Department of Adult and Vocational Education, University of South Florida.

Hernandez-Gantes, V., Brendefur, J. & J. Burrill, (1998). *MathNet: A guide for developing integrated mathematics curriculum units*. Madison, University of Wisconsin: Center on Education and Work.

Hofstader, R., & Chapman, K. (Eds.). (1997). *Foundations for excellence in the chemical process industries: Voluntary industry standards for chemical process industries' technical workers*. Washington, DC: American Chemical Society.

Hurd, P. (1998). Linking science education to the workplace. *Journal of Science Education and Technology, 7*(4), 329-335.

Institute on the Education and the Economy. (1998). A workshop on mathematical and occupational skills standards. *IEE Brief*, No. 3. IIE, Columbia University, New York.

International Technology Education Association (ITEA). (1997). *Draft technology education standards*. Reston, VA: International Technology Education Association.

Jones, D. W. (1997). Education-industry collaboration in Europe. *Journal of Science Education and Technology, 6*(13), 241-244.

Mathematical Sciences Education Board (MSEB). (1995). *Mathematical preparation of the technical work force: Report of a workshop*. Washington, DC: National Academy Press.

Mathematical Sciences Education Board (MSEB). (1998). *High school mathematics at work: Essays and examples for the education of all students*. Washington, DC: National Academy Press.

McFarland, L., & Vickers, M. (1994). The context and rationale for the reform of vocational and technical education. In L. McFarland & M. Vickers (Eds.), *Vocational education and training for youth: Towards coherent policy and practice* (pp. 7-18). Paris: Organisation for Economic Co-Operation and Development.

National Alliance of Businesses (NAB), Business Coalition for Education Reform. (1998). *The formula for success: A business leader's guide to supporting math and science achievement*. Washington, DC: U.S. Department of Education.

National Board for Professional Teaching Standards (NBPTS). (1997). *Vocational education: Standards for national board certification*. Southfield, MI: Author.

National Council for Professional Teaching Standards (NCTM). (1989). *Curriculum and evaluation standards for school mathematics*. Washington, DC: National Council for Teachers of Mathematics.

National Research Council (NRC). (1996). *National science education standards*. Washington, DC: National Academy Press.

Olson, L. (1997). *The school-to-work revolution: How employers and educators are joining forces to prepare tomorrow's skilled workforce*. Reading, MA: Addison-Wesley.

Pedrotti, L. (1996). STS in vocational areas. In R. E. Yager (Ed.), *What research says to the science teacher, Vol. 7: The science, technology, society movement* (pp. 91-96). Washington, DC: National Science Teachers Association.

Raizen, S. (1994). Learning and work: The research base. In L. McFarland & M. Vickers (Eds.), *Vocational education and training for youth: Towards coherent policy and practice* (pp. 69-114). Paris: Organisation for Economic Co-Operation and Development.

Raizen, S. (1995). Learning by doing. In *American issues for school and the workplace*. Washington, DC: Council of Chief State School Officers.

Raizen, S., Sellwood, P., Todd, R. D., & Vickers, M. (1995). *Technology education in the classroom: Understanding the designed world*. San Francisco: Jossey-Bass.

Richmond, G. (1998). Scientific apprenticeship and the role of public schools: General education of a better kind. *Journal of Research in Science Teaching, 35*(6), 583-587.

Ryan, R. D., & Ime, S. (1996). School-to-work transition: Genuine reform or the latest fad? *ERIC Review, 4*(2), 2-11.

Secretary's Commission on Achieving Necessary Skills (SCANS). (1991). *What work requires of schools: A SCANS report for America 2000.* Washington, DC: U.S. Department of Labor.

Stern, D., Bailey, T., & Merritt, D. (1997). School-to-work policy insights from recent international developments. *Centerfocus*, No. 14. Macomb, IL: National Center for Research in Vocational Education.

Stern, D., & Wagner, D. (Eds.). (1999). *International perspectives on the school-to-work transition.* Creskskill, NJ: Hampton Press.

Vickers, M., & Steinberg, A. (1998, April). *Why science educators should collaborate with school-to-work programs.* Paper presented at Conference on Secondary Science Reform, Cambridge, MA.

Vocational Instructional Materials Laboratory. (1998). *Making connections: A curriculum ideabook for teachers of applied academics and industrial and engineering systems.* Columbus, OH: Author.

Welzel, H. (1995). Implications for developing American versions of German youth. In M. Vickers & L. McFarland (Eds.), *American issues for school and the workplace.* Washington, DC: Council of Chief State School Officers.

Appendix A
More Curricula With
Workplace Connections

Chapters 4 and 5 are limited to 23 reviews to keep the size of this guide manageable. However, the authors found more curricula that make connections to the workplace, and this appendix briefly describes some of the best. (See Selection Criteria, p. 39.) The second paragraph of page 40 outlines factors that influenced whether a product was fully reviewed or described in this appendix.

NSF-Supported Materials

Before presenting brief reviews of more curricula, it is important to note some reform curricula that are not included in either the appendix or the review chapters. The authors assume that educators interested in this guide are willing to consider expanding the content and pedagogy of their mathematics or science instruction. For example, while they may lecture on traditional disciplinary concepts and run structured laboratory activities, they also want students to acquire understanding of science and mathematics applications in the real world through cooperative learning, authentic assessments, and inquiry-oriented investigations. A lot, perhaps even a majority, of recent curricula aim to incorporate such content and instructional approaches. After all, such content and pedagogy are prescribed by the recent national curriculum standards in mathematics and science. Unfortunately, however, relatively few curricula use workplace applications as real-world contexts for explaining or illustrating concepts.

To address broader reform goals, readers are referred to some curriculum materials that are progressive in revising content and instructional approaches, albeit mostly without making connections to workplace contexts: curricula funded by the National Science Foundation's Instructional Materials Development (IMD) program. The NSF-supported projects that attain commercial publication generally address well the national curriculum standards. They include rigorous content and appropriate pedagogical features. Further, the NSF matarials are designed for *all* students, including both academic and non-college-bound. Some NSF materials make workplace connections and are described in this appendix or reviewed in chapters 4 and 5. (See Main Funders column of table 3.1, pp. 41-42.)

However, readers also are encouraged to look at other NSF-sponsored materials such as the following mathematics and science curricula for middle and high school grades:

Middle School	High School
Connected Mathematics	Contemporary Mathematics in Context
Mathematics in Context	IMP (Interactive Mathematics Program)
MathScape	MATH Connections
MathThematics (STEM)	Mathematics: Modeling Our World
Middle-School Math Through Applications	SIMSS (Systemic Initiative for Montana Mathematics and Science)
Kids Network	Active Physics
Prime Science	Biology: A Community Context
Science Education for Public Understanding Program (SEPUP)	Science Links

The above list is not comprehensive. At this point in time, more mathematics than science curricula supported by NSF have become commercially available, in part because the NCTM Curriculum Standards preceded the NAS Science Standards by several years, and therefore NSF funded mathematics curriculum development earlier. Information about NSF-supported curricula can be obtained by checking the NSF Web site at www.nsf.gov. Further, NSF supports centers that assist educators in selecting and implementing the commercially available mathematics curricula it has sponsored: The Show Me Center for middle grades materials (University of Missouri, Columbia), www.showmecenter.missouri.edu; and COMPASS, Curricular Options in Mathematics Programs for All Secondary Students (Ithaca College, NY), www.ithaca.edu/compass. In 1999, NSF will support centers that will provide similar assistance for science curricula.

Reviews of Mathematics and Science Curricula

This appendix provides mini-reviews of five mathematics curricula followed by four science curricula that collectively have these characteristics:

- All but one of the mathematics curricula are intended for the middle grades, in contrast to chapter 4, where more of the mathematics materials reviewed are designed for high school rather than middle school. Similarly to those in chapter 5, most of science curricula (three of four) are targeted to students in high school or community college.

- All materials are very recent, being published in 1996-1999+.

- Six of the nine curricula were financed and developed by private companies, in contrast to the curricula reviewed in chapters 4 and 5, which generally were supported by government agencies, foundations, or corporations.

- Considerable development remains to be done for four of the curricula, whereas almost all materials reviewed in chapters 4 and 5 are fully completed and available.

- Two of the curricula can be used as entire courses or supplements (Chemistry for the Technologies and Material Science Technology), but the rest can be used only as curriculum supplements.

These short reviews identify the instructional components of the curricula and primarily discuss the curriculum features most central to this book, i.e., their mathematical or scientific content and the workplace connections used. (See category descriptions on pp. 46-47.) Because space constraints preclude much discussion of pedagogical features such as instructional approach and assessment, it should be noted that many of these curricula have less extensively developed or progressive pedagogical features than those of the majority of products reviewed in chapters 4 and 5.

Life by the Numbers *1998, grades 6-12*

Developer and Distributors	**Funders**
WQED Pittsburgh (PBS)	*NSF, Texas Instruments,*
1-800-274-1307 (PBS) for full video episodes	*several foundations*
1-800-TI-CARES (TI) for a free highlights	
video or 32 pp. workbook, www.ti.com/calc	
1-800-225-5945 for 214 pp. book @ $29.95	

This set of seven one-hour videos that were broadcast by PBS in 1998 do an exceptionally strong job of using workplace contexts to explain mathematics. Shows address some mathematics topics that are advocated by the NCTM Standards but often weakly addressed in school, e.g., pattern analysis, statistical regression, probabilities, and data analysis. The accompanying print materials, which have been reviewed by the Mathematical Association of America (MAA) and in NCTM's *Mathematics Teaching in the Middle School* (MAA, 1999, p. 488), use standards-based instructional approaches such as hands-on investigation of open-ended questions, analysis with graphing calculators, and communicating through written and oral reports. Workplace connections are limited mostly to scientific or technical careers or professional sports rather than using a broader spectrum of jobs to which a greater variety of students might aspire.

Math in the Middle *1998-1999+, grades 6-8*

Developer and Distributor	**Funder**
Satellite Educational Resources Consortium	*National Science Foundation*
Great Plains Network (GPN), 1-800-228-4630	
www.mathinthemiddle.org	
$450 per unit per school, including on-line features	

The 20-minute videos for the first two released units of this supplemental curriculum resource (Oceans, Music) both provide very detailed, interesting explanations of the uses of mathematics in various fields (e.g., oceanography, aquatic biology, music). These interdisciplinary materials also show connections with science, social studies, art, and music. The teacher's guide for each unit matches specific unit topics to the corresponding NCTM Standards and includes 12 activities that require one class period or less. Student work includes both paper-and-pencil exercises and hands-on activities. The Oceans unit's activities often are conservative (drill and practice, algorithmic), but in the Music unit, students collect and analyze data. The Web site provides sample lessons that teachers can use, links to other Web sites with related content, career profiles of experts, a chance to send questions to an expert, and an opportunity to collaborate with other classrooms on projects involving data collection.

PrimeTime Math *1997, grades 6-8*

Developer and Distributor

Tom Snyder Productions, 1-800-342-0236 or www.teachtsp.com
$79.95-$599.95 (1-20+ computers) per CD-ROM title

Students view interactive, engaging videos of dramatic contexts (putting out a fire, treating a medical emergency, and investigating a crime scene). Episodes highlight occupations requiring a range in both educational preparation and the frequency with which mathematics is used (fireman, detectives, nurses, and doctors). The programs enhance the authenticity of the workplace contexts by incorporating technical terms used in the various occupations. The use of mathematics depicted occasionally does not seem strongly authentic, although that may not be obvious to students. Students record data and then use simple mathematics to solve problems. They tabulate and graph data and make calculations with them (e.g., percentages, means, unit conversions, rates, Pythagorean theorem). All student work is paper-and-pencil and generally is quite structured, but sometimes students must show their work or explain their mathematical reasoning. Each unit requires 2-4 class periods and is composed of a CD-ROM plus a printed teacher's guide that contains reproducible student worksheets. PrimeTime Math is reviewed in *Mathematics Teaching in the Middle School* (1999, p. 480).

ProMath: Crime Stoppers *1997, grades 6-10*

Developer and Distributor

Learning Wave Communications
1-800-833-2004, www.learningwave.com
$175 for 26-minute video and 20 student activities

This video does an exemplary job of showing students how critical mathematics and science are to forensic science, detective work, and general police work. A chief medical examiner, an assistant state attorney, and several police detectives and officers recount the important uses of mathematics and science both in their daily work (e.g., fingerprints, ballistics, autopsies, traffic control, etc.) and in solving notorious crimes (e.g., the Ponzi scheme, Al Capone's tax evasion). The video showcases a variety of mathematical topics and processes, including logic, probability, time/space/distance formulas, trigonometry, calibration, matrices, etc. Because a single video cannot give in-depth treatment of these many topics, teachers will not find it useful for explaining the mathematics or science concepts. A teacher's guide contains masters for about 20 student exercises (crime "cases") that require from a few minutes to a whole class period. These activities are not linked to the video, generally are prescriptive, and cover mathematics such as arithmetic operations, ratios, and simple formulas.

ThinkSmart *1998-1999+, grades 6-12*

Developer and Distributor

Think Smart, Inc.
1-888-THINK-20, www.tsmart.com
$500-$1000 per unit, per school

The developers base these videos and their accompanying printed activities on what they identify as 75 mathematical concepts that solve 90% of the problems in the real world. Episodes address, in simple terms, some complex mathematics topics such as discrete mathematics or mathematical optimization algorithms, which are widespread in business but typically omitted from the school curriculum. The mathematics illustrations and explanations are conveyed very much through workplace contexts. Developers plan to provide additional supporting information and activities through the Web, including opportunities for live "chats" with relevant professionals. Initial topics available are "A Story of Life and Death" (use of exploratory data analysis to save an emergency room patient) and "Seconds Count: A Race to the Fire!" (mathematical procedures used to determine the shortest route to an emergency site). The price per school for each episode (including video, print, and Internet) is $500-$1,000 (depending upon the number of students).

Chemistry for the Technologies
1999+, grades 10-14

Developer and Distributor

South Carolina Department of Education
Office of Occupational Education
1-803-734-8399. Dr. Earl McConnel
draft, 200 photocopied pages, free or at-cost

The SC Department of Education developed this semester-long course because it determined that no commercially available teaching resources taught the technological aspects (versus theory) of the chemistry used in occupations such as a laboratory technician in a quality control laboratory, a process operator in a paper mill or chemical or textile plant, or a medical technologist. The course complements a traditional high school chemistry course and ChemCom. It has 14 very structured laboratories on topics such as the viscosity of motor oils, agricultural dilutions, synthesis of aspirin, esters for flavor, recycling newspapers, and gas chromatography. The curriculum advocates cooperative learning because it is consistent with contemporary industry practices. Units include job profiles and incorporate industry terminology such as *material balances, mass accountability, weight,* and *wt%.* Measurement accuracy and error analysis (e.g., standard deviations) are emphasized throughout. The draft does not provide much technical, chemical, or pedagogical background information for the teacher and emphasizes the need to draw upon standard chemistry texts while using the program.

Material Science Technology
1996-1997, grades 9-12

Developer and Distributor	Funder
Pacific Northwest National Laboratory *Energy Concepts, Inc. (ECi)* *1-800-621-1247* *$50 per unit (class master)* *$70 instructor's manual for all units*	*U.S. Department of Energy*

This set of five 5-week modules can compose a 1-year course, particularly for tech prep or other school-to-work initiatives, or be used as supplments to chemistry or other science courses. The product addresses the following topics, many of which also are treated in Materials World Modules (reviewed in chapter 5 on p. 178): ceramics, composites, metals, polymers, and solids. A dominant reason for including both of these curricula in the guide is that they cover science that is prevalent in business and industry but typically left out of school science. (See Adding Workplace Math and Science Topics to the School Curriculum, p. 22.) Most classroom time is devoted to very structured laboratory activities that require a lot of materials and apparatus, including some specialized items that need to be purchased, and occasional use of equipment typically found in various vocational classrooms. However, for each lab, considerable content explanations are provided, including descriptions of industrial processes for manufacturing materials (e.g., processing iron from ore into steel) and a glossary of industrial terms (e.g., terms for metal working - *stamping, extrusion, swaging*). Many of the student questions at the end of each lab only require short answers such as the identification of correct terms, but some require making short conclusions or predictions based upon their labs. The instructor's manual provides extensive background information for running the student laboratories.

A World in Motion *1996-1999, grades 6-8*

Developer and Distributor	Funder
Society of Automotive Engineers *1-800-457-2946 or* *www.sae.org/students/awimord1.htm, free*	*SAE, NSF*

This supplemental curriculum resource connects to workplace contexts by having students experience the technological design process that is central to engineering. (See Using Engineering Design

Principles, p. 20). Each unit is an 8-week design challenge: the first released unit, Mobility Toys, is presented as a Request for Proposals (RFP), in response to which students create and market a new toy for children ages 6-10. Activities necessarily include learning about vehicle building materials, motors and gears, conducting market research, refining their designs, and communicating their proposals. The Toys unit includes an introductory motivation video, materials for constructing prototypes, and a 300 pp. teacher's guide (including masters for student activity sheets) that thoroughly supports implementation of each step of the design activity and provides the scientific, mathematical, and technological knowledge involved. The guide indicates how activities fulfill specific national curriculum standards for mathematics, science, and technology education. The SAE provides this curriculum free to every middle school willing to establish a partnership with an area business or organization that will sponsor volunteer engineers who will help with classroom activities. One unit is available for each grade level.

WorkWise *1999+, grades 9-14*

Developer and Distributor

Institute for the Study of Family, Work and Community
Gary Hoachlander, 1-510-849-4942

Funder

U.S. Department of Education

WorkWise aims to help students in the classroom acquire science and mathematics concepts in the context of major industries through authentic work-based problems. The project plans to produce units on topics such as global trade, automotive design, manufacturing of aircraft, and urban transit. The first unit is being field tested and combines video, graphics, gaming, simulation, and text into a multimedia package.

[In the late 1990s, the Department of Education supported 12 curriculum development projects that sought to integrate academic and vocational education, including several that emphasized mathematics and science. The authors thought it important for this book to note these efforts even though the Department was unable to award later years of the intended funding because Congress did not provide sufficient money. Only a few of the projects were able to find other funding to continue, and they are proceeding at a slower pace. WorkWise still plans to produce materials that will be sufficiently developed for wider use.]

Appendix B: Getting Ideas for Making Your Own Materials

The tips briefly presented in this appendix will help teachers create curriculum materials that put school learning in the context of the workplace. However, novice curriculum developers should first carefully consider the trade-offs between the pros and cons of using commercially available curriculum materials versus creating their own materials. Our greatest caution is that it is challenging to make curriculum materials, especially ones that connect fields. It is extremely laborious to make good ones that incorporate solid subject matter as well as best practices in teaching and learning. And most teachers do not have the resources needed to create lessons that are sufficiently developed for use by educators elsewhere. The difficulty of creating materials is, of course, one of the major reasons why educators look for existing materials that best fit their local needs, even though they may need to be adapted.

On the other hand, local educators are the people who can create lessons that best match the specific curriculum needs of their students and that can take advantage of their community's resources. Teachers in school-to-work, tech prep, career academies, and similar programs especially need curriculum materials that connect their students' academic learning with the jobs, careers, businesses, or industries in their area. So, this appendix will help local educators develop curricula for use in their own classrooms, schools, or districts. But remember that even when curriculum materials are well developed, they may not meet the needs of teachers in other districts or states, e.g., your materials may focus on paper mill processing when no such industry exists in another school's area.

The biggest initial barrier for creating curriculum materials that connect mathematics and/or science to workplace contexts, the one addressed in this appendix, is not having adequate knowledge of specific connections. Most teachers have had little exposure to workplaces during their teacher preparation and career. So, here are two central tips for gaining the knowledge needed to create such curriculum materials:

- Science and mathematics teachers should collaborate with teachers of vocational courses, school-to-work, or tech prep programs, etc., and vice versa.

- Collect examples of curriculum materials that make connections and guides that provide specific tips on how to much such materials.

- Learn about workplace contexts by obtaining available information, job shadowing, more limited workplace observations, interviewing, etc.

Collaborating With Other Kinds of Teachers

Some of the curricula we saw as having the strongest "connections" resulted when teachers from different subject areas but within the same school collaborated for the first time. A mathematics teacher at a conference enthusiastically described her discovery that the instructor who taught plumbing used the Pythagorean theorem as a mainstay for determining how to angle pipes in building construction. Plumbers are required to know and use this mathematics as part of their licensing. By collaborating, the two instructors created a unit that helped each other's instruction. She used the plumbing context in her mathematics class for applying the Pythagorean theorem. The vocational instructor beefed up the academic treatment of his pipe calculations to show that it was a specific example of the Pythagorean theorem, which could be employed in many other life and work situations.

Go down the hall or across the campus to become familiar with what other kinds of teachers are doing. You may even need to go across the district if vocational, school-to-work, and other programs are located in different schools. It is a tragedy that American teaching conditions and culture cause most educators to work in isolation, seldom conferring with other teachers. It is especially rare for mathematics or science teachers to confer with faculty teaching entirely different courses, such as home economics, metal working, etc. But vocational and other technical education teachers often have knowledge of workplace connections that could be valuable for your curriculum development. Hurdle the practical and political barriers (including stigmas about the status of some fields versus others) that too often stop teachers from benefiting from the expertise of other teachers.

While it takes a good bit of work to cross these barriers, it takes even more time to collaborate on producing new lessons. When collaborating, you not only have to work on learning the connections in the substance of what you teach, you will somewhere along the way also need to take time to understand each others' professional backgrounds, course constraints, and even different teaching vocabularies. But the enhanced connections of your resulting jointly produced curricula certainly can be worth it.

Collect Sample Curricula and Guides for Developing Materials

Readers can use this guide to look for materials they might use, but they also can examine the sample pages to prompt ideas for developing their own materials. Further, the authors collected over 200 examples of curriculum materials that make connections between mathematics and/or science and workplace contexts. Many of the examples could not be included in this resource guide because they either were not sufficiently applicable for teachers across the country or were not polished enough for widespread use. But some of them would be terrific for educators trying to think of connections that they could use when developing their own materials. We collected a lot of these materials by going to conferences that a science or mathematics educators would not typically attend, such as meetings of the Association for Career and Technical Education (ACTE, formerly the American Vocational Association), school-to-work or tech prep conferences, and the *High Schools That Work* conferences of the Southeast Regional Education Board (SREB). We looked for sessions that suggested these educators were trying to infuse more academic science or mathematics into their programs and asked them to send samples of their materials. Admittedly, this strategy is more realistic for curriculum supervisors than classroom teachers. But anyone could obtain descriptions of instructional programs that make connections (e.g., Center on Education and Work, 1996a, 1996b) or guides with detailed suggestions for creating your own materials (e.g., Hernandez-Gantes, V, Brendefur, J & J Burrill, 1998; Vocational Instructional Materials Laboratory, 1998). Also, consider joining ACTE to obtain their periodical, *Techniques*, and scan it for articles describing programs that make connections. Write these programs to request samples of any curriculum materials they have developed.

Discovering Workplace Connections

The most powerful way of teaching oneself about connections is gaining direct knowledge about the workplace. Here are several strategies, listed by their increasing order of effort:

- Obtain industry literature, especially those prepared for K-12 educational purposes.
- Bring industry experts into class as speakers or facilitators of activities.
- Interview professionals about the mathematics or science they regularly use in their jobs.
- Observe professionals at work and look for applications of math and science.
- Intensively observe professionals by job shadowing over a period of time.
- Work at some other occupation during summer teaching breaks.

Obtaining industry literature is particularly easy today. A lot of companies are interested in helping the schools in communities where their employees' children go to school and their future employees are being educated. Most teachers have received industry-produced educational brochures or units in their mailboxes without asking for them. Never forget that such industries are producing literature not only as a public service but also to cast the producer in the best possible light, even to the point of picking and choosing what science to enlist in making their points rather than presenting all available scientific evidence. Nevertheless, this literature sometimes can give you tremendous ideas on the applications of science and mathematics. Besides taking a closer look at whatever arrives in your mailbox, you can contact businesses and industries that you predict are particularly likely to have many and/or strong uses of mathematics and science. Try asking for whomever is in charge of educational outreach (sometimes they are in public relations departments) and/or professional training. Looking at a company's Web site might give you a head start.

You could also benefit from arranging for professionals to visit your class. So many people are willing to do this, especially if you invest the time to prepare them by familiarizing them with what your students know and are currently studying so that they can think of connections. A mere career awareness talk will not help make connections. If you have multiple conversations with your contact, perhaps they will work with you to develop some instructional activity which they could help facilitate in your class. At this stage, you at least have a resource for creating a curriculum activity if not a potential collaborator for writing it. Even if your local circumstances make it hard to take students to the workplace for field trips, this is a way you can bring the workplace to the class.

When guest speakers or facilitators are at the school, arrange for time to interview them about the mathematics and/or science they regularly use in their jobs. They may find it difficult to remember the content of "school" mathematics or science. So, show them student textbooks as a prompt for them to consider how they could be making direct or indirect use of the content in their work. However, be aware that their use of mathematics and science may be so routine, contextualized, and embedded in their functions that they have difficulty making the connections.

If possible, make arrangements to go observe professionals in their work setting. You may better be able to spot their uses of math or science, increasingly so as you spend more time there. Most teachers will not be able to spend large amounts of time doing observations and interviews. So, ask workers about their entire range of job activities to try and make educated guesses about what and when observations would be most fruitful. If you do have considerable time (in the summer, for example) to observe, you could "job shadow" by following a worker around for a day or more.

The ultimate way to discover connections can be working at some other occupation yourself during the summer. A lot of companies are willing to hire teachers in the summer. If you are a frequent participant in summer workshops for teachers, consider this alternative experience that also could enrich your teaching (and provide some summer compensation). While this is a rich approach, it could be narrow. Concentrating on one particular job will probably yield a narrower range of connections than spending an equivalent amount of time surveying many different jobs through the approaches mentioned earlier. The advantage of summer employment, however, is that you will be immersed deeper into a field and gain stronger insights about the connections that can make it easier to develop curriculum materials.

All of these approaches involve considerable work over and above regular instructional responsibilities. That should not be surprising, however. As a curriculum developer, you are a type of author. We commonly accept that authors (even of fiction) have to do considerable research in order to gain the insights they need to convey ideas to their audiences. Whether the hard work of doing research to find connections is for students in one class or school, or for a district or state, or the whole country, it can be fun and professionally rewarding for you and educationally enriching for students.